Open access edition supported by the National Endowment for the Humanities / Andrew W. Mellon Foundation Humanities Open Book Program.

© 2019 Johns Hopkins University Press
Published 2019

Johns Hopkins University Press
2715 North Charles Street
Baltimore, Maryland 21218-4363
www.press.jhu.edu

The text of this book is licensed under a Creative Commons Attribution-NonCommercial-NoDerivatives 4.0 International License: https://creativecommons.org/licenses/by-nc-nd/4.0/.
CC BY-NC-ND

ISBN-13: 978-1-4214-3330-1 (open access)
ISBN-10: 1-4214-3330-3 (open access)

ISBN-13: 978-1-4214-3328-8 (pbk. : alk. paper)
ISBN-10: 1-4214-3328-1 (pbk. : alk. paper)

ISBN-13: 978-1-4214-3329-5 (electronic)
ISBN-10: 1-4214-3329-X (electronic)

This page supersedes the copyright page included in the original publication of this work.

ENTREPRENEURIAL VERNACULAR

CREATING THE
NORTH AMERICAN LANDSCAPE

Gregory Conniff
Edward K. Muller
David Schuyler
Consulting Editors

George F. Thompson
Series Founder and Director

Published in cooperation with
the Center for American Places,
Santa Fe, New Mexico,
and Harrisonburg, Virginia

ENTREPRENEURIAL VERNACULAR

Developers' Subdivisions in the 1920s

CAROLYN S. LOEB

THE JOHNS HOPKINS UNIVERSITY PRESS
Baltimore and London

© 2001 The Johns Hopkins University Press
All rights reserved. Published 2001

2 4 6 8 9 7 5 3 1

The Johns Hopkins University Press
2715 North Charles Street
Baltimore, Maryland 21218-4363
www.press.jhu.edu

Library of Congress Cataloging-in-Publication Data
Loeb, Carolyn S., 1948–
Entrepreneurial vernacular : developers' subdivisions in the 1920s
/ Carolyn S. Loeb.
p. cm.
Includes bibliographical references and index.
ISBN 0-8018-6618-9
1. Land subdivision—United States—History.
2. Housing—United States—History. 3. Real estate
development—United States—History. I. Title.
HD1390.3.U6 L64 2001
333.77—dc21
00-011508

A catalog record for this book is available from the British Library.

Frontispiece: 335 Valdez displays the basic elements of the architect's modular design system in the speculative subdivision of Westwood Highlands, San Francisco.

For Dick

In Memoriam L.A.L. and S.M.L.

CONTENTS

List of Illustrations   xi
Acknowledgments   xv

INTRODUCTION
THE ENTREPRENEURIAL VERNACULAR SUBDIVISION   1
    Entrepreneurial Vernacular   2
    The Emergence of a Housing Solution in the 1920s   5
    The Subdivisions and Their Builders   10
    Agency, Form, and Meaning   14

PART I.
THREE SUBDIVISIONS AND THEIR BUILDERS

CHAPTER 1.
THE FORD HOMES: The Case of the Borrowed Builders   19
    The Ford Homes: Background and Overview   20
    The Ford Homes: Design and Construction   30
    The Development of Industrialized Building   43
    Relations of Production   47
    Modeling Efficient Development   51

CHAPTER 2.
BRIGHTMOOR: The Case of the Absent Architect   55
    Brightmoor: Background and Overview   55
    B. E. Taylor and the Development of Brightmoor   61
    The Absent Architect   71
    Situating Brightmoor   81

CONTENTS

CHAPTER 3.
WESTWOOD HIGHLANDS: The Rise of the Realtor — 88
  Westwood Highlands: Background and Overview — 90
  The Role of Style — 107
  The Principles of Organization — 108
  Realtors: The Professional Project — 123
  Realtors as Community Builders — 128
  Rationalizing Development — 136

PART II.
AGENCY, FORM, AND MEANING

CHAPTER 4.
THE HOME-OWNERSHIP NETWORK:
Constructing Community — 143
  The Prevalence of the Single-family Detached Suburban House — 144
  The Home-ownership Network — 149
  The Neighborhood Unit Plan — 163
  Communities on the Ground — 176

CHAPTER 5.
ARCHITECTURAL STYLE: The Charm of Continuity — 180
  The Ford Homes — 182
  Brightmoor — 186
  Westwood Highlands — 187
  Stylistic Pluralism — 191
  The Charm of Continuity — 200

CONCLUSION:
ARCHITECTURE AS SOCIAL PROCESS — 204
  Distilling a New Vernacular — 205
  Entrepreneurial Vernacular and the Landscape of Exchange — 208

Notes — 215
Bibliographical Note — 259
Illustration Credits — 261
Index — 263

ILLUSTRATIONS

1. Graphic Analysis of Residential Construction Activity, 1915–1969   8
2. Map of Detroit Indicating the Locations of the Ford Homes and Brightmoor   22
3. Diagrams of Neighborhood Plans by Albert Wood, 1918   26
4. Exterior of Model A, Ford Homes, Dearborn, 1920   34
5. Exterior of Model B, Ford Homes, Dearborn, 1919   35
6. Exterior of Model C, Ford Homes, Dearborn, 1919   35
7. Exterior of Model D, Ford Homes, Dearborn, 1919   36
8. Exterior of Model E, Ford Homes, Dearborn, 1919   37
9. Exterior of Model F, Ford Homes, Dearborn, 1920   37
10. View of Typical Bathroom, Ford Homes, Dearborn, 1919   38
11. View of Typical Living Room, Ford Homes, Dearborn, 1919   39
12. View of Typical Kitchen, Ford Homes, Dearborn, 1919   39
13. View of the Early Stage of Construction, Ford Homes, Dearborn, 1919   42
14. Diagram of the Details of Balloon Frame Construction, 1923   44
15 a and b. Two Views of Brightmoor Streets, Detroit, 1924   64
16. View of Living Room, Brightmoor, Detroit, 1924   68
17. View of Bedroom, Brightmoor, Detroit, 1924   69
18. View of Kitchen, Brightmoor, Detroit, 1924   69
19. Exterior and Plan of Model 614, Brightmoor, Detroit, 1924   70
20. Exterior and Plan of Model 514, Brightmoor, Detroit, 1924   72

ILLUSTRATIONS

21. Plan of Model 714, Brightmoor, Detroit, 1924   73
22. Exterior View of an Appalachian Cabin   85
23. Map of San Francisco Indicating the Location of Westwood Highlands   89
24. Topographical Map Indicating the Street Plan of Westwood Highlands, San Francisco   92
25. Map of the Proposed Subdivision, Woodcrest, San Francisco, 1922   96
26 a and b. Renderings of Entrance Features for the Proposed Subdivision, Woodcrest, San Francisco, c. 1922   98
27. Entrance Features Built for Westwood Park, San Francisco   99
28. Signage Defining the Boundary of Westwood Highlands, San Francisco   100
29. Advertisement for Nelson Bros., Builders, and Westwood Highlands, San Francisco, 1925   101
30. Exterior of 185 Westwood, Westwood Park, San Francisco, Under Construction   104
31. Exterior of 591 Wildwood, Westwood Park, San Francisco, Under Construction   105
32. Exterior of 25 Northwood, Westwood Park, San Francisco, Under Construction   106
33. Two-module-type House, Ridgewood between Joost and Mangels, Westwood Highlands, San Francisco   110
34. View of Corner House, 250 Hazelwood, Westwood Highlands, San Francisco   111
35. Four-module-type House, Yerba Buena between Brentwood and Hazelwood, Westwood Highlands, San Francisco   113
36. Four-module-type House, Hazelwood between Yerba Buena and Brentwood, Westwood Highlands, San Francisco   113
37. Three-module type House, 325 Colon, Westwood Highlands, San Francisco, 1927   114
38. Three-module-type House, Hazelwood between Los Palmos and Brentwood, Westwood Highlands, San Francisco   114
39. Exterior, Interior, and Plan of 944 Monterey, Westwood Highlands, San Francisco, 1925   116

ILLUSTRATIONS

40. View of Corner House, Intersection of Hazelwood and Brentwood, Westwood Highlands, San Francisco   117

41. Plan of Two-bedroom House, Westwood Highlands, San Francisco   119

42. Exterior and Interior Views, 225 Valdez, Westwood Highlands, San Francisco, 1925   121

43. Interior of 944 Monterey, Westwood Highlands, San Francisco, 1925   122

44. Advertisement for the Services of a Subdivision Site Planner, 1923   135

45. Advertisement for the Own Your Home Campaign, 1920   156

46. Diagram of the Neighborhood Unit Plan by Clarence A. Perry, 1929   168

ACKNOWLEDGMENTS

Even a modest project incurs great debts, and one of the pleasures of seeing it through to the end is being able to acknowledge them. Many people were generous with their time, knowledge, and encouragement, and I am grateful to have the opportunity here to thank them in some small measure.

Descendants of some of the developers and architects whose work this book is about kindly gave me access to information and documents. My thanks to Moyer Wood, Mari Shaw, James T. Hughes, and Bert E. Taylor Jr. for their generosity and trust. I also received helpful leads from Joseph Oldenburg, who researched the Ford Homes for landmark designation.

For their encouragement of this project at an early stage, I thank Elizabeth Blackmar and Gwendolyn Wright. I am also grateful for encouragement by the late Eugene Santomasso and the late Hanna Deinhard.

This book shares with many recent works an interest in how and why particular patterns of built form become commonplace; it also shares a method of approach that considers how architectural design can be affected by cultural, social, historical, and economic developments as well as by aesthetic decisions. For me, the bases for these perspectives were nurtured during my early, formative years as a scholar, when a generation of students struggled to make sense of the institutions they confronted. As to the work at hand, I owe an intellectual debt to many scholars of vernacular architecture and design who have made this field one of the richest and most dynamic in recent years. I have tried to acknowledge these throughout the text, but I apologize in advance to those inadvertently overlooked. The work and collegiality of those associated with the Vernacular Archi-

ACKNOWLEDGMENTS

tecture Forum and the Society for American City and Regional Planning History have been especially valuable. In particular I thank Laurence Gerckens, founder of the latter, for creating a welcoming environment for scholars from all disciplines, and R. Eugene Harper for his service as a commentator on an early version of part of this book.

My colleagues in the Art Department at Central Michigan University have been steadfast in their support, for which I thank them. Two leaves of absence from my teaching responsibilities enabled me to launch this project. I appreciate grants I received from CMU's Faculty Research and Creative Endeavors Committee that enabled me to present segments of this work at national and international conferences.

I am grateful for the support and editorial labors of David Schuyler, a consulting editor of the Creating the North American Landscape series, as well as those of George F. Thompson and Randall Jones of the Center for American Places, which nurtured this project through its final stages of development. My thanks, too, to anonymous reviewers and their insightful critiques. All responsibility for advice both gratefully taken and stubbornly rejected is my own.

I thank Katherine McCracken for sharing her editorial expertise, and Cheryl Dusty-DeLauro, graphics production coordinator at CMU, for help with illustrations.

Finally, my deepest thanks to comrades Fran Nesi, Gail Radford, Linda O. Stanford, and Marjorie Thau for their solidarity; to Ann Peterson; and to Richard Peterson for his companionship on all the journeys.

ENTREPRENEURIAL VERNACULAR

INTRODUCTION

THE ENTREPRENEURIAL VERNACULAR SUBDIVISION

> I remember once in London I saw a picture of an American suburb, in a toothpaste ad on the back of the *Saturday Evening Post*— an elm-lined snowy street of these new houses, Georgian some of 'em, or with low raking roofs and— The kind of street you'd find here in Zenith, say in Floral Heights. Open. Trees. Grass. And I was homesick! There's no other country in the world that has such pleasant houses. And I don't care if they *are* standardized. It's a corking standard!
>
> Sinclair Lewis, *Babbitt*, 1922

We can still recognize Babbitt's Floral Heights in subdivisions encountered from Maine to California, from the Great Lakes to the Gulf of Mexico. With a few modifications, Floral Heights could have been the model for several decades of suburban subdivisions, for Sinclair Lewis's characterization is prescient: the novel is set in 1920, just before the first great wave of speculative suburban residential subdivision development broke in mid decade. The familiarity of Floral Heights—with streets, slicing through a former apple orchard, lined with "Cheerful Modern Houses for Medium Incomes"—invites us to wonder whether those subsequent real-life near replicas were also created by figures like realtor George Babbitt and his cronies in Zenith's Boosters' Club. A question very similar to that one led to this study.

Curiosity about suburban subdivision housing and design arises from the dominance of this residential type in the United States. How did it become so widespread and why did it take the form that it did? The experienced eye can detect some of the more familiar, formative, nineteenth-century influences, such as the early suburbs of Riverside, Illinois, and Llewellyn Park, New Jersey, and the introduction of later

INTRODUCTION

English garden-suburb design concepts. But it is unclear how or by whom these were translated into the distinctive housing idiom that marks much of the North American residential landscape. Understanding the evident success achieved by suburban subdivision development is valuable for its own sake, as well as for the insight it provides about the limits to alternative housing possibilities that prevailed in the United States.

This book pursues answers to these questions by examining subdivision housing schemes from two different vantage points. One provides a close-up view of three representative speculative suburban subdivisions that have not previously been studied: the Ford Homes in Dearborn, Michigan; Brightmoor, in Detroit; and Westwood Highlands, in San Francisco. Analyses of their histories and design produce a vivid picture of the developers of these projects, the circumstances they were working within, the way each project was formed, and the distinct features that make up the pattern of subdivision development. The other vantage point highlights the historical context for these typical subdivisions and the scores of others they represent. This wider perspective takes account of the histories of housing professionals in the United States in the nineteenth and early-twentieth centuries and how these professionals framed and responded to housing issues.

Using this two-pronged approach—considering both local and particular housing histories and the impact of nationwide institutional and social-structural changes—brings into sharper focus the essential features of subdivision housing, how these features were defined, and who was involved in their broad circulation.[1] What emerges is a view of single-family suburban subdivision development that shows it as the product of a diffuse array of social, historical, and design concerns. These were articulated through a distinctive pattern of built form that was both flexible and controlled; it is a housing solution that can be described as "entrepreneurial vernacular."

Entrepreneurial Vernacular

Vernacular describes not a style but a category of building. It generally designates "ordinary" building, the commonplace fabric of architectural forms that evolve within a context of local needs and conditions. The term encompasses not only the design features of built form in a particular time and place but also that form's methods of construction, materials, production relations, spatial organization, and functions. The creators of vernacular architecture are frequently characterized as indigenous, signaling their debt to local traditions and circumstances rather than to the benefits of professional training in a more cosmopolitan cultural center. The flexibility of the term that allows it to be applied to geographically and historically diverse examples of ordinary built form can create confusion; perhaps as vernacular studies advance, the term will be replaced by more precise designations. But this flexibility has the virtue of providing a way to interpret the design, construction, and meaning of a broad, but historically overlooked and undertheorized spectrum of the built environment.

Suburban residential subdivision development can be characterized as vernacular, first of all, in that it is pervasive and dominant as a housing solution in the United States. Recognizable by its distribution of single-family houses set in the middle of green lawns—formal space facing the public street, private yard or garden in back—its variations are legion, in scale of development, size and cost of lots and houses, and architectural style. Discussions of such housing have often focused on elite suburbs; by examining more modest, and more typical, subdivisions, this study considers the creation of a vocabulary of ordinary building and locates a pattern of shared forms underlying these variations.[2] It describes how subdivision developments used specific construction, design, and planning devices to achieve a balance of visual unity and variety, an image of historical continuity, and a sense of neighborhood. Wider social, economic, historical, and aesthetic developments informed the choice of these devices and the meanings they conveyed. This interaction between social practices and built form is also characteristic of the vernacular.

Another feature of vernacular architecture is that it is frequently either documented poorly or documented in unconventional ways. Its creators generally function outside established architectural institutional frameworks. Records are sparse or nonexistent. The researcher must rely on the built forms themselves as documents and as guides to

INTRODUCTION

alternative lines of inquiry that can shed light in the absence of key records. This reliance on built form is necessary in the case of subdivision developments. Much can be learned about planning and design decisions from close study of the projects, as will be clear from the analyses here of three selected subdivisions. The interpretive framework for these analyses, however, draws on a wider range of sources, including local histories and patterns of urban development.

Vernacular architecture often seems at first blush to be anonymous. Its creators' identities are generally unknown beyond the region or community in which they have built. A particular vernacular system of design and construction may minimize, diffuse, or obscure authorship, in contrast to the star billing often received by a professionally trained designer. This study examines the authorship of suburban subdivision housing and finds that although there were roles for building-craftsmen and architects, the primary shapers of these projects were real-estate developers. This becomes clear through consideration of the three representative subdivisions selected for close analysis. In connection with these, I trace the histories of all three parties—building-craftsmen, architects, and realtors—and their relationships to small-house design. These histories indicate what the social and economic changes in the building industry were that placed realtors, rather than architects or building-craftsmen, in a position to determine the shape and direction of subdivision development. Structural shifts in the nature of work and the rise of professionals enabled realtors to champion a type of housing they were ideally suited to create.[3]

By studying the evolution of building practices and the emergence of realtors as professionals, it is possible to discern the entrepreneurial skills that such a housing solution required and that realtors were in a singular position to provide. Their entrepreneurial skills underlie and symbolize this process of housing provision as a whole and the built form that is its product. Not only did realtors organize and manage a construction process; they also integrated aspects of existing suburban projects with contemporary views about housing that were being expressed and promoted by a network of early-twentieth-century housing professionals with which they were associated. As we consider the institutions and interests of this housing network, it becomes evident how suburban residential subdivision development addressed the concerns of planners, housing reformers, and social theorists about such issues as urban dislocation, housing shortages, and the need for community. In other words, realtors organized and managed a crucial set of ideas bearing on problems of contemporary housing provision, as well as administering the nuts and bolts of a construction process.

Suburban subdivision development also represents an entrepreneurial housing solution because it both entailed the business of risk management and physically embodied this bid to control investment outcomes. The realtor-developer embraced risk in the first instance by undertaking the organization and construction of a housing tract. However, by considering such diverse aspects of these projects as financing and the meanings of design elements, it becomes apparent that risk management was generalized throughout the development as a whole. Familiar legal instruments such as zoning and deed restrictions served to perpetuate housing patterns,[4] but the planning and design features of a subdivision also addressed risk through the ways in which they physically represented the idea of community. To the extent that spatial organization and design amenities contributed to neighborhood definition, these features fostered a sense of the subdivision's continuity and thus reassured home owners about the security of their investments. Community became an emblem of continuity, allowing these housing schemes to signal control over unpredictable and disruptive market and social forces. Suburban residential subdivisions achieved success, ultimately, because they were designed to transfer the original risk associated with entrepreneurialism from the developer to the home owner. A number of factors made this possible. Their result, however, was the manipulation of house design and neighborhood identity to assert the stability of the community, so that the safety of everyone's investments would at least seem to be ensured.

The Emergence of a Housing Solution in the 1920s

Entrepreneurial vernacular, then, describes the residential pattern that realtors negotiated by means of their patronage of building-craftsmen and architects, their association with a network of other housing professionals, their knowledge of the housing field, and the new organizational skills they brought to the process of urban development. But at what historical point did the numerous strands of housing design, building practices, and theories of housing need and provision become interwoven to create the recognizable warp and woof of this residential fabric?

In order to follow the evolution of each contributing aspect of this housing history, this book's story ranges over the decades of the late-nineteenth and early-twentieth centuries. The subdivisions selected for close analysis, however, date from the 1920s. During this decade there was a surge in housing construction, stimulated by increased demand for new housing as a result of the movements of population caused by World War I. The concentration on production in war industries had meant both that production to meet peacetime needs was postponed and that industrialized urban areas saw a great influx of newcomers to work in their factories. Once the national economy recovered from postwar depression, the residential construction industry began to respond to the housing shortage. Housing production peaked in 1925, and by the end of the decade, when a new economic crisis forced the cessation of construction, an average of 703,000 new dwellings per year had been built (fig. 1).

There was a great deal of diversity in housing types to meet the demands created by the housing shortage in this period, including apartment buildings and smaller multifamily dwellings.[5] But the majority of units were detached, single-family houses, constructed in the expanding rings of suburbs at the urban fringes. This eruption of suburban development offers the student of residential architecture a wide range of possibilities for close scrutiny. The fact that this housing could be provided in such quantity, and so rapidly, also suggests that the agents, mechanisms, and formal solutions necessary for its construction were already in place.

Another impetus for focusing on 1920s residential developments is the challenge to the contemporary status quo presented by the critical, modernist tradition in housing studies within the United States during this period.[6] In the face of post–World War I housing needs and what they regarded as an inefficient response to it, a small but articulate group of critics proposed alternative solutions through their writings and a handful of model developments. Critical of the wasteful redundancy of single-family housing constructed within conventional suburban subdivisions, writers such as Edith Elmer Wood, Catherine Bauer, and Lewis Mumford urged coherent planning strategies and unified designs that would yield affordable, stable, and integrated environments adapted to modern needs. They analyzed residential construction in the United States and the achievements and pitfalls of large-scale developments such as company towns and wartime housing, and they studied ambitious European undertakings, especially in the Netherlands, the United Kingdom, and Germany, as precedents for nonspeculative approaches to the building of new communities.

The attitude of these critics toward existing patterns of speculative residential development in the United States and toward the real-estate developers who built these projects can be summarized in the words of planner Henry Wright, co-designer of Radburn, New Jersey, one of the progressive models that embodied these critics' ideals. "Housing progress in this country is impossible," he wrote in 1933, "because of the inadequacy, amateurishness, and incapacity of those groups to whom it has been entrusted as a side-line to land merchandising and the mortgage business."[7]

Deserving of such criticism as real-estate developers may have been, however, it is their work that students of built form encounter as they look at the mass of subdivision design in the 1920s. Contemporary critiques of existing practices do not illuminate how or why these practices succeeded. Sensitive though they are to the social, environmental, and aesthetic costs of developers' practices, these critiques miss the structural changes in the construction field that were affecting relationships among building-craftsmen, architects, and newly professionalized realtor-developers. Furthermore, these critiques do not address the recognizable patterns of development created by 1920s developers. Searching and sophisticated, these critiques countered existing practices with an ideal of planning that was inherently radical and a challenge to free-market conceptions of urban develop-

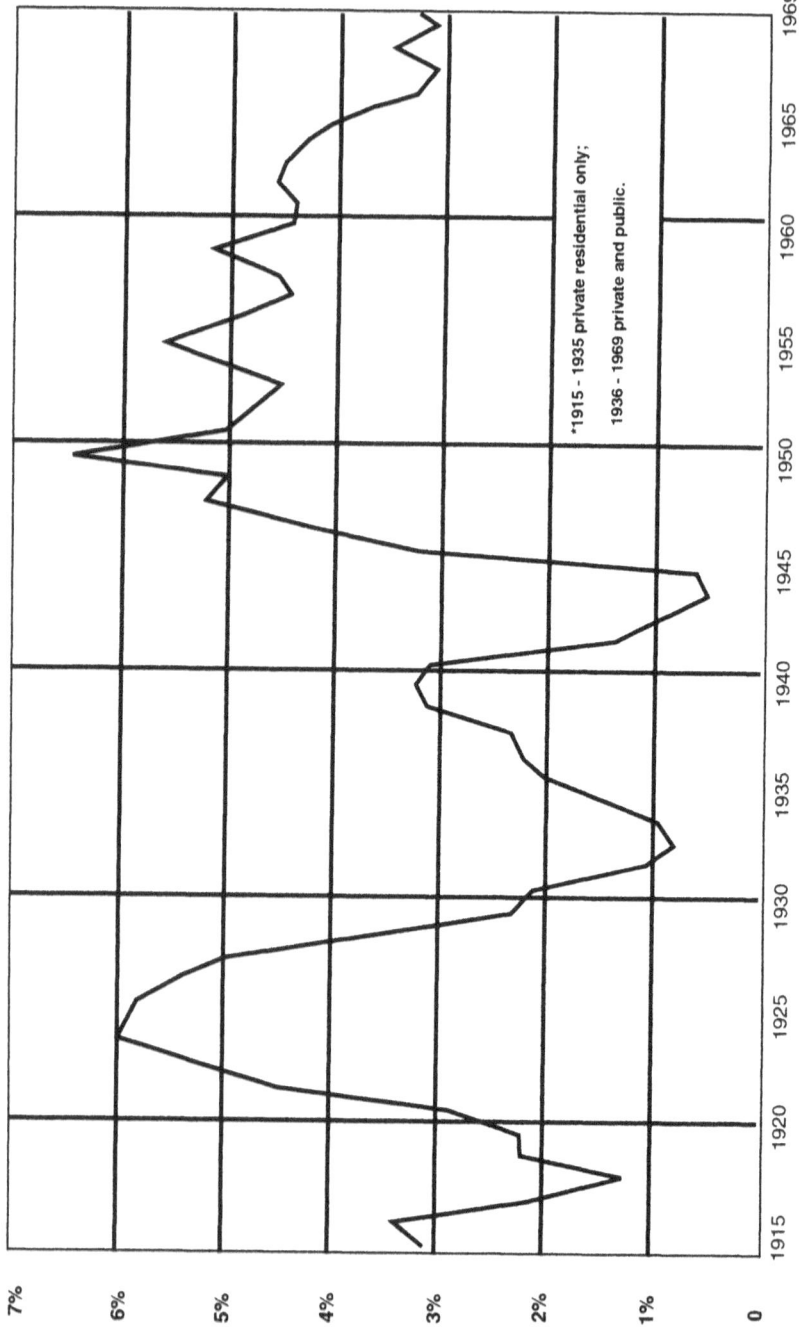

ment. Measured by the standards of this ideal, contemporary procedures were incoherent and undisciplined as well as wasteful in both social and material terms. And yet, apparent similarities in design and organization among 1920s subdivisions seem to belie the absence of planning.

In other words, the prevalence of a pattern of detached single-family suburban subdivision development in the 1920s suggests a level of coherence and rationality within the housing industry of the period. This rationality was at odds with the critics' planning ideal, but it succeeded in shaping an important dimension of the built environment. It is this underlying rationality—the mobilization of a form of planning that had the appearance of its opposite, a lack of planning—that this book explicates. It is a measure of the achievement and endurance of this rationality that the critics' proposals remain ideals. To the extent that one may still wish to see these ideals realized, it is worth exploring a seemingly incoherent landscape to locate the actors—along with the methods they used and the institutional structures they created—who succeeded in determining the pattern of residential subdivision development in the United States.

These actors and the organizational strategies that guided their relationships were also in place by the 1920s. Both grew out of the Progressive Era, when leadership by experts was extolled as the way that democratic society would advance. The pursuit of professional status by realtors, for example, which stems from this period, responded to this widely held conviction. In the 1920s, Herbert Hoover, first as secretary of commerce and then as president of the United States, was the most visible champion of a management model that linked realms of expertise through networks of voluntary associations. The housing

---

Figure 1. New residential construction as a percentage of gross national product, 1915–1969. This graphic analysis indicates changes in the strength of housing within the economy. The rise in housing production during the 1920s can be seen in relation to the slumps of the earlier war years, the succeeding Great Depression, and the next housing boom following World War II.

INTRODUCTION

network that professional realtors joined, along with other experts in fields concerned with housing issues, exemplified just such a linkage. Decentralized but operating nationally, the housing network was the conduit for ideas and information between experts and local practitioners. This book, by tracing this network's diffuse structure, brings to light the planning system that led to the dominance of entrepreneurial vernacular as a housing form.

Entrepreneurial vernacular resulted from an amalgam of cultural and historical resources inherited from the nineteenth and early twentieth centuries, and it contributed a specific housing solution that gave contemporary social developments a physical form. This solution was not necessarily the only one possible, as the models offered by Catherine Bauer, Henry Wright, and other critics were intended to demonstrate. But the evolution of the housing network, the way its members regarded the past, and how they construed present needs led to entrepreneurial vernacular's achievement of dominance as a housing idiom. This meant that subdivisions like Babbitt's Floral Heights came to set the standard, shape the image, and control debates about American housing.[8] Through the success of entrepreneurial vernacular, the type of housing understood as representing "the American Dream" was unambiguous and virtually uncontested.

The Subdivisions and Their Builders

The three selected subdivisions presented in part I are examples of relatively large-scale residential projects in which developers undertook the entire process of subdivision, design, and construction. Although large-scale development is often associated with the suburban construction surge following World War II, its prerequisites were in place by the 1920s. While the practice of selling both unimproved lots and lots with only infrastructural improvements—such as streets and sewers—within subdivisions was widespread in this period, there was also a trend toward large-scale, speculative residential building.

Two examples of such large developments are Brightmoor in Detroit and Westwood Highlands in San Francisco. A sporadic series of articles on these and similar projects that ran during the 1920s in

Building Age, a builder's journal of the period, indicates that this kind of large-scale development was significant within the housing industry, although no systematic overview of such projects was conducted. The third subdivision discussed is the Ford Homes in Dearborn, Michigan.

Each of the subdivisions took a different form, both physically and in terms of the specific housing needs it was created to meet. The Ford Homes project was developed by the Dearborn Realty & Construction Company, an organization staffed by associates of Henry Ford and established for the task of building 250 houses near Ford factories. It was not conceived as a company town; as I indicate, it was intended to stimulate private-sector real-estate development by creating a model of efficient construction procedures based on the principles of standardization and assembly-line production pioneered in Ford's plants. Although the architect commissioned to design the houses had innovative ideas about community design, few of these were realized in this project. Instead, the Ford Homes scheme was intended as a model for conventional subdivision design. If the developer wanted to break new ground, it was in achieving efficient results through rationalized production. Spurning innovative design solutions, this tract exemplifies features of subdivision design that were typically considered desirable, including a balance between architectural unity and variety and the overall identification of the subdivision as a distinct community.

The building practices that enabled construction of the Ford Homes to proceed using assembly-line and mass-production techniques are a focus of chapter 1, which examines trends within the construction industry that diminished building-craftsmen's skills. This overview places the nature of building-craftsmen's work and their production relations in their historical context. Against such a backdrop, it is possible to evaluate the Ford Homes project's commitment to furthering industrialized construction methods and to assess the role that building-craftsmen played in general in residential development in the 1920s.

In contrast to the Ford Homes, which were affordable to skilled workers and middle-class professionals, the houses at Brightmoor, the subdivision described in chapter 2, were designed for unskilled workers from rural areas who were attracted to jobs in Detroit's growing industries. Built by real-estate developer B. E. Taylor, the thousands of houses of the district did not meet minimal standards and had few amenities. Nevertheless, Taylor drew commercial and social services to the area to provide for community needs and development, and he succeeded in forging a lasting neighborhood identity. Although the housing he constructed may seem to place him at the margins of the realty profession, Taylor enjoyed respect among his peers and, after the period with which we are concerned, he went on to develop middle-class subdivisions.

Having considered, in the chapter on the Ford Homes, the historical development of building-craftsmen's relationship to housing construction, when the study shifts to Brightmoor the anonymity of the workforce and its diminished conceptual contribution to the construction process will already be familiar. At Brightmoor, however, these features are joined by the lack of any professional architectural involvement in the project. In the case of the Ford Homes, the architect's contribution was substantial but circumscribed; to understand the significance of the absence of an architect from the Brightmoor project, we must look at how the architectural profession historically distanced itself from problems of small-house design. Individual architects wrestled with solutions to these problems, but conflict between architects with such interests and the professional architectural elite limited the role that architects played in determining the shape of subdivision development.

While both the Ford Homes and Brightmoor may seem to be special, even limiting cases, they are not isolated examples. There was a good deal of attention focused within the construction industry in this period on production processes and ways to maximize rationalized building practices to reduce costs. The Ford Homes project has its unique history, but it is also representative of this concern within the housing industry. Similarly, Brightmoor is representative of the vast majority of housing built for the working poor, which was typically substandard. Yet, it is possible to see that Brightmoor also advanced significant mainstream trends in suburban residential development, including the establishment of neighborhood identity, the construction of an image of historical continuity, and the extension of formal methods of housing provision to groups of people who traditionally met their needs independently through community and owner-builder patterns of construction.

Westwood Highlands, in San Francisco, is perhaps the most conventional subdivision of the three in its development and the market for which it was created. It was developed by a prominent realty firm, Baldwin & Howell, in a district in which the earliest suburban development had seen the construction of residential enclaves for the affluent. Once public transportation linked the area to downtown, middle-class subdivisions followed, including an earlier tract by this firm called Westwood Park. At Westwood Park, lots were sold to buyers who individually commissioned architects and builders to design and construct their houses. Westwood Highlands represents the consolidation of Baldwin & Howell's sense of the market for housing in the district—a sense gained from their Westwood Park experience. In the later tract, they worked with one of the builders and one of the architects from Westwood Park and built speculative housing.

Baldwin & Howell's experiences at Westwood Park and Westwood Highlands reveal some of the processes by which realtors were becoming self-conscious, as well as often self-promoting, suburban developers. The histories of building-craftsmen and architects traced in chapters 1 and 2 chart these groups' diminishing roles in shaping residential development; by contrast, chapter 3 looks at the historical emergence of realtors, the group that had become dominant and determinant. Arising as a profession at a point when organizational skills became more valuable than craft-based abilities, realtors staked their claim to professional status largely on the basis of their self-description as community builders. Following models established by pioneering suburban developers of the nineteenth century, the profession absorbed ideas from designers working in romantic suburb and garden-suburb traditions, but saw these ideas as part of an arsenal of sound development practices aimed at controlling property values. In addition, realtors increasingly became patrons of building-craftsmen and of architects, organizing their artisanal, intellectual, and artistic forms of expertise to suit development demands, as Westwood Highland's history shows.

Westwood Highlands is also the most ambitious of the three subdivisions in its design. It incorporates curvilinear streets that suit its hilly topography, and varying house sizes. Its architect, like the designer of the Ford Homes, used a modular system to generate diversity from a limited number of plans and elevational elements.

From this brief overview, it is clear that the range of subdivisions constructed in the 1920s was quite broad and that the history of each is particular to its time and place. Yet, as different as each of these three subdivisions is, there are also common notions and goals of residential planning that undergird their design.

Agency, Form, and Meaning

What remains unclear from looking only at individual subdivisions is how a shared body of shaping ideas was transmitted and absorbed. In order to understand how such ideas were circulated, chapter 4 analyzes broader historical trends in the residential construction industry and among those interested in housing issues. It looks at the way in which realtors joined with other housing professionals in a network of associational progressives to shape patterns of suburban development.[9] Enjoying the sponsorship of the federal government, this network promoted single-family home ownership through a variety of private-sector programs, including the Own Your Home and Better Homes in America campaigns, and culminating in the 1931 President's Conference on Home Building and Home Ownership. These linked the activities of realtors, planners, architects, building-craftsmen, engineers, housing reformers, financiers, and other groups interested in residential construction, at both national and local levels. Through this network, too, the emphasis on community that had developed among urban reformers received wide attention in the form of Clarence A. Perry's neighborhood unit plan inspired by the garden suburb. The proposals this network embraced, including standardization, suburbanization, and the development of a sense of neighborhood, correspond to the patterns of built form analyzed in the three subdivisions.

Chapter 5 delves deeper into the role of architectural style, both in the subdivisions that have been analyzed and within the broader context of the needs of community development in the 1920s. It examines both the characteristics and meanings of the stylistic pluralism that typifies subdivision design and its relationship to modern architectural practice. Here it emerges that in addition to creating a balance between unity and diversity and contributing to the articulation of neighborhood identity, architectural design served as a visual anchor for the subdivision's claim to continuity, positing roots in the past and reaching toward a controllable future. In the face of dynamic social changes, of which housing shortages and subdivision solutions both were parts, architectural style helped reassure home owners and investors that familiar patterns of residential organization would persist.

Identification of the organizational agents, institutional mechanisms, and design meanings of subdivision developments clarifies how a distinctive pattern of built form—the entrepreneurial vernacular—was constructed and became widespread. The entrepreneurial vernacular consolidated numerous strands of social and architectural development. Insofar as the entrepreneurial vernacular was innovative, it was as a particular distillation of these strands and their synthesis as distinctive residential environments.

PART I

THREE SUBDIVISIONS AND THEIR BUILDERS

CHAPTER 1

THE FORD HOMES

The Case of the Borrowed Builders

Architect, building-craftsman, developer—which of these three groups was, in the case of the Ford Homes, the *builder*? The source of the ambiguity here lies in the use of the term in general, not just in relation to the Ford Homes. Traditionally, the builder was the artisan, or building-craftsman; today, the developer typically is referred to as the builder, although the term can also apply, especially on smaller jobs, to building-workers. By the turn of the twentieth century, *builder* had already become a contested term. This reflected conflicts among those involved in the production of buildings, conflicts that arose from the transformation of the nature of labor in the construction industry. Thus, in order to understand who were the builders of subdivision developments such as the Ford Homes in the 1920s, we need to consider not only the personnel involved in each individual project but also each group's historical relationship to housing construction and to the other groups involved in residential construction.

This chapter examines the building-craftsman's history, since the workforce assembled to construct the Ford Homes epitomizes the process by which craftsmen were replaced by less-skilled building-workers. This housing project literally borrowed its workforce from Ford's nearby factories, signaling the diminished role that skilled construction labor had come to play in the production process. By tracing the historical changes in the nature of building-craftsmen's work, it is possible to see how the evolution of building practices made the Ford Homes labor arrangement possible.

In a sense, the Ford Homes subdivision borrowed its developer, too. The Dearborn Realty & Construction Company, charged with the construction of the Ford Homes, was established by Henry Ford and his close associates to provide housing near Ford plants in Dearborn, just west of Detroit. Ford and his associates were not building company housing, nor were they professional real-estate developers. Rather, they intended the tract of 250 modest single-family houses to demonstrate to real-estate professionals the benefits of applying industrialized building methods to the problem of subdivision development. At a time when realtors were constituting themselves as a profession, the Ford Homes developers focused on some of the same issues of efficiency and organization that real-estate developers were concerned with as part of their claim to professional status. The ability of Ford and his associates to draw on their manufacturing experience to organize efficient housing construction reinforces the view that construction problems had become sufficiently abstract by the 1920s that building-craftsmen, despite their hands-on knowledge and experience, could be displaced from the central role in building.

Before examining the history and design of the project and how these shifting relations of production are evident in the Ford Homes subdivision, it is useful to step back and look at the social and historical context to which it was a response, and at some of its architect's ideas about housing development.

The Ford Homes: Background and Overview

Detroit is the fourth link in a chain of cities that grew in size in response to the expansion of manufacturing beginning in the last quarter of the nineteenth century.[1] From Pittsburgh to the lakeshore cities of Buffalo, Cleveland, Detroit, and Milwaukee, the westward spread of industry resulted in the successive transformation of these settlements into metropolitan areas. Still a compact "walking city" at the turn of the century, even its boundaries accessible on foot, Detroit grew at an accelerating rate over the next three decades.[2] By the middle of the 1920s, it was the fastest growing metropolitan area in the United States, and it had become the fourth largest.

A range of industries, from stove manufacturing to pharmaceuticals, contributed to Detroit's early growth, but the 1903 founding of the Ford Motor Company initiated the development of what would become the "Motor City." Detroit would probably in any case have shared proportionately in the trend of population flow to urban, industrial areas in these decades, but the growth of the new automobile industry ensured that the city would become a magnet for thousands of people. Of the 528,000 that more than doubled Detroit's population to 994,000 between 1910 and 1920, roughly four-fifths were newcomers to the area from elsewhere in the United States and abroad.[3] They were drawn to Detroit by the evident need of this young industry for workers, expressed in news stories about ever-increasing production, or in ads and flyers distributed by the Ford company in poorer, less-industrialized states to entice migration northward. Ford's notorious creation of the five-dollars-a-day wage in 1914, in the middle of the winter of a year of economic depression, lured tens of thousands of people to the city before it became clear that this largesse was not intended for all.[4] The industrial boom created by World War I added to the incentives for moving to Detroit.

In 1918, Dearborn, just west of Detroit, still had the appearance of a country village with scattered clusters of houses dotting acres of farmland.[5] The only industrial intrusions into its rural landscape were the tracks of the Michigan Central Railroad, heading westward toward Chicago from the center of Detroit, and the Henry Ford & Son tractor plant. Ford had built this plant in 1915, south of the tracks, and by 1918 it employed about four thousand men.[6] Because little housing was available nearby, many of these workers had to undertake long commutes to their jobs from expensive rented quarters in Detroit that cost as much as $75 per week.[7] In 1919, Henry Ford supported the idea of building housing in Dearborn itself to ameliorate this problem and to promote cost-effective construction in this period of building inactivity following World War I. The Dearborn Realty & Construction Company, established for the creation of Ford's housing development, bought a tract of land west of the tractor plant and built 250 houses between 1919 and 1921, before itself succumbing to the vagaries of the general economy (fig. 2). By September 1920, the tractor plant had foundered, as agriculture entered a decade-long depression. The plant was dismantled, its machinery and workforce moved to the River Rouge works under construction farther to the east in Dearborn.[8] Home sales in the Ford subdivision slowed, and

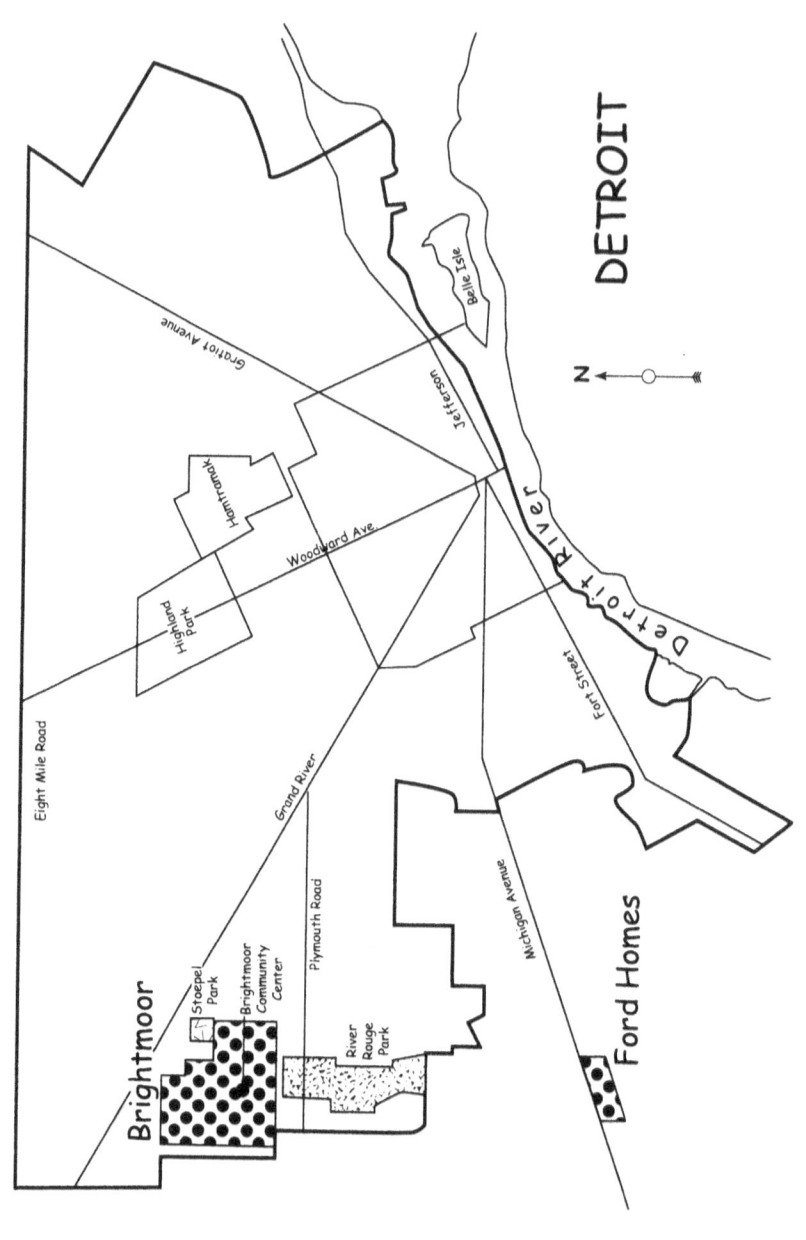

new building ceased. A second project that Ford considered in the years 1918–1920 for a more elaborate scheme called Fordson Village, to the east of the Ford Homes, was abandoned, probably owing to the downturn in the economy.[9] By the time Ford's Rouge plant was completed, the construction industry had revived and Dearborn shared in the house-building boom of the mid 1920s. Ford's involvement with housing provision was no longer necessary.

Although Ford supported the Dearborn housing project, it is not clear that he initiated it. He had certainly been interested in the mass production of dwellings from at least 1913, when he considered building houses according to the system patented by his friend Thomas Edison in 1908. Edison's scheme, which involved pouring concrete into reusable cast-iron molds, produced a house in six hours, though four more days were needed to allow the concrete to harden. Interest in his idea was great, and the national press tracked its evolution beginning in 1906. Though Edison conceived this as a solution to urban housing ills, one early skeptic connected it with another industrial product when he reported that "Mr. Edison says that he is going to make it possible to build a $25,000 house for $500 by simply forcing concrete into molds. Many people hope, however, that he will give us that $500 automobile first."[10] In 1914, another newspaper account announced that "Henry Ford, the automobile builder, wants 3,000 [houses]" to be built using a variation of Edison's technique, substituting steel for cast-iron molds.[11] Although Ford had abandoned this technology by the time he embarked on the Dearborn project, it is certainly possible that this venture was inspired by what one scholar has described as Edison's "ability to apply industrial concepts to housing; he understood that the efficiencies and economies

---

Figure 2. Map of Detroit showing locations of the Ford Homes and Brightmoor, both within the metropolitan area. The map also shows the relative distance of each subdivision from the Highland Park and Hamtramck industrial hubs. The Henry Ford and Son Tractor plant was to the east of the Ford Homes, as are the River Rouge works.

inherent in mass production could benefit working-class families."[12] The Ford Homes demonstrated a similar lesson.

Ford's interest in community development antedated his attraction to Edison's scheme. In August 1891 he joined the Citizens' Committee of Fifty to promote the development of Oakwood, south of the area that would become the site of the Rouge plant.[13] Almost thirty years later, the need for affordable housing in this region was much more pressing.

In his reminiscences, E. G. Liebold, Ford's personal secretary and the president of the Dearborn Realty & Construction Company, claims to have proposed the Ford Homes venture.[14] It is also highly possible that the architect Albert Wood, who worked for Ford on an earlier Detroit project, the Henry Ford Hospital, before becoming the Ford Homes designer, introduced the idea to Ford. Wood's contribution to the project, as built, is not emphasized in contemporary published accounts, and perhaps any role he might have played in initially fostering it may have been glossed over as well. His interest in housing, however, is evident from a booklet entitled "Community Homes" that he wrote and had privately printed in 1918.[15] In this work, Wood sketches the great immediate need for decent housing and proposes models for single-family residential developments. Because there are no documents that establish whether Ford or the members of the Dearborn Realty & Construction Company were aware either of Wood's booklet or of Wood's strong interest in the housing issue, it is impossible to credit him with the inspirational role in the development of the housing scheme that was actually built. But this remains a provocative possibility, given the booklet. What program for housing did Wood set out in "Community Homes," and how close to realizing it did the Ford Homes come?

Writing before the 1918 Armistice and in the context of the demand for housing created by the war industries' sudden need for thousands of additional workers, Wood favored placing the responsibility for housing development with independent agencies. He argued against the formation of a central authority, either governmental or corporate, to control the provision of housing. The existence of such authorities, which he considered "autocratic" and "paternalistic," undermined, he felt, the "true spirit of democracy."[16] Wood also stressed the importance of providing hygienic housing. He had found, while working on the Henry Ford Hospital, under construction at the time of his writing, that "thousands of families live among disease-breeding surroundings while fortunes are spent in the erection of hospitals which are mostly monuments to our inefficient methods of combating disease."[17] He also emphasized the formative moral role that decent housing can play, referring both to the recent success of the Prohibition movement and to the achievements of Hull House. The latter served as a model for instilling democratic, spiritual, and moral virtues within the home and the neighborhood. Indeed, Wood was not alone in his appreciation of the Chicago settlement house; B. E. Taylor, the developer of the Brightmoor subdivision in Detroit, established a settlement house there. Such a presence, and such a model for development, may be unexpected in residential suburban tracts. The larger context that made this plausible will be clarified in chapter 4.

Along with centralized authority, Wood also rejected the wasteful system of speculative subdividing and building and the inefficiency that results from jousting among prospective home owners, contractors, and architects. Instead, he proposed development, or stock, companies that would allow people who otherwise could not afford to buy homes to do so. By joining together, they would especially enjoy the advantage of scale that would increase efficiency and bring down the costs of house building.[18] Short of the establishment of development companies, he wrote, "the few farsighted real estate operators who are making it their business to plan and develop a property in its entirety, from the subdivision of the acreage to the completion of all the improvements, including the houses, should be encouraged."[19]

The scheme that Wood offered in his booklet "Community Homes" to demonstrate his ideas built upon the already widespread, grid-derived rectangular block as the design unit as well as the social and, ultimately, political unit (fig. 3). He was not concerned in this text with the design of individual houses but with the organization of a neighborhood and its services in an extendable, modular form. Within a block in which ten to thirteen single-family houses, depending on

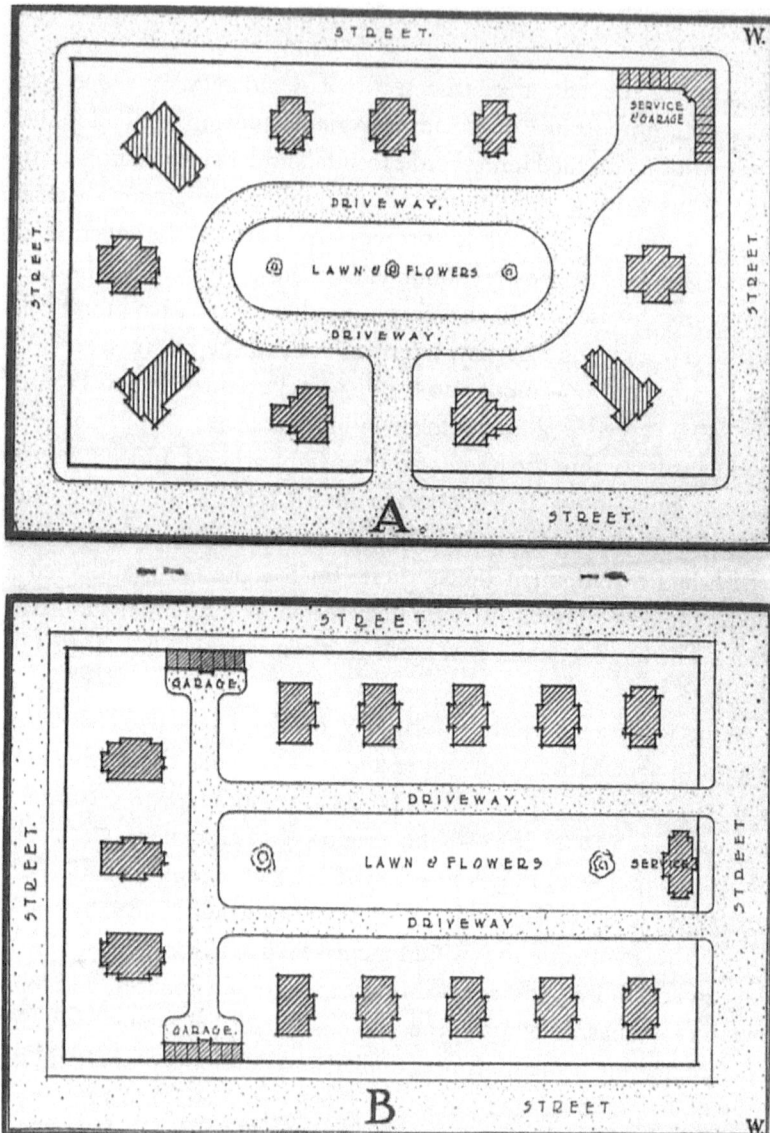

Figure 3. Albert Wood, architect for the Ford Homes, published these diagrams for clustered housing in his 1918 pamphlet "Community Homes." The layouts show ways to reorganize the typical block to create a sense of community among neighbors. Shared amenities include landscaped islands, the services of a caretaker, and a bank of garages. In their abstraction from local topography and house design, Wood's diagrams reflect the period's tendency to create models capable of being adapted to diverse local conditions.

costs, marked the perimeter, a common landscaped court was set aside for general use and as a protected children's play area. Garages were clustered, eliminating the need for individual driveways. A service building was included that would house a caretaker who would run the centralized heating plant and garbage incinerator and who would serve as a sort of concierge for the block, taking deliveries and providing other services for the housing group. Wood thought that the block might even develop beyond a functional unit into a civic unit: "If the scheme included a large number of adjacent blocks, the owners could, by appointing a representative from each block, secure a committee who would thoroughly understand the requirements and be competent to provide for the advantageous development of schools, playgrounds, civic centers, and other necessary improvements. And why could we not develop a better, more efficient, community political system as a result of this co-operation?"[20]

Wood's ideas were not unique in this period. His scheme reflects many of the same ideals that shaped, for example, Clarence A. Perry's neighborhood unit plan, which had not yet been published. Rather, what is significant about Wood's proposals is the fact that they do share a number of the assumptions that characterized contemporary housing discussions.

The Ford Homes project certainly did not fulfill the ideal sketched in "Community Homes." But it is possible that Wood's convictions regarding the centrality of decent housing to the physical and moral well-being of American citizens may have appealed to Ford as yet another challenge to his ability to get things done, and contributed to the decision to support the undertaking.

Wood's ideas may have affected the Ford Homes project in other ways. He may have influenced the institution of the policy whereby Ford employees received preference as house buyers, but nonemployees were also encouraged to buy homes there. Writing to a business correspondent in 1919, Wood explained that this policy was intended to avoid creating the feeling of a company town.[21] Albert Wood himself moved into one of the first houses to be completed in 1919, and he lived there until 1925. The head of mechanical work for the project, Harry C. Vicary, also bought one of the houses and lived there until 1978.²² George Ebling, Ford's industrial and family photographer, bought one of the houses, and his descendants lived there as recently as 1990.²³ Prices were too high for unskilled workers to afford, ranging from $6,750 to $7,750 in 1919, a figure that by the middle of 1920, when costs increased, had risen to $8,750 to $9,550.²⁴ Selling prices of the houses included 10 percent of the materials, labor, and overhead costs as profit; they were sold directly to purchasers, without the involvement of banks, at the customary rate of 6 percent interest. By the end of 1921, the houses were not selling as quickly and prices may have fallen, but full financial records for the development have not survived.

These prices are considerably higher than the average contemporary cost of a new single-family house in the United States, which was $4,320 in 1920 and $3,972 in 1921, according to housing reformer Leifur Magnusson.²⁵ They are also somewhat higher than prices in a comparable development for auto workers in Flint, Michigan, built in the same years by General Motors. There, prices ranged from $3,500 to $8,500, with the majority selling for $5,000–5,500.²⁶

Wood's claim for the efficiency of large-scale projects undertaken by a single developer also would have complemented Ford's general outlook and approach to his endeavors. The Dearborn Realty & Construction Company was organized according to the pattern of "the few far-sighted real estate operators" that Wood commended. Although the final profits over its twenty-four years of existence seem to have amounted to more than $600,000,²⁷ an early statement by the developers asserted that "this is strictly a non-profit plan. We are interested solely in enabling our workmen to live in Dearborn without paying the excess tax which all real-estate speculation imposes on home buyers."²⁸ The sole restriction that applied to the buyer, stipulating that the house could not be resold for at least seven years, was also intended to eliminate the possibility of speculative activity.

The company's reservation of the right to buy back a house within the first seven years of occupancy if the buyer was considered to be "undesirable" reflected the tradition of surveillance in Ford's enterprises more than it advanced Wood's vision of civic development.²⁹

And the two social improvements that the company committed itself to—provisions that would have reflected Wood's conception of the needs that a neighborhood committee might undertake to redress—were only partially carried out. One was a park and playground area, originally allocated to the strip of land at the northern boundary of the tract, bordering the Michigan Central Railroad tracks. This aspect of the project was never completed, and the area remained undeveloped, without special equipment or landscaping. However, this did not prevent it from functioning, at least minimally, as an open and informal green space.

The Dearborn Realty & Construction Company did contract with the school district to build an elementary school: Southwestern (now DuVall) School, at Beech and Military, opened in September 1921. It had ten classrooms to serve the subdivision and to relieve overcrowding elsewhere in the school district. By 1928, 320 children were attending grades kindergarten through six. Contemporary ideas about the importance of such facilities to neighborhood design will be explored later, but it is worth noting here the limited community role conceived for this school. While it met the minimal needs of the schoolchildren, it was not originally equipped with a gymnasium, a library, or a kitchen to prepare hot food.[30]

The establishment of community amenities was not a priority for the Ford Homes developers; they placed greater emphasis on providing modern services. Electricity and telephone connections reached each home from utility poles located in alleys behind the houses. Streetlight wiring ran underground, following the progressive "boulevard" lighting system. As one might anticipate, the design of curbs was carefully considered; they were curved so that auto tires would not rub against them. And house purchasers were given the option of requesting construction of a garage.

The promise of the Dearborn Realty & Construction Company as the sort of agency Wood had had in mind when he wrote "Community Homes" was not met, then, by many aspects of the Ford Homes project. But what of the design of the subdivision as a whole, and of the design of the houses? Although documentary accounts of the project often refer to design ideas inspired by Henry Ford or by Liebold, who authored many of these accounts, Wood's contribution is never emphasized.

The Ford Homes: Design and Construction

Although he was still a young architect, Wood was well prepared by 1918 for the Ford Homes commission. Albert Gardner Wood Jr. was born in New York City in 1886.[31] His father was a builder and cabinetmaker, his mother a teacher and pianist. Wood attended Bunker Hill Grammar School in Boston, then apprenticed as a carpenter with his father. At seventeen, he traveled to the Pacific Coast and worked in a variety of locations, eventually joining the architectural office of A. Warren Gould in Seattle.

Gould's background, like Wood's, reflected an alternate route into the profession, one that contrasted with the educational program set out by the architectural elite. Gould (no relation to Seattle architect Carl Gould) had had no academic architectural training; his background was in building and contracting.[32] He worked in Boston in the late 1890s and arrived in Seattle in 1903, around the same time as Wood. It is not known whether the two had had any contact before Wood entered the firm. Gould's practice specialized in the design of office blocks, through which he introduced new steel-frame and ferroconcrete building techniques to Seattle. This would have prepared Wood for the institutional commissions he took on in Detroit. Gould also had an interest in civic planning.

While he worked for Gould, Wood studied architecture at night school and through correspondence courses; when he left Seattle, he had progressed from draftsman to designer and then to associate of the firm. He moved to Detroit sometime after 1912 and worked in an architectural office where one of the clients was Henry Ford. When Ford began plans for the Henry Ford Hospital, he hired Wood for the job. Often referred to in Ford records as chief of construction for this project, Wood also was its architect.[33] He became a member of the American Institute of Architects in 1919.[34] After his work on the Ford Homes, Wood left Ford to establish his own firm in Detroit; his commissions included houses, schools, and hospitals in the region. He moved to New York in 1932, where he continued to work as an architect and, in 1934, founded an interior design and crafts firm, Albert Wood and Five Sons, that continued until 1988 to specialize in the design of church and synagogue interiors. Wood died in 1970.

Given this background, and his developed interest in housing, Wood was ready to design the 250 Ford Homes, a commission he carried out between late 1918 and the beginning of construction in May 1919. Between May and November 1919, 94 houses were built; the remaining 156 were constructed in 1920, with some of the work possibly carrying over to 1921. As in the consideration of the genesis of the scheme to build housing, so too in the attempt to assign responsibility for design concepts: the records permit only speculation that some of the ideas for which Ford and Liebold took credit were influenced by Wood's suggestions. At the very least, however, he was responsible for the integration of his colleagues' desires into workable and competent designs.

The land bought by the Dearborn Realty & Construction Company for their housing project had already been subdivided. Wood was presented with a preexisting grid of nine blocks interrupted by alleys and divided into lots that measured typically 50 by 125 feet. The only device used by the developers to shape the organization of houses so as to avoid uniformity and create smaller clusters of neighbors was to set houses at staggered intervals from the street. Groups of three or four houses were placed alternately twenty-four and thirty-two feet from the street, but all aligned parallel to it. Liebold claimed that this had been his idea, although it is clear from "Community Homes" that Wood had been interested in ways to cluster houses.[35]

From the beginning, Liebold stated, the developers intended to avoid "the error of other towns where rows of houses, all looking alike, giv[e] a monotonous tone to the neighborhood."[36] To achieve this end, three strategies were used: (1) Wood designed six different models of houses; (2) the models were allocated to lots in a varied order; and (3) several exterior claddings and colors of roofing shingles were used. The second strategy meant that the purchaser could select the house model, but not necessarily the lot. The exteriors were wood clapboard siding in two widths, brick veneer, or cedar shingles, and combinations of these.

The diversity achieved in these ways was balanced by the scheme's overall design unity and by the use of modular elements to organize the design of the facades. Wood used simplified colonial forms to articulate the surfaces and the massing of the houses (figs. 4–9). Their rectangular boxiness was relieved by bold, asymmetrical rooflines, accented by large, unified dormer windows, gables, and a centrally placed chimney. The few decorative features chosen conveyed economically the aura of colonial style: shutters flank second-floor windows facing the street; small fanlights mark the attic; columns or pilastered posts frame the porch; a carved hood in either an arched or pedimented form marks the front entrance; and wood trim—around doors and windows and, especially, in a broad band above the first-floor windows—unified each composition. Colonial elements such as these were in wide use by this period.

The six models that Wood developed were referred to simply by letter designations, reminiscent of the familiar tags for early Ford automobiles. Wood created these models by juggling the shapes and orientation of the roof and by manipulating the basic modular elements of the first-story elevation. He pivoted the roof, setting the gable either parallel with or perpendicular to the street, and used cross-gables, dormers, and modified hipped roofs to vary the massing of the houses. These features complicate the roof-line silhouettes, adding visual interest to the otherwise broad and planar surfaces.

The basic modular elements of the first-story elevation consist of the entrance, porch, and windows. Wood varied their placement and relationships, and the number of windows, to produce six different combinations of these elements.

The plans of all models correspond to the notion of the small, efficient house that had evolved from the turn of the century.[37] Thirteen houses were built with four bedrooms, using a variant of model D. All the others had three bedrooms. The dimensions of the master bedroom averaged fifteen by ten feet, and the smaller bedrooms were about ten by ten feet. The single bathroom, which like the bedrooms was on the second floor, measured about eight by four feet; it was tiled and fitted with porcelain-enameled, cast-iron fixtures (fig. 10). This equipment, its arrangement, and the tiling of bathroom surfaces had become typical by World War I, although built-in bathtubs began to replace footed tubs in the 1920s.[38] On the first floor, the living room, with fireplace, averaged twelve by eighteen feet, the dining room about ten by fifteen feet (fig. 11). The kitchen was about ten by twelve feet, a size typical for the period (fig. 12). A small entrance vestibule and the porch completed the array of rooms, which conformed to the complement of rooms recommended for a laborer's cottage by contemporary experts in household economics.[39] All houses had full basements. Every model contained these elements, although the arrangement of spaces varied. As Liebold recalled, "they were all based on one central plan and just altered in details."[40]

The flexible plan for interiors and the modular system that Wood used to generate the range of house models constitute his major contributions to this subdivision scheme. The other housing issues and ideas that animated him in "Community Homes" did not figure in the Ford Homes project. Clearly, the Dearborn Realty & Construction Company valued Wood's ability to design housing that could be produced efficiently. This criterion is evident as well in the construction process and personnel marshaled for the project. Looking more closely at these aspects of the development, it becomes clear just how central a concern efficiency was and why so few of Wood's ideas came to fruition in the project.

The Dearborn Realty & Construction Company was incorporated on January 10, 1919. Henry Ford was not officially involved in the firm, possibly so that the project "could succeed on its own merit"[41] rather than through the influence of Ford's presence, but his connections to it were never in doubt. E. G. Liebold, Ford's personal secretary, was the president of the company, and Edsel Ford, his son, was vice president.

By April 1919, the Dearborn Realty & Construction Company purchased 312 lots in a subdivision west of the Ford tractor plant. The entire tract had been bought in 1890 by J. B. Molony, who immediately subdivided it into 502 lots, measuring for the most part, as noted above, 50 by 125 feet, on nine blocks divided by eight sixty-

Figure 4. Model A (*above*) of the Ford Homes presents in their purest form the elements that architect Albert Wood manipulated to create the subdivision's panoply of houses. The gable that faces the street embraces the second-story windows. On one side, the smooth slope of the pitched roof is uninterrupted; on the other side, a cross-gable rises from the first floor and intersects the main mass. The modular elements of the first-story elevation are present in their simplest form: entrance, windows, and porch.

Figure 5. Model B (*top right*) compresses the modular pattern used in Model A. At the first-story level, two of the three modules are superimposed; thus, this model reads visually as two modules wide. The porch is located within the perimeter of the house, as a kind of loggia, with the entrance set at its rear. The gable faces the street but is treated asymmetrically, emphasizing the reduction of the width of the house by one module.

Figure 6. Model C (*bottom right*) also compresses the three modules of Model A into a two-module-wide facade. Windowed doors are set at the back of the broad porch. The roofline is rotated so that the slope of the roof with its centralized dormer presents a symmetrical image to the street side.

Figure 7. Model D (*above*) contains aspects of both the compressed variation (models B and C) and the expanded version (models E and F). It includes two sets of window modules, but its entrance is placed within a loggia-like corner porch. The truncated hipped roof is broken by a projecting flattened gable on one side of the street facade, underscoring its asymmetry.

Figure 8. Model E (*top right*) expands the modular pattern found in Model A. Two sets of first-story windows flank the entrance, one large and one small. This asymmetry is reinforced by the modified hipped roof, which extends over the porch to embrace it within the silhouette of the main mass of the house.

Figure 9. Model F (*bottom right*) stretches the configuration used in Model A by setting large windows on both sides of the entrance. A pitched roof is superimposed on the hipped roof; the truncated gable end visually joins the porch to the body of the house.

Figure 10. A typical bathroom (*above*) from the Ford Homes. Bathrooms, located on the second floor, used standardized fittings.

Figure 11. The typical Ford Homes living room (*top right*) included a fireplace, oak floors, and wood trim. All materials were standardized and assembled in shops located at the building site.

Figure 12. The typical Ford Homes kitchen (*bottom right*), with built-in cabinets, measured ten by twelve feet and was standard for the period.

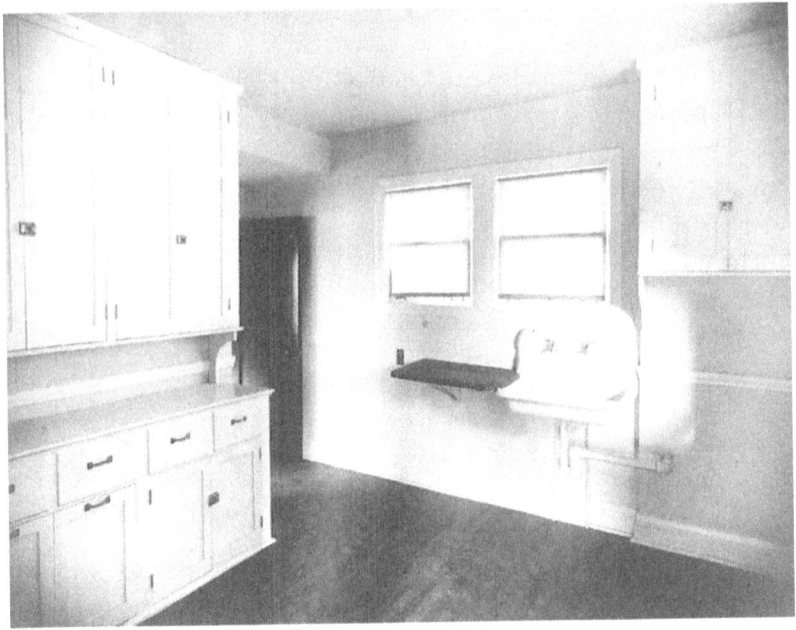

THREE SUBDIVISIONS AND THEIR BUILDERS

foot-wide streets and including twenty-foot alleys in the center of each block.[42] Only a few of these lots had been sold when, in 1898, the previous owner of the land foreclosed on Molony's unpaid deed. In 1910, the land was bought by Henry Ford, from whom the Dearborn Realty & Construction Company subsequently purchased it.

The workforce for the construction of the subdivision was drawn from the ranks of Ford employees. At any one time, from 250 to 500 men were at the work site. Some of them had worked on earlier Ford construction projects, such as the recently completed Henry Ford Hospital in Detroit.[43] As Liebold wrote, "This is in accord with Mr. Ford's belief that men ought to spend part of the year outside factory walls."[44]

Once the project was under way, the first structure to be built was the office, located on Nowlin between the railroad tracks and Park Street.[45] In the next block of Nowlin, between Park and Nona, a planing mill, lumber warehouse, and plumbing and tin shop were erected. Brick, lumber, piping, and ducts for the heating system were bought in bulk and transported to the site on the Michigan Central tracks. In the shops, these materials were cut to standardized sizes and then taken to the building sites in narrow-gauge railway cars pulled by horses. The windows, casings, moldings, frames, doors, and fixtures were completely standardized and were assembled in the shops.

The purchase of materials in bulk and the standardization of parts reduced costs. According to one account, "$300 is being saved on the heating systems alone in each home, while the economy in lumber construction will be even greater."[46] Such savings helped offset the cost of the relatively high-quality materials that were used, such as oak flooring, which was installed until it was judged too costly, and a steel beam that was employed in each basement to support the superstructure.

Construction was organized according to the principles of assembly-line production. "Each crew has its own specialized work to do on a house," Liebold wrote in a 1919 *Detroit Journal* article. "In this way, experts in their particular line are kept entirely on their own work, making both for efficient construction and speed."[47] An excavation crew first dug the basements, using Ford tractors. A second crew laid the foundations. This crew was followed by one responsible for erecting the framework (fig. 13). Next, the interior finishing crew saw to the installation of plumbing and heating fixtures, electrical wiring, glazing, trim, and painting. The last crew finished the exterior, including landscaping. Liebold summed it up: "That was mass production applied to building."[48]

Far from contributing to the overall design of the subdivision or its individual houses, the workers employed to construct the Ford Homes were only peripherally connected to building trades at all. Borrowed from their regular jobs in Ford's factories, assigned to specialized tasks on the construction site, they contributed their manual labor in quantifiable units of time on the site and units of materials processed. Did the Dearborn Realty & Construction Company transform housing construction with this project, as Ford had transformed the nature of work in general with the introduction of the assembly line to automobile production?

The developers of the Ford Homes were in fact taking advantage of changes that had occurred in the building process over a number of decades. Moreover, they were not alone in observing these changes. Their recognition that the role now open to the traditional building-craftsman was circumscribed is echoed, for example, from a very different perspective, in a contemporary observation by the writer of a *House and Garden* article entitled "Local Materials and Local Labor." In this piece, the prospective home owner is urged to express her individuality not by imposing favorite historicist styles on inappropriate environments—"building a Spanish Mission villa in a New England village"—but through sensitivity to the characteristics of local building types and materials. Yet, while the virtues of searching out and respecting a prevailing local heritage are extolled, the writer assures the reader that this will not mean dependency on potentially idiosyncratic local builders. "Today, from the nature of the newer order of specialization in the building trades, local labor is generally no more than incidental."[49] The ironies of this fact were lost on the writer, but they accurately reflect the process of rationalization that integrated builders within a nationally controlled supply network developed over the preceding hundred years.

THREE SUBDIVISIONS AND THEIR BUILDERS

Figure 13. This view of the early stage of Ford Homes construction indicates the orderly succession of specialized crews, who were assigned to excavate, lay foundations, frame, and finish rows of houses. Horse-drawn, narrow-gauge railway cars brought materials, precut and assembled, from on-site shops to the building site.

In the course of the nineteenth century, the process of building changed, the identity of builders was transformed, and the relationship between builders and other figures involved in construction became more complex. Many of the changes that occurred in building and in the role of builders first took place and had their strongest impact in the field of commercial construction, especially in connection with the rise of skyscrapers, where the effects of new technologies and new materials were most visibly dramatic. Nevertheless, the trends that intensified with the introduction of skyscraper construction had been in evidence for several decades; as large-scale residential development became a more general practice, the impact of rationalized building procedures also became more widespread. The combined effects of industrialization—mechanization, standardization, and specialization of construction practices—changed builders' work.

The Development of Industrialized Building

The route toward industrialized building begins with the balloon frame, created in the Midwest in the 1830s.[50] This new framing system relied on the ability of the steam-powered circular saw to produce thin lengths of wood rapidly and in quantity, combined with the availability of machine-cut nails manufactured from rolled iron plates. In contrast to traditional timber framing, with its heavier members and hand-cut joinery, balloon framing not only reduced building loads and the total amount of wood needed for a frame but also required less labor to erect. Over the succeeding decades, refinements were made to the details of balloon-frame construction, culminating in the 1920s when the western, or platform, frame began to supplant it.[51] An offspring of balloon framing, the western frame had been developed around the period of the Gold Rush in California. Instead of using studs that ran the full height of the structure, western framing treated each floor as a self-sufficient, stackable unit. This system established an eight-foot vertical module and made construction even faster (fig. 14).

Although significant, in itself the balloon frame was not responsible for the industrialization of building, despite its reliance upon standardization and mechanization. As vernacular architecture scholar Dell Upton notes, balloon framing can be seen as "another in the lengthy list of popular adaptations of traditional practices."[52] Craft traditions were not static; they embraced improved techniques that increased flexibility and labor efficiency. Some of the elements of balloon framing had been used since the seventeenth century, so it was possible for nineteenth-century craftsmen to see "the new forms . . . as modifications of the old."[53]

Furthermore, recent scholars of regional building practices have found that where local markets were large enough to support mass production of building parts, carpenters established steam-powered

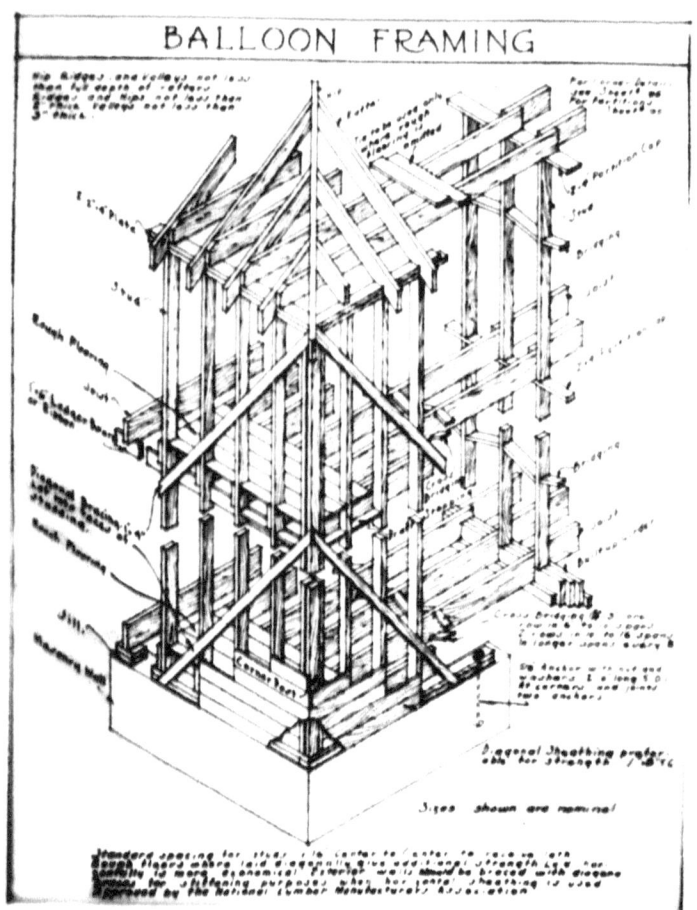

Figure 14. The balloon frame was developed in the 1830s to take advantage of new industrial processes that produced lighter, thinner lengths of wood and cheaper nails. It supplanted traditional timber framing, becoming the most widespread method of housing construction and continuing to be refined into the 1920s. This illustration from the April 1923 issue of *Building Age* indicates its basic principles. The standardization and mechanization that balloon-frame construction promoted laid the basis for the evolution of industrialized building practices following the Civil War.

factories for the manufacture of window sash and blinds as early as the 1840s.[54] These evolved from the earlier practice on the part of some carpenters of laying in a stock of "shop work," consisting of window sash, venetian blinds, panel doors, and other items, for their own use as well as for sale to others. From the 1820s on, such work was produced with the aid of a steady accumulation of specialized woodworking machines, created by both mechanics and carpenters.[55] The introduction and continuous refinement of planing machines, molding machines, lathes, and numerous other mechanical devices attest to carpenters' interest in reducing repetitive labor.

Balloon framing and woodworking machinery provided the necessary technological basis for the evolution from craft to industrialized building practices. But the pace and quality of the changes that these early developments toward mechanization and standardization introduced were initially controlled by craftsmen and the needs of the relatively small markets they served. Tendencies toward standardization and mechanization in the mid nineteenth century were fully exploited only in the years following the Civil War. At that point, with the general increase in industrial and overall economic development in the last third of the century, rationalized practices penetrated the building process more profoundly than they had through either the invention of the balloon frame or the introduction of woodworking machinery into local shops.

Thus, the 1888 *Report of the 10th Census on Power and Machinery Used in Manufacturing* found that, after 1871, woodworking machinery had displaced thousands of carpenters.[56] The transformation of labor-saving devices that had evolved through craft processes into labor-eliminating ones that were themselves mass-produced took place once an efficient transportation network ensured access to widened markets. This occurred with the establishment of the rail system, which allowed not only lumber but, even more importantly, finished wood—trim, sashes, and other building parts—to be sent great distances cheaply and safely. Rail transport supplanted the former method of transporting lumber along waterways, which damaged finished wood. Also, with the spread of rail transport in the 1880s and 1890s, species other than the ubiquitous white pine became marketable; unlike white pine, woods such as ash, oak, hickory, and maple do not readily float.[57] Taking advantage of this revolution in wood transportation, lumber companies increasingly installed woodworking machinery and expanded their production to include finish work in a wider selection of woods. Diversification to create more products also stimulated further invention; of the twenty-five hundred patents for saw and mill improvements on record in 1895, more than seven hundred were filed in the decade of the 1870s, and more than eight hundred in the ten years from 1885 to 1895.[58]

Economic expansion through diversification, however, also led to the concentration of the industry, for the increased costs of such machinery put smaller mills out of business.[59] The value of the goods produced at the 31,560 sawmills recorded in the 1840 census was only $400 per mill. Diversification allowed lumber companies to increase the value of their raw materials, first in the Great Lakes states and then, as timber resources were consumed, along the Pacific Coast. In 1884 in the West, "rough lumber hardly paid its cost, but the application of skilled labor and machinery in the process of planing increased the value of this same lumber by 100 percent, in the manufacture of doors by 200 percent, in the manufacture of sash 300 percent, and in the production of mouldings 500 percent."[60]

The impact of machine-made woodwork on builders was obvious to many, but one 1895 writer expressed the situation succinctly: "Indeed, the very houses that shelter us no longer represent the skill of the joiner, for the mill has usurped his place, and the carpenter only assembles its work."[61]

The large, diversified mill both supplanted the builder and transformed the nature of his work. By manufacturing standardized doors, windows, trim, moldings, and other woodwork, the lumber companies deprived the craftsman of work he had performed in the winter, when on-site construction was not possible. Furthermore, woodworking machinery took little skill to operate and was often run, in the early years, by "greenhands"—women, children, and other unskilled laborers.[62] And, as machine-made materials became available, employers introduced piecework, paying builders not by the day but according to a quantity of work completed. Accompanying the move to piecework was the trend toward specialization, making routine for individual workmen the assembly or installation of machine-made windows, doors, floors, and trim.

The savings in labor and cost were great. One compound carver, or lathe, for instance, could replace sixty carpenters, and a planing machine could do in eighty-three minutes the amount of work that it took 110 hours to execute with a hand plane.[63] The output of each worker continued to increase as improvements were made to machinery—both at the mill and, with the introduction of power tools, on the site—and as there was further standardization of materials and specialization of work. The impact of these changes can be seen even as late as the 1920s when, between 1921 and 1928, productivity in contract construction increased 25 percent.[64]

For the craftsman, however, this process meant that his skills had become obsolete. Both the knowledge of complex calculations needed, for example, to build a staircase, and the subtle awareness of a wood's grain needed for hand drilling were unnecessary, once standardized elements were available from the mill and power tools were introduced.[65] Also, the craftsman's role became attenuated, since he primarily assembled or installed materials from the mill that formerly he had produced himself. Accordingly, with specialization, the builder's contribution to the conception and integration of the structure as a whole decreased.

Thus, although the invention of the balloon frame established the formal basis for standardization and mechanization, the particular course of development that these took was shaped by larger, more complex processes. And as the building-craftsman's work was transformed by industrialized construction practices, the definition of the builder was also changing, as were his relationships with others involved in building.

Relations of Production

The builder's identity was increasingly in flux. In the late-nineteenth century, ambiguity arises regarding whose activities are being referred to when the term *builder* occurs in the literature. The process of subdividing building practices into discrete, specialized tasks—one of the features of industrialization—also resulted in the differentiation of roles and the establishment of a new hierarchy. As the craftsman's responsibility for overall construction diminished, other people assumed control over the management and organization of building endeavors. The term *builder,* thereby, came to refer to the person who performed these latter tasks rather than the manual labor of construction.

The skills of the "practical builder" of preindustrial times, whether he was called a carpenter, housewright, mason, or mechanic, had been honed within the traditional, guild-based system that led from apprenticeship to the position of journeyman and then to master builder.[66] At its best, this system maintained an adequate supply of builders whose skills encompassed the entire range needed for construction, including the assessment of materials, the design of structures, and the organization of the work schedule, as well as knowledge of the techniques of building.

Strains within this system appeared in urban centers in the early years of the Republic, when increased land values led to higher building costs.[67] As master carpenters were unable to afford the entire cost of building projects, speculators arose as financial middlemen. Master carpenters then became labor contractors and, in the 1790s, the earliest journeymen's trade unions were founded. In labor disputes, however, it was not always clear who the employer was: was it the master carpenter–contractor or the middleman? Some master carpenters allied themselves with the speculators, others with the journeymen. Something of this ambiguity can be seen, for example, in an 1825 statement regarding a labor dispute addressed by some Boston middlemen to the journeymen on behalf of the contractors, and signed "Gentlemen Engaged in Building."[68] By the end of the century, the stratification of roles that was still variable in 1825 became more deeply entrenched, but the developer, or "builder," and the general contractor of the later period have their origins, it seems, in the financial middleman and master carpenter–contractor of the earlier one.

During the nineteenth century, many organizations formed to redress problems of pay, working hours, or itinerancy that affected building-workers. They tended to be both local in scope and short-lived. In 1881, however, the United Brotherhood of Carpenters and Joiners was created, a national union whose founder recognized that "only real national power . . . could cope with real national economic forces."[69] The union arose in response to the inroads industrialization had made in the transformation of building practices. The use of greenhands to run woodworking machinery and the imposition of piecework wages that resulted from the availability of standardized, machine-produced elements were among the primary issues that the union addressed. Its supporters well knew that "an Ohio machine threatened the Chicago carpenter and the Philadelphia carpenter equally."[70]

In the face of the loss of building-craftsmen's livelihoods caused by mechanization and standardization, the union attempted to preserve wages and jobs. Its founder, Peter J. McGuire, a Lassallian socialist, forged the union to spearhead the struggle for the eight-hour day in 1886; success in achieving reduced hours won new members and led to a lasting role for the union in the leadership of the American Federation of Labor, which McGuire helped establish. The importance attributed to this strategy can be seen in an incident in 1884 in which the union leadership denied a request from the Amalgamated Iron and Steel Workers that urged the union to discourage the increasing use of mass-produced steel nails since this new technology reduced steelworker employment. The General Executive Board replied that "while our Brotherhood sympathized with them, they did not deem it advisable to fight labor saving machinery, and recommended the Iron and Steel Workers to struggle for a reduction of the hours of labor to offset the evil."[71] If hours were reduced, more men would have to be hired to do the original amount of work, thus returning to the workforce those who had been laid off through mechanization.

In addition to saving carpenters' jobs through the eight-hour struggle, the union sought to preserve work that was threatened by the hiring of greenhands. In 1882, the craft qualifications for membership in the union referred only to carpenters and joiners; by 1886, "stair builders, millwrights, planing mill bench hands or cabinet makers engaged at carpenter work, or any carpenter running woodworking machinery were admitted."[72] By 1890, the union included twenty-one locals of planing mill hands, five locals of stair builders, and three locals of sash, blind, and door makers.[73] By embracing industrialized work, the union ensured that the workers so employed would receive carpenters' wages and work carpenters' hours; carpenters, thus, would be hired for the jobs instead of unskilled laborers. This goal continued to be pursued through the union's fight against dual unionism and through its struggle for union labeling of construction materials that guaranteed that union labor had been used in the mills.

These actions were successful, and through them the United Brotherhood of Carpenters and Joiners became the largest of the building trades unions. In a number of cities, including San Francisco, the Building Trades Council, under the leadership of the carpenters' union, became the voice for all labor around the turn of the century. And yet it is, at the least, a measure of the magnitude of the forces facing building-workers that the issue of jurisdiction became the preoccupation of the union in the early decades of the twentieth century. Although the union determined that, "once wood, it is always the right of the carpenter to install it, no matter what the new material is," it became impossible to predict what innovations might pose a challenge to the carpenters' jurisdiction.[74] As the union's general executive board acknowledged in 1915, "owing to the rapid change in the building industry in the last few years, the substitution of one material for another in construction work, as well as the methods of construction, a detailed statement of our claims today may need changing tomorrow or the next day."[75]

While the union protected the livelihoods of many of the workmen engaged in diverse aspects of the construction industry, it could do nothing to affect the splintering of builders' work that mechanization, standardization, and specialization created. Rather, it seems that by organizing the building-trades workers, the unions, of which the United Brotherhood of Carpenters and Joiners was the largest and most powerful, reflected the new division of labor that industrialized practices gave rise to. They implicitly ratified the separation of manual work from the managerial, financial, and design aspects of the building process.

As specialization increased and as new trades, such as plumbing and electrical work, arose, the need for overall coordination of the building process at the planning stage increased, too.[76] Depending upon the complexity and cost of the job, this managerial role was undertaken by contractors or developers. Both of these groups evolved in the course of the nineteenth century from their origins as master carpenters–contractors and speculators, respectively.

Contractors often allied themselves with building-workers. When the carpenters' union initiated its campaign against piecework, for example, contractors supported its efforts.[77] On smaller jobs, including the majority of nineteenth-century residential construction, there continued to be a certain fluidity between roles, carpenters especially having the opportunity to gain contracting experience.[78] As the scale of both commercial and residential projects grew, however, the line separating the roles of building-worker and contractor became less permeable.[79]

Developers, on the other hand, were generally consistent in their opposition to the claims of building-workers. In 1890 and 1891, for example, organized as an employers' group called the National Builders' Association, they defeated workers' efforts to win the eight-hour day in several cities.[80] As the name of this early organization suggests, this group also challenged the worker's role as a builder. At the same time that building-workers' jobs were becoming industrialized, developers increasingly took responsibility for the planning and financing of larger-scale developments. The skills needed for these activities had little to do with direct knowledge or experience of any particular building craft, but depended more on organizational and entrepreneurial acumen.

Modeling Efficient Development

Thus, by the end of the nineteenth century, the nature of construction practices had been transformed and a new system of stratification was evolving that reallocated control over the building process from the building-craftsman to the builder-entrepreneur. The professional rise to prominence of the latter will be considered later; for now, it is possible to see that the ability of the Dearborn Realty & Construction Company to employ the labor power of industrial workers to construct the Ford Homes resulted from the diminished role that traditional builders' skills and activities played in the construction process.

Nevertheless, given the very different kind of work involved, how well suited to their tasks were those employees who were drafted for Ford's building project? The borrowed builders remain anonymous, but two contemporary features suggest their competence despite the novelty of their work site. First, it is possible to speculate that some of these workers were familiar with the basics of housing construction as owner-builders.[81] These were often recent arrivals to the city for whom home ownership was a high priority; Detroit's newcomers included a high percentage of settlers with this goal. Second, it is useful to remember the diversity of job categories required for Ford's automotive operations. Painters, woodworkers, and electrical workers were employed along with steelworkers, molders, glassmakers, welders, and other more typically industrial craftsmen. Routine maintenance of Ford's factories included regular painting as well as cleaning; woodworkers were employed to build models; electricians worked on self-starters.[82] Thus, when the Dearborn Realty & Construction Company drew on the Ford automotive workforce, they may have relied upon their workers having at least cognate skills adequate for the job.

Deskilling due to specialization and mechanization did not eliminate craft skills altogether. It curtailed them and reduced the worker's ability to contribute to conceptual problem solving. This is reflected in the Ford Homes by the decisive role played by the Dearborn Realty & Construction Company. The developer set the parameters within which both building-workers and architect fulfilled their tasks.

Historical changes in the construction process that allowed for the employment of borrowed builders also affected the structures designed for this project. Extending the standardization inherent in balloon-frame construction, all materials, fittings, and trim were standardized and cut or assembled on site. The architect's use of a modular system to generate house designs accommodated this uniformity, while it varied the dwellings' massing, elevations, and surface textures to reduce monotony. The simplicity and legibility of the scheme's colonial revival vocabulary of architectural forms contributed to Wood's ability to balance standardization with the modular arrangement of parts.

The Ford Homes project was not the only development aimed at providing much-needed housing for factory workers and others in a community that was undergoing rapid growth through industrialization. The Modern Housing Corporation, a General Motors' subsidiary, for example, built 950 houses for workers in Flint in 1919 and 1920.[83] In these developments, the companies were taking up the slack for private developers during a period of building inactivity. W. C. Durant, president of General Motors, tried to reassure professional developers when he announced that the company would build houses in Flint: "Our whole purpose in taking up the enterprise is not to enter the real estate field in a competitive way, but rather to stimulate general activity in building to relieve congestion that must constantly grow worse unless the most radical steps are taken to overcome it."[84]

The Ford enterprise, like others, was intended neither to establish a company town nor as philanthropy. Rather than creating a model community in either the architectural or the social sense, the Ford scheme was intended as a model for realtor-developers. Perhaps influenced by the achievements of the federal government's housing projects built under the pressure of World War I for workers in war-related industries, and eager to ensure that construction revert in peacetime to the private sector, the Ford developers were concerned principally with issues of speed and numbers.[85] The goal was to streamline construction in order to produce more housing faster, enabling developers to reduce costs in time, labor, and materials without sacrificing amenities for the home owners. The process itself would put a brake on excessive speculation, it was felt, because the risks of building would be minimized by controlling the development of an entire neighborhood; profits would be guaranteed by the cost reductions resulting from this large-scale construction. By seizing opportunities inherent in the transformation of the construction process, the Ford Homes developers intended to demonstrate ways to control speculation. Were realtors to absorb this lesson, they argued, home owners, workers, industry, and society as a whole would benefit.

This may explain why most of Wood's proposals, as he formulated them in "Community Homes," were not realized in the Ford project. The developers were concerned more with highlighting trends in the production process than with experiments in community design. They wanted to create a demonstration project that would extend assembly-line procedures into a new industrial setting. The Ford Homes intended to put to the test the methods of production with which Ford's name was synonymous, and that many increasingly saw as applicable to the housing field. One architect noted in a 1920 article entitled "Standardized Small Houses," "The principle which Mr. Henry Ford has so successfully applied to the production of automobiles can be worked out for the homebuilder."[86] The processes of auto production had come to set the standard for all production, seizing the imaginations of creators in diverse fields. Where shortages existed, the efficiencies of rationalized production would create abundance. The Ford Homes responded to the clamor to solve the housing problem in just this way.

When Model A is mentioned, however, it calls to mind an ancestor of the Tin Lizzie, not one of the Ford Homes. Despite their sponsor, the Ford Homes claimed only local attention. Among other reasons for this is the fact that, by the 1920s, efforts to apply rationalized procedures to housing production were relatively widespread. The construction industry itself was already being reshaped by new technologies and methods of organizing production that were identified internationally by the 1920s as Fordist. The exceptional use of borrowed builders to construct the Ford Homes provides a window through which to view trends that were becoming typical.

CHAPTER 2

BRIGHTMOOR

The Case of the Absent Architect

The use of borrowed construction workers on the Ford Homes project signals dramatic changes that occurred over the previous decades, reshaping building-craftsmen's role in housing development. Perhaps the lack of professional architectural involvement in Brightmoor's creation points to a similar historical shift in that group's experience. At the Ford Homes, Wood's contribution was important but also more limited than the one he had been prepared to offer; his abilities or interests determined his involvement less than the developer's needs. Brightmoor's developer went a step further and dispensed with the services of an architect altogether. The absence of an architect at Brightmoor draws attention to the role architects played in suburban residential development and how this role changed. What impact did the absence of an architect have on Brightmoor's development?

Brightmoor, like the Ford Homes project, is located in the Detroit metropolitan area. Its creation responded to some of the same needs for housing for newly arrived workers attracted to the city's expanding industrial sector that was noted in chapter 1. This project assumed, however, a specific niche within Detroit's housing market—one that makes its similarities to the other subdivisions examined here that much more intriguing and suggestive. It is useful to return to the consideration of Detroit's development to begin to see how Brightmoor fit into it.

Brightmoor: Background and Overview

The massive growth of Detroit's population in response to industrial development put such severe pressure on the housing stock of the old city that it mounted to crisis proportions. The *Annual Report for the*

THREE SUBDIVISIONS AND THEIR BUILDERS

City of Detroit for the Year 1919 estimated that there was a shortage of 30,402 dwellings, a figure that historians consider conservative.[1] In 1920, 30 percent of the families in Detroit were underserved by existing housing, a situation that led to overcrowding and the use of inadequate structures.[2] Few initiatives were taken to deal with this problem even after it became an issue of public discussion. Instead, it was left to market forces, which finally responded in the years between 1923 and 1926 with an unprecedented surge in subdividing and construction activity. At this point, according to Detroit historian Sidney Glazer, "realty subdividing became highly specialized, calling for large capital requirements. Builders developed models for the construction of single-residence homes on a mass basis."[3]

Many studies of Detroit's response to this housing crisis have focused on the "wave of excessive subdividing" that outdistanced actual construction.[4] One work published by the Michigan Planning Commission compared the speculative mania of the period to that which took place contemporaneously in Florida, the symbol of runaway speculation. It noted that during the three years from 1924 to 1926 alone, "54.3% of all lots of record, representing 45% of all acreage subdivided in the entire history of the [Detroit] metropolitan area, were platted."[5] The *Northwestern Business Booster* reported in October 1925 that "at present, plats are being filed at the rate of ten to twelve daily, a figure unprecedented in the history of the country."[6] The surplus of subdivided lots could be inferred from the relation between the 479 percent increase in population in the metropolitan area between 1900 and 1930 and the 1,105 percent increase in subdivided acreage for the same period.[7] Analysts felt that such speculation undermined the provision of sound housing, since it drove prices up without assuming responsibility for the coordination or improvement of neighborhoods and resulted in pockets of vacant land when the economy turned toward depression.

Few writers, however, examined the housing that, too, was a product of this boom period.[8] Little has been written on the "models for the construction of single-residence homes on a mass basis" that Glazer refers to in the above quotation. The 1920s saw a succession of record-breaking years for suburban building, beginning in 1923 with the construction of eleven thousand houses between Detroit's city limit and the twelve-mile arc from downtown.[9] Many builders contributed to this process, and there has been no close analysis of the impact of their work on the formation of the built environment in the Detroit area.

Aspects of the activities of realtor B. E. Taylor, the developer of Brightmoor, bear out some of the critiques of rampant subdividing that were made in studies of real-estate development in Detroit in the 1920s. The scale of his enterprise was enormous. As one account from the early 1920s states, "Mr. Taylor has developed and improved building lots in the Grand River Avenue district which total one-third of all present vacant improved building lots in the city of Detroit under fifteen hundred dollars in value."[10] Between 1921 and 1925, Taylor bought twenty-eight parcels of land in this district and subdivided them into 15,511 lots, not including areas subdivided for light industrial uses. As late as 1938, only 25 percent of these 4,580 acres of lots had been developed, indicating that many of the lots were bought for purposes of speculation alone and resulting in numerous pockets of vacant land.[11] Taylor encouraged this by requiring home buyers to purchase one and sometimes two lots in addition to that on which their houses would be built.[12]

These facts represent only part of Taylor's activities, however. He also built houses, enticed businesses to the area, and constructed neighborhood facilities. In March 1922, the first family moved into Brightmoor; by the end of 1925, the district had a population of 11,319 living in 3,958 houses, and there were 190 businesses in operation.[13] A number of the neighborhood institutions that Taylor fostered continue to operate today. These include the local newspaper and the community center, the latter having been established in 1922 as a settlement house. Although construction of Interstate 96 in the post–World War II period physically divided the neighborhood, its identity remained intact.

Partly as a result of the presence of its settlement house, Brightmoor was an object of study—mainly conducted by social workers—almost from its inception. A 1925 study by the Michigan Department of Health found a high incidence of diarrheal infections in Brightmoor children due to the lack of adequate sewage disposal.[14] Taylor's houses did not include indoor bathrooms; as late as 1938, only three-quarters of Brightmoor homes had flush toilets.

Brightmoor houses were not unique in their lack of amenities. In its 1939 *Study of Subdivision Development in the Detroit Metropolitan Area*, the Michigan Planning Commission analyzed the efficacy of existing patterns of building restrictions. It found that there were no attempts to insure minimum standards for the 91 percent of houses citywide that cost less than $3,000, more than half of which were constructed without furnaces, bathrooms, or basements.[15] Brightmoor houses included none of these features.

Minimal standards characterized suburban housing elsewhere in Michigan. In Flint, for example, this pattern continued into the 1940s when, one scholar notes, "half the fringe area homes had no running water; three-quarters had no flush toilets."[16]

Clearly, Taylor's willingness to build in this way was not an isolated phenomenon. J. C. Nichols, a prominent realtor and later developer of Kansas City's Country Club District, built his first houses in 1903 and 1904; small cottages for workers, they did not include indoor plumbing.[17] Indeed, an address delivered to the 1915 National Conference on Housing reflects the professional acceptance of such a lack of amenities in workers' housing. Discussing standards for low-cost housing, one architect referred to the need for light, air, and usable space; none of the amenities missing from Brightmoor were included among his minimal requirements for working-class homes.[18]

At its start, Brightmoor had no paved streets, no street lights, and no water connections; water was provided by a water wagon. By 1924, water was piped in from the city of Detroit and electrical connections were installed. This conforms to the pattern of urban expansion in the United States in the 1920s analyzed by historian Jon Teaford. In the case of Detroit, he notes that the city "did not annex Hamtramck with its massive Dodge plant, Highland Park with its huge Ford factory, or the string of Grosse Pointes with their handsome mansions. Instead it absorbed miles of open country to the northwest with a low tax valuation and with no water mains, paved streets, or street lights."[19]

This latter area includes Brightmoor; in that part of Brightmoor not annexed by Detroit in 1926, and included today as part of Redford Township, the streets remain unpaved. In other words, developers such as Taylor purchased less-expensive unincorporated acreage and avoided infrastructural costs by relying on its eventual absorption by the municipality for the permanent provision of essential utilities and services.

The houses in Brightmoor cost just less than $2,000 in 1924—a price affordable to the working-class population that Taylor attracted.[20] A typical ad for the subdivision in the *Detroit Free Press* in April 1924 mentioned among its features that "Twelfth Street (paved)"—one of the main streets of the neighborhood—"runs directly to the front door of the Ford Highland Park plant."[21] The plant lies about seven miles due east from the intersection of Twelfth (now Fenkell) and Burt Road (see fig. 2).

As noted earlier, the Detroit area was a magnet for people looking for work in the industrial sector in the period before and after World War I. In the years from 1920 to 1930, most of these newcomers were between the ages of fifteen and thirty.[22] In 1920, although 29.6 percent of the population of the United States was between the ages of twenty-five and forty-four, in Detroit 40 percent of the population was in this range.[23] Thus, Detroit attracted settlers who were in their prime working years and beginning to establish families.

Within this broad group of newcomers, it appears that Brightmoor primarily attracted migrants from within the United States, especially from Appalachia and southern states. According to the Fifteenth Decennial Census of the United States in 1930, 7.6 percent of the total native white population of Detroit was born in those regions, and almost all of the 79,274 individuals represented by this figure came north in the decade of the 1920s.[24] At least one ad for Brightmoor describes it as a "100% American neighborhood," suggesting that foreigners were not encouraged to settle there.[25] As late as 1938, the foreign-born accounted for more than 10 percent but less than 19 percent of the registered voters of this area.[26] A report written by the Wayne University School of Public Affairs and Social Work in

1941 described Brightmoor as a predominantly white, Protestant, working-class community.[27] In his talk at the first annual convention of the Homebuilders and Subdividers Division of the National Association of Real Estate Boards in 1923, Taylor stated that the sale of Brightmoor houses was restricted to whites.[28] Taylor also may have actively solicited migrants from other states. One account claims that he hired salesmen in distant cities and "Greyhound busses, six or ten a week, would bring people from Ohio, Kentucky, Michigan and farther to Detroit. They would be put up in a nice downtown hotel, taken to a good dinner and show, and the next morning they would be brought to Brightmoor to look over the propositions that had been made to them in their home towns."[29] Such courting of prospective home buyers has its roots in nineteenth-century town boosterism.[30] It also recalls practices during the early years of the auto industry aimed at overcoming the shortage of workers, when "the Employers' Association [of Detroit] systematically exerted itself through agents, circulars, and news stories to draw men to the city."[31]

Relatively young families, then, usually from rural, undeveloped areas, were among the early purchasers of homes in Brightmoor.[32] The conditions they found there may not have been substantially different from those they had left, but the threats that a lack of amenities posed to public health in a denser, urban setting were both more visible and potentially more dangerous. To some extent Taylor recognized this, for in May 1924 he commissioned the Committee on Nursing Activities of the American Red Cross to operate at the community center. The center also provided recreational programs for children, cooking, sewing, gardening, and other classes for women, a small library, and counseling by social workers to integrate the residents of Brightmoor into a new environment. It is useful to recall that Albert Wood's proposals for community design were inspired by the achievements of the Progressive Era social reform movement at Hull House. At Brightmoor, Taylor introduced a settlement house to provide a focus for neighborhood activities and to support newcomers' assimilation to urban life. Taylor's experience and his outlook on housing shed light on his use of this feature and his conception of Brightmoor.

B. E. Taylor and the Development of Brightmoor

Burt Eddy Taylor was born in Sandusky, Ohio, in 1877.[33] He graduated from Ohio Wesleyan University in 1899. His business career began at the American Crayon Company, in Sandusky, where he rose to vice president. Beginning in 1908, he surveyed real-estate projects and possibilities in large Great Lakes cities and determined that, as a result of the new automobile industry, Detroit held the greatest potential for growth. At some point, in Sandusky, he had sold bicycles on the installment plan, and he thought that the same principle could be applied successfully to the sale of real estate and housing.[34] It is not known whether Taylor was aware of the activities of W. E. Harmon in Cincinnati, whom realtors considered to have been the first to introduce real-estate sales on the installment plan in the 1880s, or of Chicago developer Samuel E. Gross's use of the installment plan in the same decade.[35] Installment sales of autos, by comparison, emerged as a strategy in 1910.[36]

It seems that Taylor developed subdivisions along these lines in Akron, Ohio, and in Kentucky.[37] Around 1913–14, Taylor settled in Detroit and began to purchase tracts of land near Grand River Avenue close to the Detroit city limit.[38] His enterprise flourished and grew and he extended his activities throughout the northwestern section of the area. In 1922, his career as a realtor was sufficiently established locally for him to serve as general chairman of the Detroit Better Homes and Building exhibition.[39] He addressed the Homebuilders and Subdividers Division of the National Association of Real Estate Boards at their first annual national convention in 1923 and again in 1925.[40]

A listing of Taylor's subdivisions totals ninety-five tracts, including the twenty-eight that became Brightmoor.[41] In the course of the 1920s, Taylor developed higher-priced properties, including some that were contiguous with golf courses, and his firm hired architects to design the houses for these.[42] These later subdivisions follow more closely the precedent established by Kansas City developer Nichols's influential Country Club District. The business suffered reversals during the Great Depression, but began to revive just before World

THREE SUBDIVISIONS AND THEIR BUILDERS

War II. Taylor's son, Burt Eddy Taylor Jr., continued the work of the firm.

In a report written in 1925, Taylor explained that in creating Brightmoor he was "trying to do (without any comparison at all) what Henry Ford has done in the manufacture of the Ford car.... The greater part of his [Ford's] success has been due to the fact that he made something that the masses could buy.... There is not so much personal pride in building the inexpensive home, and developing and building such a community of homes, but it is a real service and one that is soul-satisfying to us."[43] Taylor's goals, like Ford's in both housing and automobile production, were efficiency and cost reduction. Many of the decisions Taylor made concerning the provision of services and amenities were calculated with those ends in view. What was their impact on the overall site of Brightmoor as well as on its houses?

Brightmoor lies about twelve miles northwest of the Detroit City Hall, its streets, for the most part, conforming to the direction of the rectilinear grid that characterizes all but the oldest part of the city. Whereas early French settlement was oriented to the riverfronts, the street plan of most of the Detroit metropolitan area followed the section lines of the territorial land survey that began in 1815 and was oriented to the points of the compass.[44] The River Rouge, one of the few geographical features of this flat expanse, snakes through the western part of Brightmoor. The band of parkland flanking it is the northern extension of River Rouge Park, whose development was completed in the 1920s.

In 1921, when Taylor began to buy tracts for what would become Brightmoor, this area was farmland. Located within Redford Township, its eastern edge was about a mile from the Detroit city limit. In January 1926, Detroit concluded its geographical growth by annexing a block of land that included Brightmoor as far west as Telegraph Road, which remains virtually the city limit.[45] This brought Brightmoor residents under the umbrella of city services, such as police and fire protection; before annexation, the latter had been provided by a volunteer company, but there had been no police or governmental structure.[46] Other benefits of annexation included paved streets and streetlights.

BRIGHTMOOR

The Pere Marquette (now C&O) railroad tracks marked the southern boundary of Brightmoor. When Brightmoor was developed, the fastest access to downtown was along Grand River Avenue, one of the radial thoroughfares that follow original Native American trails, widened by the territorial governor, Lewis Cass, in 1830 to serve as military roads. Now, Interstate 96 provides a direct route to downtown, as well as connections to other directions, though it also segments the neighborhood. Aside from thoroughfares following the section lines, the other major road linking Brightmoor with various sectors of the city is Outer Drive. This forty-five-mile boulevard grew out of a proposal made by Edward A. Bennett in the city plan that he prepared for Detroit in 1915. It runs an eccentric course, weaving through the grid from the Detroit River at Ecorse, through Dearborn and along the River Rouge, across northwestern Detroit, and ends at the traditionally fashionable north-central section of the city. It was completed in the 1920s.

The location of Brightmoor on lots that originally were farmland and at some distance from built-up areas helped keep Taylor's costs down. This made it possible for him to target the working-class market for which Brightmoor was well sited, equidistant as it was from the Ford plants at Highland Park to the east and at River Rouge to the southwest. Taylor ensured that workers with modest incomes could travel easily from Brightmoor to their jobs by subsidizing a bus system; it operated for two years, until a local bus company took over its routes.[47] Perhaps Taylor was aware of the importance of linking working-class housing to industrial sites based on the failure of developments such as Benjamin J. Rosenthal's 175-unit tract constructed in Chicago in 1919; its isolation resulted in high turnover and instability.[48]

Taylor had bought thirty-three parcels of land before he purchased his first Brightmoor tract, the plat for which he registered in June 1921.[49] He filed each of the twenty-seven succeeding subdivisions under the name Brightmoor, usually using the names of farmers from whom he bought the land as subtitles. He subdivided each tract into uniform lots that generally measured from 30 to 34 feet by 100 to 125 feet; business lots, on the major streets, typically measured 20 feet,

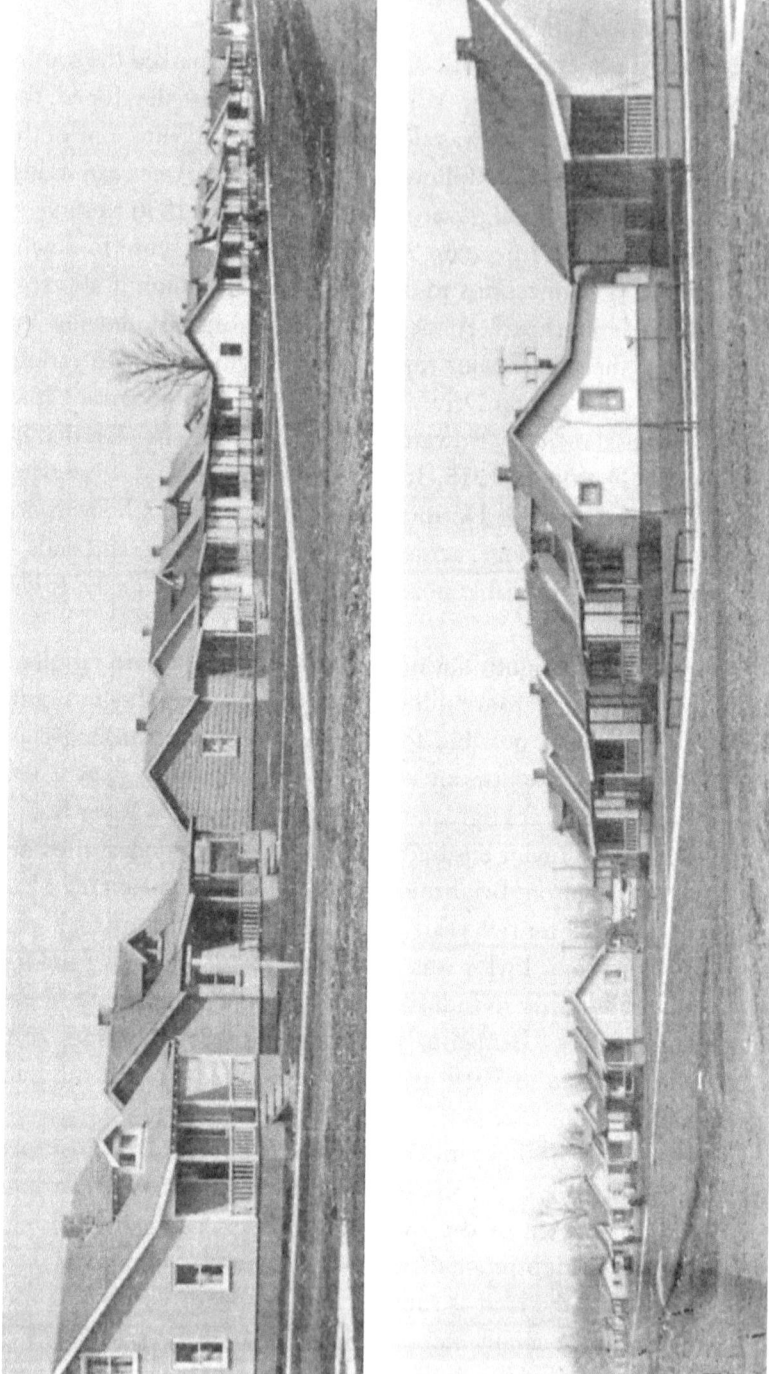

although corner lots were larger. The smallest tract, Elmoor, was filed in August 1921 and yielded 175 lots; the largest, Mercier, was registered in February 1925 and amounted to 1,440 lots. Central alleys generally divided blocks, which were laid out according to "the speculative gridiron ... the most ubiquitous method of urban edge expansion prior to World War II."[50]

Lots could be bought without improvement, as an investment, or by speculative builders, but many purchasers had Taylor build a house on their lot (fig. 15, a and b). According to the account of the development published in *Building Age* in April 1924, "the cry for houses swelled and swelled until the construction department [of the Taylor firm] had to work feverish overtime hours to keep abreast of the demand."[51] However, house purchasers were required to buy one or two lots in addition to the one they were building upon. As Taylor explained this strategy to a group of fellow developers in 1923, "I build the houses to sell the lots. ... It just happens that there is a great big demand in Detroit for houses and there is more demand for houses than there is for lots, so like the standard [*sic*] Oil company I am taking advantage of the situation by selling three lots with a house."[52] This was a recognized practice among realtors. As one of the early professional texts noted in 1923, "the building of homes greatly facilitates the sale of lots."[53]

Taylor had bought the land for about $1,000 per acre; he sold each lot for $1,000.[54] Using a house that cost $1,595 as his example, Taylor outlined his financing procedures in 1923. After a down payment of from $300 to $350 on this house and two lots, monthly payments came to $38, well within the range of contemporary rental costs.

Taylor contracted with carpenters for the construction of the houses. Each contracted carpenter hired from three to eight men, and at the

---

Figure 15, a and b. These Brightmoor streetscapes from the April 1924 issue of *Building Age* provide overviews of the standardized houses that B. E. Taylor constructed. Gaps between houses indicate additional lots purchased by home owners. This was one of Taylor's sales strategies; as he said, "I build the houses to sell the lots."

peak of construction as many as thirty-two carpenters' crews were at work in the subdivision. Separate contractors handled plumbing, wiring, painting, and paperhanging.

Taylor provided all of the materials used in the construction of the houses, buying them in quantity to reduce costs. The houses were built to plans that followed as closely as possible the standard sizes of materials so as to expend the minimum amount of time preparing them and to minimize waste.

The houses were built on cedar posts and timber foundations and did not include basements. Taylor was questioned about this practice at the 1923 Housebuilders and Subdividers conference, but he did not see it as problematic. The exchange that is recorded in the transcript of the discussion is worth recounting:

> Mr. J. J. Swartz (Plainfield, New Jersey): You stated a moment ago that you put these houses on cedar posts. That does not seem to be conducive to a real good healthy proposition, especially in Detroit, does it? Don't they require foundations under their houses out there? It gets pretty cold there, doesn't it?
> Mr. B. E. Taylor: Who do you mean require?
> Mr. J. J. Swartz: Why, the occupants of the home.
> Mr. B. E. Taylor: No, these homes have gone through two winters. I never heard anybody say they were cold. (Laughter.)[55]

The only word that concerned Taylor here was "require"; short of building-code standards to ensure full basements and foundations, there was no obstacle to keeping costs down by using Taylor's methods.

Plans were designed for houses with four, five, and six rooms. This included the kitchen; there were no indoor bathrooms. All the bungalows (as Taylor and the press called these houses) had a front porch. Living rooms generally had two windows, but bedrooms were designed with one window even when it would have been feasible to install another on an adjacent wall (figs. 16, 17, and 18). One window per room was one of the "minimum criteria for clean, safe, and comfortable working-class housing" established by Lawrence Veiller in the "Standards Recommended for Permanent Industrial

Housing Developments" that he created for the United States Housing Corporation during World War I. Indoor bathrooms were also recommended.[56]

The massing of these undecorated houses is consistent, shaped by the main pitched roof and porch extension. The only variation derives from the orientation of the ridgeline—parallel to the street in some houses, in others perpendicular so that the gable end faces the street. Regardless of this shift, the plans are the same (figs. 19, 20, and 21).

The approach that Taylor took toward efficiency and cost reduction, it is clear, was different from that taken by the Dearborn Realty & Construction Company at the Ford Homes. The houses at Brightmoor were very small; the four-room models measured 440 square feet, and the six-room model slightly less than 600 square feet. Only the largest approached the dimensions of four-room houses built by cost-conscious federal agencies during World War I, which varied from 616 to 943 square feet.[57] In addition to trimming size, however, Taylor also cut back on infrastructural elements so much that Brightmoor houses contributed to their inhabitants' physical discomfort and, ultimately, health risks.

But it is possible to note similarities between Brightmoor and the Ford Homes. Both provided single-family houses with garden space within a neighborhood that was defined in part by local institutions or amenities put in place by the developer. Brightmoor was a much larger-scaled subdivision, however, with a wider array of neighborhood services and organizations supporting its population.

Brightmoor, in short, offers a seemingly contradictory housing solution. On the one hand, it exemplifies the roughly 45 percent of Michigan housing in this period that was constructed without meeting minimum standards, including the lack of furnaces, bathrooms, and basements.[58] Yet in contrast to the indifference to inhabitants' welfare that this suggests, Taylor did foster a neighborhood identity and solicit a range of institutions to locate there to support home owners' social, educational, and commercial needs.

What accounts for the discrepancy between these two sides of Taylor's development activity? To answer this question we must look

Figure 16. This Brightmoor living room (*above*) is described as "neat and comfy" in the April 1924 issue of *Building Age*. As the table indicates, it doubled as a dining room. The other focus of attention within the room is the stove, the main source of heat in the house.

Figure 17. In a typical, compact Brightmoor bedroom (*top right*), ca. 1924, *Building Age* noted that there is "nothing crowded." Taylor finished all rooms but the kitchen with wallpaper.

Figure 18. Brightmoor kitchens (*bottom right*) came equipped with a sink and a freestanding cupboard with a drop shelf. They typically measured eight by ten feet.

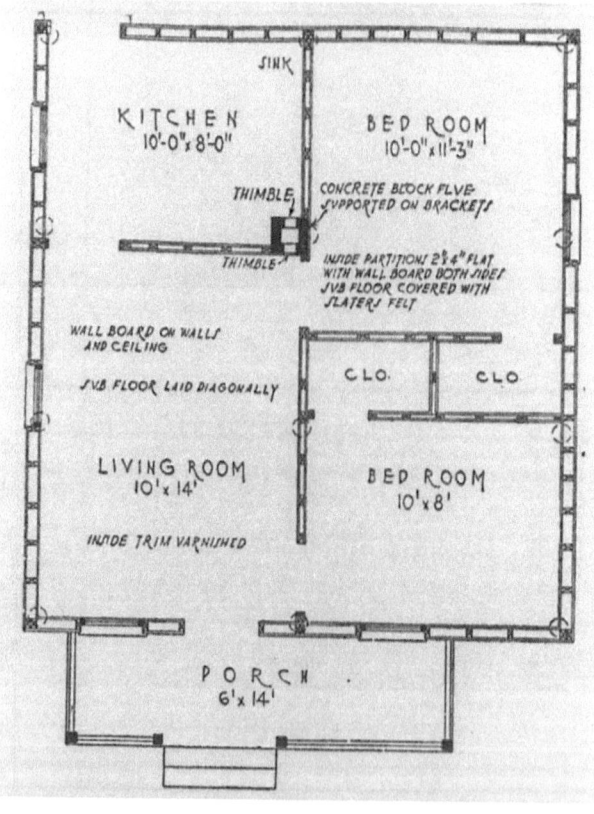

more closely at the kinds of activities developers typically engaged in. Chapter 1 considered how responsibilities for conceptualizing and organizing construction processes were increasingly transferred from building-craftsmen to developers. At Brightmoor, the developer also assumed responsibility for house design; Taylor was able to dispense with the services and advice of an architect. By considering the relationship of architects to small house design, we gain a clearer view of the evolution of architects' interactions with developers.

The Absent Architect

How architects defined their profession's concerns affected their involvement in residential development. The view of the profession presented through its press and by recent scholars suggests that the process of professional self-definition was a contentious one; agreement tended to be based on narrow definitions of the profession's role.[59] The bases for the stresses that shaped the history of the architectural profession in the West go back to the seventeenth century.[60] Here it is sufficient, however, to focus on the development of the profession in the late-nineteenth and early-twentieth centuries in the United States.

From the time of their founding the American Institute of Architects (AIA) in 1857, leaders of the architectural profession allied their field with the traditions of Beaux Arts theory and practice. These derived from the rigorously classical and systematizing orientation toward the visual arts and architecture promoted by the Ecole des Beaux-Arts in Paris. Calvert Vaux's suggestion, around 1865, that a special membership category of the AIA be created for painters, carpenters, masons, and others involved in architecture was opposed because "it would amount to a confession that the Institute members

---

Figure 19, a and b. The gable end of Brightmoor's model 614 faces the street; inside the house, the partitions that divide the interior lengthways are aligned with the ridgeline. This four-room model measures 440 square feet. Despite the general lack of amenities, every house included a porch.

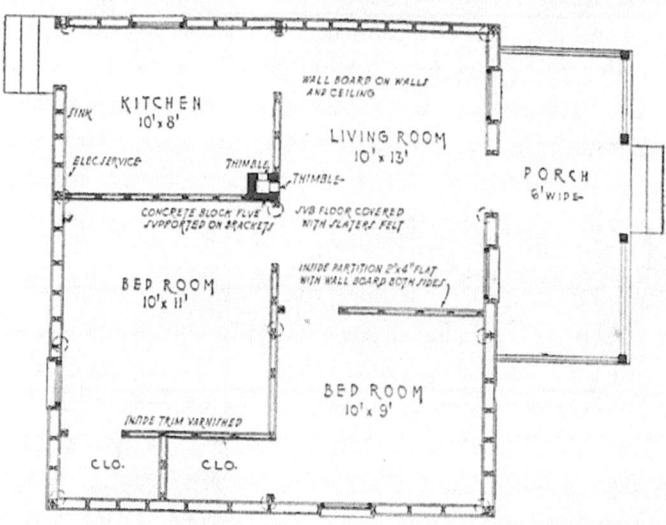

Figure 20, a and b. Model 514 is the same size as 614; it differs only in the disposition of spaces. The ridgeline parallels the street and the bisecting wall divides the interior equally between front and back. Broad, stark external wall surfaces reflect the general practice at Brightmoor of including only one window per room.

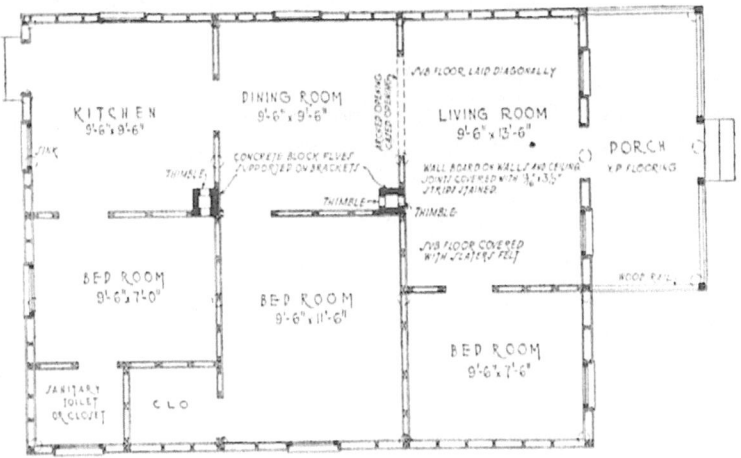

Figure 21. In Brightmoor's largest, six-room model, measuring slightly less than 600 square feet, all room sizes were reduced to contribute to the creation of the additional two rooms. The compact, side-by-side plan of abutting spaces, without transitional zones or hallways, remains the same.

were in need of the information supposed to be imparted by the technicians and craftsmen."[61] Instead, by emphasizing academic principles, architects defined their activities so that, as one put it, "real architectural interest is almost as esoteric and professional as an interest in abstract law or medicine."[62] The terms of the definition distinguished architects from both building-craftsmen and engineers, whose activities, however, accounted for the majority of actual construction. As late as the teens of the twentieth century, roughly sixty years after the initial organization of the profession, it was estimated that almost 90 percent of the buildings in the United States were constructed without the aid of architects.[63] And yet this situation had been created, in a sense, both by the narrow theoretical and aesthetic definition of architecture and by the devaluation of types of buildings that were seen as unsuitable to receive the attention of architects.

For our purposes, it is of special interest that the architectural profession tended to assert itself not through residential design for the middle and working classes, but through the design of public and monumental structures and homes for the wealthy. Architectural historian Gwendolyn Wright admirably charts the devaluation of domestic building by the architectural elite during the last quarter of the nineteenth century. Building-craftsmen dominated the residential field, challenging architects' claims to professional recognition on the basis of a special competency.[64] Architects articulated their expertise in different terms, designing public monuments that lent themselves to the application of classicizing formulas that made use of their Beaux Arts training. They also distanced themselves from the activities of building-craftsmen both by disparaging the mass of housing produced through their efforts and by relegating housing as a form to a realm beneath the concern of architects. An 1876 editorial in the *American Architect and Building News,* for example, used this disdain for domestic architecture to diminish the professional contribution of women who specialized in such areas: "The planning of houses, at least so far as the convenience of their arrangement is concerned, though a very necessary part of an architect's duty, is not architecture at all; and the ability to arrange a house conveniently does not in the least make an architect."[65]

By the 1890s, this attitude was entrenched within the leadership of the profession. *Inland Architect,* a major journal for the Midwest, announced in 1894 that it would no longer carry notices of buildings under construction that cost less than $5,000, which included the majority of domestic building. The ideal architectural firm became Daniel Burnham's, in which specialized aspects of the commissions that came from municipalities and from the business community were allocated to staff architects and to the one hundred draftsmen employed by the office, and little residential design was undertaken.[66]

The devaluation of housing, however, created tensions within the architectural profession. The type of construction that was most widespread and with which most people would come into contact throughout the course of their lives was designed by individuals who were able to call themselves architects, and yet who had neither the training nor the ideals recognized by the professional elite. On the other hand, a young architect who modeled his career development on the pattern of the elite had difficulty acquiring small residential commissions using professional standards, since building-craftsmen dominated the market for modest dwellings. Around the turn of the century, professional dismay with the work of building-craftsmen and new efforts to tighten professional controls yielded a solution that heightened these tensions.

The first strategy to secure control over architectural standards was to achieve state endorsement for architects through licensing. In 1897, Illinois passed the first state licensing law. Other states followed suit, although it was not until 1951 that all states had instituted licensing requirements.[67] The criteria for registration included education in an accredited architectural school or success in an examination. Although aimed at regulating the design of structures that involved new and complicated technologies, licensing also addressed housing. Only the design of single houses was exempt from architectural control; the purpose of this exemption was to protect owner-builders. A speculative builder who constructed more than one house a year was required to enlist the services of an architect or to apprentice to qualify to take the licensing exam.[68]

Monitoring the education of architects was another avenue to the establishment of tighter professional controls. In 1907, the AIA's Committee on Education recommended that an architectural degree be conferred only on those who demonstrated a proficiency in Latin, completed a year of preparatory study and four years in a school of architecture, had at least a year of advanced study in ateliers in Paris, Rome, or the United States, and traveled for at least a year in Europe. Reflecting this emphasis on formal education, twenty-one new architectural programs were established between 1893 and 1914, bringing the total in the United States to twenty-eight, and their "curriculum and methods of teaching were either directly controlled by 'imported' French architects or dominated by Beaux-Arts programs."[69] This type of training was not designed to address the kinds of problems encountered in the field of small-house construction, nor was it created to attract to the study of architecture students who had an interest in that field.

In 1909, the AIA drew up a canon of ethics that also was designed to regulate professional activities. It included an injunction against architects engaging in the building trades. This mechanism was intended to ensure the disinterestedness of architects by prohibiting the possibility of seeking financial gain through the construction process. It also formalized the desire of the professional elite to separate the role of the designer from that of the builder.

Significantly, this ethical position was not incorporated into state licensing laws because it was opposed by many practicing architects and builders.[70] There was also opposition to licensing proposals. The actions of the professional elite met resistance from the many architectural practitioners whose relations with building activities did not conform to the Beaux Arts ideal. In tightening professional controls, the elite was widening the breach between design and building and forcing many designers to choose between entering the ranks of the profession or working outside it by supplementing their design activities with commercial endeavors. Many architects, working in small and still-rugged communities throughout the nation, chose the latter route, rejecting professional distinctions in order to design and build within the framework of existing commercial realities.[71]

Conflicts within the AIA over the Architects' Small House Service Bureau (ASHSB) in the 1920s underscore the tension created by defining the architectural profession in these ways, a tension that was especially strong in the area of housing. Architect Edwin H. Brown, of Minneapolis, founded the ASHSB in 1919 as a limited dividend corporation with the participation of eighty-five small architectural firms. It published a plan magazine, *Small House,* and sold stock plans. The basis for the controversy over these activities lies in the tradition of such plan books and in the independence of building-craftsmen and clients from architectural oversight that they fostered. Throughout the nineteenth century, published pattern and plan books provided building-craftsmen with stylistic and construction guidelines. Stock plan services, beginning with the magazine *Godey's Lady Book* in 1846 and continued by lumber companies and building-supply dealers into the twentieth century, offered drawings for model home designs.[72] Access to these plans enabled building-craftsmen to keep up with changing styles and meet the needs and desires of their clients. They were, in other words, an important mechanism for the transmission of architectural ideas.[73] From the standpoint of the architectural elite as they embarked upon the project of professionalization, they were also an important mechanism for maintaining the independence of building-craftsmen from architectural control. Armed with a stock plan, the builder or prospective home owner did not need to hire an architect. Designers from a variety of backgrounds produced the plans, but even when architects created them, the process of populist dissemination of architectural ideas was anathema to the elite. And the stock plan turned the process of design into a commodity, whereas, as Magali Larson notes, "professionalization movements are attempts to subtract certain areas of social life from the naked operation of market forces."[74] Selling the design "product," as opposed to being involved with the individual commission from beginning to end and designing for the particular situation, ran counter to the definition of professional service that architects were striving to enforce.

The activities of the ASHSB raised these issues once again. As Arthur Holden wrote in his defense of the project in the *Journal of the American Institute of Architects* in 1925, the AIA was the "moral sponsor" of the organization, although their endorsement, as this suggests, was controversial.[75] Indeed, in their statement of support the board of directors of the AIA made clear the limits of their endorsement by asserting that the AIA "approves the idea only."[76] A clear distance was maintained from the concrete work of the ASHSB, for this organization represented an attempt to reclaim a large portion of the built environment for the profession by acknowledging and reaching an accommodation with existing market arrangements. Accepting the practices of building-craftsmen, however, and working with them as designers of stock plans, was still repugnant, and even unethical, to many professionals. To preserve the "morality" of the profession in this sense, the elite was prepared, at the least, to deny professional recognition to dissenting fellow practitioners, if they could not also succeed in withdrawing professional services from the small-house field.

This tension was evident in the documents of the ASHSB itself. In his introductory remarks to a compilation of plans, for example, one writer felt constrained to remind potential homebuilders of modest means that the ASHSB "is not a complete service. That can only be obtained from the individual architect who is engaged to manage the home building operation from first to last."[77] As a result of the firmness with which professional boundaries were asserted, the ASHSB was forced to tread a very fine line and to acknowledge the limitations of their project to those very clients for whom any alternative architectural advice was beyond financial, and perhaps even geographical, reach.

While there was conflict within the profession, then, over architects' involvement in stock plan services, another definition of the profession in relation to housing evolved during the first decade of the twentieth century. Instead of focusing on the design of individual houses, this approach concentrated on the overall planning of entire residential communities. Wright discusses this development, noting that when architects had designed whole communities in the nineteenth century, as, for example, Solon Beman did in the Chicago area, their work received no recognition in the professional press.[78] By 1913, the year of the Chicago City Club competition and exhibition of schemes for a model suburb, and the year in which a regular feature on town and city planning was added to the monthly *Journal* of the AIA, the attitude within the profession had changed. Single residential commissions for the wealthy continued to be presented as unique and individualized objects, but the profession began to conceive of housing for the middle and working classes in terms of aggregates. Beaux Arts principles that architects applied to the design of civic centers could also determine the design of neighborhoods and subdivisions. Other planning principles were formulated and rapidly disseminated following the turn of the century, notably garden-suburb design and, later, neighborhood unit planning.[79]

Albert Wood's booklet "Community Homes" exemplifies the recasting of the profession's concern with housing into planning terms. His scheme is characteristic of the new emphasis in the way it ignores the design of individual houses and concentrates on the organization of space on a larger scale, embracing many units (see fig. 3). It looks to the development of the neighborhood for the creation of an environment nestled in nature, separated from the flow of traffic and commerce, instead of trying to achieve this ideal in terms of individualized dwellings.

But who would be the clients for these planning services provided by architects? By reconceiving their role as designers of residential totalities, architects shifted the issue of patronage from individual home owners, who relied upon building-craftsmen more than architects, to necessarily corporate bodies capable of organizing community building on a large scale. Albert Wood, it is useful to recall, urged the creation of development companies, associations of prospective home owners whose pooled resources could finance the services of an architect at the same time as they would achieve the design of more amenities through economies of scale. Despite wide discussion of such ideas following World War I, these did not evolve in the United States.[80] Nor did philanthropic entities, such as the Russell Sage Foundation, sponsor of the model development of Forest Hills Gardens, emerge in significant numbers. In the aftermath of the strife at Pullman on Chicago's edge, employers were less likely to undertake community development, unless they included a number of controls to avoid the appearance of establishing a company town, as in the Ford Homes. Instead of these, the major client became the developer, the realtor who engaged in building large-scale subdivisions. The next chapter considers more closely the rise of the professional realtor and the nature of his role as a developer. For now, it is possible to note that the reconceptualization of the architect's contribution to housing as a planner had its parallel in the reformulation of the role of the speculative realtor as a community builder, which took place at the same historical moment. When projects were developed at very low cost, as Brightmoor was, the realtor assumed the architect's role as well.

The only other body that had the potential to serve as client for such a scale of architectural services was the state. Earlier discussion noted that the profession did look to the state for legitimation through the establishment of licensing laws around the turn of the century. Otherwise, however, relations between the architectural profession and government tended to be conflictual. The principal issue was the profession's struggle to eliminate the role of governmental staff architects in favor of assigning state commissions to architects working in private practice.[81] Although by 1912 this dispute seemed to have been resolved for federal projects, on the state level it continued to be a point of contention. An editorial in the first issue of the *Michigan Architect and Engineer* in 1919, for example, opposed a bill in the state legislature that proposed the creation of an office of state architect. Such an office "would deprive the taxpayers," the editor wrote, of the "specialized experience, expert knowledge and individualized master architectural technique" of Michigan's private practitioners.[82]

During the crisis of World War I, the architectural profession was able to enforce its position in favor of independent practice. Paradoxically, however, its experiences at that time seemed to move it further along the route of collaboration with large-scale developers. A number of architects served in the federal agencies that were responsible for the development of housing for war workers; for example, a principal in the firm of McKim, Mead, & White was the general manager of the United States Housing Corporation, and an architect who later served as president of the AIA headed the Emergency Fleet Corporation.[83] However, whereas the government had intended to use its staff architects to design the needed housing, the AIA persuaded it to commission private architectural firms for this work.[84] The general principle of maintaining the separation between public and private sectors was observed: federal war housing was designed by architects not employed by the government; it was also built by private developers.

Nevertheless, this context provided many more architects with firsthand experience of large-scale housing projects. And it seems to have impressed upon them the values of efficiency, of businesslike organization, and of collaborative work with engineers and builders. Articles in the professional press following the war reflect these new emphases. In 1919, one writer urged, "Let us cease to be artists and become builders, losing our desire for individual fame in the greater desire of perfect production."[85] Another acknowledged that engaging in such residential projects required abandoning "the desire for aloof professionalism."[86] Few looked to the government as a patron for large-scale enterprises. The architect who directed one of the most successful war-worker housing projects observed that this had been "an outstanding opportunity . . . for the Government to produce an industrial community which should be, as far as reasonable economy and the urgency of the case would permit, an example to private enterprise throughout the land."[87] The experience that the profession had had within the context created by the state prepared it for closer relations with private developers in the future.

The absence of an architect at Brightmoor, then, grows out of the longstanding practice of the architectural elite of devaluing the small house as an arena for the establishment of professional competence and prestige. Typically, building-craftsmen and not architects were involved in the design of the modest home; Taylor's design of Brightmoor's houses follows this tradition. Although he was not a trained building-craftsman, he may have assumed that he could block out the designs for structures as simple as the ones he planned to put on the market. Conversely, working on his own without the advice of an architect, Taylor encountered neither restraints on nor alternative low-cost solutions to the minimal dwellings he constructed.

Given the scale of Brightmoor as a new residential district and the neighborhood services and facilities with which Taylor provided it—both of which reflect Taylor's ambitions as a self-described "community-builder"—questions remain concerning these minimal dwellings. How did such impoverished housing succeed in anchoring this new subdivision? Looking at the historical distance that the architectural profession maintained from small-house design suggests the vacuum that existed in this field, but it does not indicate the needs filled by Brightmoor's housing—beyond their low cost—that made the development viable. There are other features of Taylor's activities as a developer that can establish what the context was that made this possible.

Situating Brightmoor

Simplicity of form, lack of detailing, small size, and absence of amenities characterize the "bungalows" that Taylor built at Brightmoor. Despite these features, Taylor was able to use them to undergird and promote sales of Brightmoor lots and the establishment of a residential neighborhood. Two historical contexts for these dwellings illuminate further meanings embodied in Brightmoor's houses that help us to situate this subdivision and Taylor's role as its developer in a larger analytic framework. By considering the market for which Taylor built these houses, it is possible to see that such structures represent an intersection of folk-traditional and working-class cultures with mass production.

One of the aspects of the history of housing in Detroit that historian Olivier Zunz discusses in his study of community building is what he calls the "dual housing market," consisting of the formal housing market, on the one hand, and of owner-builders on the other.[88] He finds that home ownership was prevalent throughout the period of his study, 1880 to 1920, especially within ethnic working-class neighborhoods often made up of recent immigrants. The formal housing market, composed of realtors, architects, and professional building-craftsmen, served the middle and upper classes, but hiring these experts was too expensive an undertaking for the majority of those who wanted houses. Their desires for houses did not go unmet, however: an alternative system developed, within the ethnic communities, to provide housing. This drew somewhat on local craftsmen and businesses, but principally it was forged by the home owners themselves, who built their own houses. Zunz found that the commitment to home ownership was so strong within these communities that house building was the focus of peoples' energies. Amenities such as pavements and sewer connections, which would have increased basic expenses, were secondary considerations, and often were not installed until years after houses had been constructed. In contrast, the formal housing market used such infrastructural elements to shape the growth of the city into new areas, such as along the Woodward corridor, in advance of residential construction. And, as historian Ann Durkin Keating has shown in relation to typical developments elsewhere, this uneven availability of infrastructure shaped urban growth socially as well as physically, helping to establish class-segregated neighborhoods.[89]

Seen in the light of this historical context, Taylor's development at Brightmoor represents the merger of these parallel activities. Taylor used professional resources to reproduce the level of very basic house building that traditionally characterized working-class neighborhoods. The housing that he provided was not substantially different from what people had constructed for themselves within their ethnic neighborhoods. But by subdividing and building on a large scale, he extended the services of the formal housing market to a class that had previously been independent of it, aligning its access to housing to the structure of speculative real-estate development. Detroit's rapid growth in population and the accompanying housing crisis made this more feasible in the 1920s than it had been earlier. At the same time, by limiting his development's amenities, he preserved the stratification by residential area that the uneven provision of infrastructural services created. Also, Taylor addressed a migrant group that did not already have a developed neighborhood network into which its members could fit. Taylor's activities as a "community-builder," which was how he characterized his business, supplanted the matrix of neighborhood institutions usually built up over time with a combination of ready-made commercial and welfare facilities.

The houses at Brightmoor thus share features with those historically constructed by working-class owner-builders within evolving ethnic communities in Detroit. What differentiates them from this tradition, however, is their assimilation into the processes of the formal housing market, which simultaneously took over the responsibility for shaping neighborhood life. In light of this analysis, the housing developments that Brightmoor might seem to resemble are company towns, in which housing and community facilities are created from scratch for a population of newcomers. The trend in company towns, in the aftermath of Pullman, was in fact to minimize the control of the employer and to try to approach as closely as possible the free-market model of speculative development. Also, period discussions of company towns, as in the essays collected by Leifur Magnusson in *Homes for Workmen*, emphasize the garden-suburb tradition in which the design of the neighborhood and houses is seen to contribute to the moral development of the residents, obviating the need for more direct paternalistic interventions. Taylor, on the other hand, preserved many of the deficiencies of working-class owner-builder housing, which were also found in some of the company-provided housing critiqued by reformers such as Magnusson.[90] Taylor solicited already-existing institutions—churches, businesses, and especially the state, for its educational and welfare services—to mold the subdivision into a community.

The specific form that Brightmoor houses took suggests a relationship to another aspect of the tradition of owner-builder housing. It is possible that Taylor built houses that would be familiar in a number of respects to the people who would be buying them, many of whom came from Appalachia. Evidence linking Taylor himself with the Appalachian region is sketchy—he seems to have worked in Kentucky before settling in the Detroit area—and no definite source for the Brightmoor houses can be specified. But in a number of ways, they recall the folk-traditional architecture of the rural upland South, the region extending from western Arkansas to eastern Pennsylvania.

Scholars have documented Appalachian housing. While it is not possible to say that Taylor's houses drew on such specific models, there are significant parallels between the house type found at Brightmoor and the type that Henry Glassie refers to as the southern mountain cabin.[91] This was constructed of log or frame, built as a single square or rectangular unit, and stood less than two stories high. While Glassie is concerned with defining this type and tracing its origins, others explore this housing's evolution, as Charles Martin does in his study of Hollybush, a small community in eastern Kentucky that existed from 1881 to 1960 (fig. 22).[92]

Far from claiming that the houses at Brightmoor reflect any architectural source with precision, the comparison between Taylor's design and the Appalachian cabin tradition can only be suggestive; even folk-traditional buildings underwent significant change, especially over the decades flanking the turn of the century. One of the achievements of Martin's study is his discussion of the transformations in Hollybush's architectural forms as a result of the change in livelihood of its residents from self-sufficiency to wage labor, and their concomitant greater contact with town life. Some changes occurred when

Figure 22. A 1949 house from the Appalachian community of Hollybush, photographed in 1979 by Charles E. Martin. Southern mountain cabins like this may have served as models for the severe simplicity of Taylor's Brightmoor houses. Their small scale, lack of amenities, combination of roof pitches, porches, plain exterior surfaces, and papered interiors are echoed at Brightmoor, but there these features were mass-produced and made with commercial materials.

Hollybush people embraced new forms (such as board-and-batten exteriors) that they became familiar with outside the community, either nearby or in industrial centers further north. It is possible that Brightmoor, as a type of Appalachian community in the north, represents one link in this chain of mutual influences. Thus, its forms can be seen as echoing Hollybush's, but also as altering them in ways that then may have affected later building in Appalachia.

It is possible to identify five features that seem to link Brightmoor's dwellings and Appalachian cabins: scale, amenities, silhouette and massing, interior treatment, and the appearance of the exterior. Southern mountain cabins were small; Glassie documented a range in size from 300 to 416 square feet. The houses at Hollybush were often smaller than 300 square feet. Brightmoor's bungalows, if larger than these, are also small, measuring from 440 to 600 square feet and divided into from four to six rooms. Rectangular cabins were usually divided into two rooms; Hollybush's houses frequently consisted of only one room, although there was a trend toward dividing this during the later part of the area's history. Beyond a fireplace or stove, there were no indoor amenities at Hollybush.

In massing and silhouette, the houses studied by Glassie and Martin are strongly echoed by Brightmoor's. All are simple rectangles with gable roofs and few windows. Most telling are the different slopes at which all three groups of houses set their pitched front porch and main roofs.

The spareness of Brightmoor's interiors, too, becomes inflected in the context of Appalachian practices. In Appalachian examples, the principal ornamental elements were paper. Glassie notes that walls and ceilings were papered with newspaper. At Hollybush, pages from catalogs and magazines were carefully applied and arranged on the walls;[93] single pictures were sometimes centered or otherwise highlighted within the composition of a wall, but patterns were frequently created through the arrangement of colors, and other decorative effects were achieved by rubbing granulated white sandstone into floorboards and door and window facings, creating a clean appearance; interior cabin walls were whitewashed. At Brightmoor, kitchens were painted and the other rooms hung with wallpaper, commercial equivalents of the Appalachian practices.

Appalachian exteriors received no decorative treatment. Visually, one was confronted with the strength and simplicity of the raw wood and of the craft techniques that were used to shape it. The lack of decoration of Brightmoor's exteriors achieves the same effect in relation to a different technology, for it allows a clear reading of their standardized and machined elements.

It is possible, then, to see Brightmoor as a project that, at a particular historical moment, accomplished a rather complex series of acculturations, through its creation of neighborhood institutions—its settlement house, but also the other social and commercial services that Taylor drew to the development—and through its architectural forms. Its housing reproduced qualities that would have been familiar to its residents, including scale, lack of amenities, and lack of embellishment. But these were taken out of their previous context of owner-builder processes and community resources and rendered, instead, through the formal real-estate system and standardized construction practices. This recast them in terms that were urban, commercial, and mass-produced.

It may seem that Taylor operated at the margins of the realty profession by adding to the stock of excess lots, by relying on eventual annexation for the provision of utilities and other services, and by building houses that did not meet minimal standards. And yet it is possible to note that he achieved a measure of prestige within both local and national professional organizations. In fact, his ability to shape a new neighborhood, designed for a specific market, exemplifies the goals that inspired realtor-developers in this period. The next chapter looks at how these goals were formulated and achieved within a more conventional subdivision.

CHAPTER 3

WESTWOOD HIGHLANDS
The Rise of the Realtor

The development of Westwood Highlands, a subdivision located in the district south of San Francisco's Twin Peaks (fig. 23), took place during the interwar period when much of the so-called Outside Lands, including the nearby Sunset District, was built up.[1] The process of its creation testifies to the self-consciousness and sophistication of West Coast realtors at this early point in their profession's evolution.[2]

The realty and development company of Baldwin & Howell shaped this scheme, working with one builder and one architect to see it through from land subdivision through house building and landscaping. The architect's role here was similar to Wood's at the Ford Homes, generating an array of housing types through the design and deployment of modular elements. Close study of this system reveals how the architecture itself articulated the new neighborhood's identity and its relationship to nearby tracts.

In the course of creating Westwood Highlands, Baldwin & Howell engaged in a number of practices that began to be recognized as marking successful residential developments in this period. Among the most significant of these were the firm's reliance upon the expertise it had accumulated through its earlier work in the district, its promotion of municipal improvements that aided the district's transformation, its integration of the new subdivision within the pattern of development of the district as a whole, and its marshaling of efficient and economical design and construction practices to provide new housing for a middle-class market. Baldwin & Howell's use of these tactics enabled the firm to help define the character of this sector of the city as a district of residential suburban subdivisions.

WESTWOOD HIGHLANDS

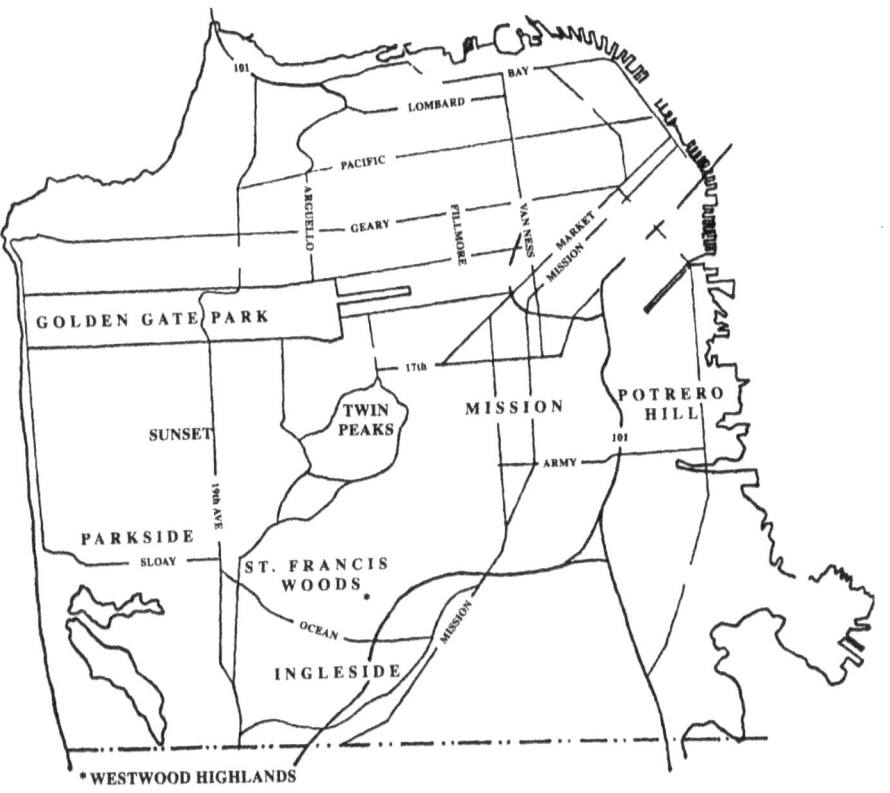

Figure 23. Westwood Highlands, in the southern part of San Francisco, is part of the "newer city" of subdivisions created during the 1910s and 1920s. The opening of a mass-transport tunnel through Twin Peaks in 1918 brought this area into the orbit of downtown. This sealed its transformation from ranchland to residential neighborhoods.

Through such activities, Baldwin & Howell acted as a de facto planner. How did this role emerge from the evolution of realtors' practices? What were the implications for the definition of the real-estate business of the dominance of the developer within the subdivisions that this study examines? To answer these questions, this chapter looks at the construction of the professional identity of the realtor-developer of the 1920s, as well as at the construction of Baldwin & Howell's Westwood Highlands subdivision in San Francisco.

THREE SUBDIVISIONS AND THEIR BUILDERS

Westwood Highlands: Background and Overview

So far as domestic architecture is concerned, San Francisco is best known for its lacy, fanciful Victorian houses and its warm, craftsmanly shingled structures in the Bay Area tradition. Perhaps the least flattering image of San Francisco housing, on the other hand, derives from the linear bands of post–World War II tract houses marking its southern hills and those of Daly City, across the city and county line, immortalized in Malvina Reynolds's song as "little boxes made of ticky-tacky." But between these extremes lie other forms of housing that, while neither as picturesque as the former nor as clumsy as the latter, nevertheless stamp the character of large areas of the city. Westwood Highlands lies in one of these zones.

Racecourses and roadhouses enticed nineteenth-century San Franciscans to journey westward from the city over the old toll road that ran through the pass between Twin Peaks and Mount Davidson. That 1860s road became Portola Drive in the second decade of the twentieth century, part of the city-wide scenic route.[3] The only trace of the former amusements of this district that can be found today amidst the rows and contoured rings of dwellings spreading from the hills to the edge of the ocean is in an occasional interruption in the street pattern (fig. 24). Ingleside Terrace preserves the oval of the racetrack it replaced, and another oval at Westwood Park marks the site where a greyhound racetrack had been.[4]

The character of the area beyond Twin Peaks began to change in the years just before and after the 1906 earthquake and fire, when those who owned the land promoted its subdivision and development. In 1911, the heirs of Adolph Sutro sold his holdings in what had once been the 4,500-acre San Miguel Rancho. The A. S. Baldwin Residential Development Company bought 725 acres and, selling some to other developers, immediately began to put residential lots on the market.[5] First Forest Hill, then Mason-McDuffie's Saint Francis Wood in 1912, followed by Fernando Nelson's West Portal Park and Baldwin & Howell's Westwood Park: each major realtor in the city carved a subdivision into the land south of Twin Peaks.[6] Spurred by competition with rival cities, these realtors and other commercial interests felt that "'San Francisco's outlying residence districts' should be designed to have 'the winsome beauty and strong attractiveness of suburbs across the bay and the towns of Southern California.'"[7]

Using census data from 1910 and 1920, Margaret Goddard King calculated that the population density in the area southwest of Mount Davidson doubled in those years.[8] A finer-grained instrument would probably show that the bulk of that growth occurred only in the last few years of the decade. The newly subdivided tracts were slow to sell until the City of San Francisco made the district beyond Twin Peaks more readily accessible to the downtown area by extending the public transportation system (the Municipal Railway, or Muni).[9] One city supervisor stated, "Our hills must be tunnelled to open up new districts to the home seeker."[10]

The transformation of this district from farms and dairy ranches punctuated by raucous recreational spots to neighborhoods of suburban domesticity resulted from the combined efforts of real-estate interests and local government. The city engineer from 1912 to 1934, Michael M. O'Shaughnessy, promoted the Muni as a tool for, as he wrote, "developing the city's growth in well-ordered and predetermined directions."[11] O'Shaughnessy was well acquainted with suburban development, for he had laid out two areas of Marin County, Mill Valley and Belvedere, in 1889–90, and Hillsborough, on the southern peninsula, in 1893–94.[12] The opening of the Panama Canal heightened expectations for San Francisco's expansion and lent urgency to the desire to shape the direction of its growth.[13] Extending Muni service to the districts west and south of Twin Peaks required boring a tunnel 2.27 miles through the hills.[14] Although the first developers of housing in the district had expressed interest in such a tunnel as early as 1908, once planning for it began in earnest under O'Shaughnessy, realtors and developers formed the Twin Peaks Property Owners Association. The Twin Peaks Tunnel was dedicated on July 14, 1917, and on February 4, 1918 the first Muni streetcar passed through it. With Mayor Rolph serving as motorman, the guests on the car included A. S. Baldwin, a recognized pioneer "of the movement which led to the building of the tunnel." Ironically, at the opening celebration "the Twin Peaks Property Owners Association met the crowded

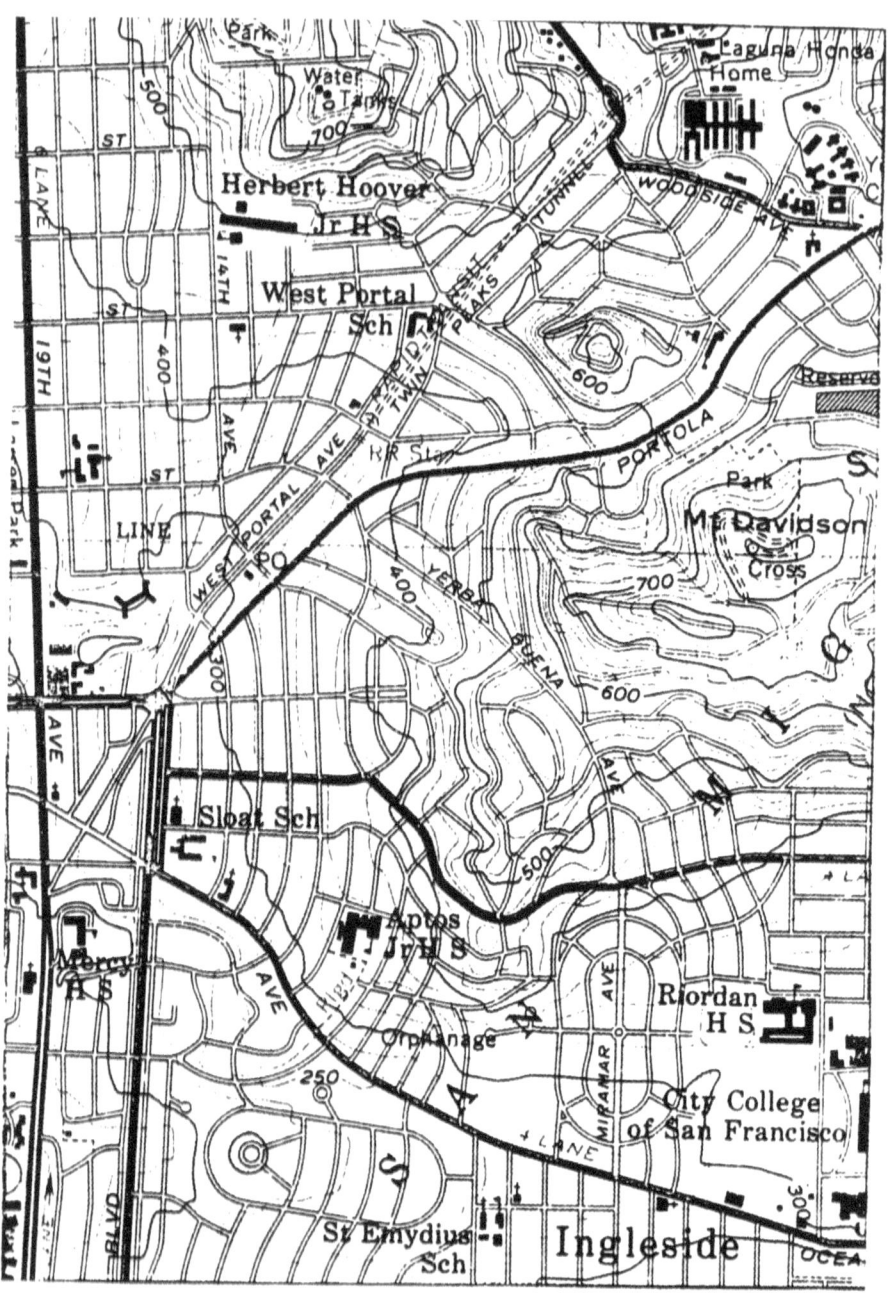

streetcars at West Portal with their automobiles and seized on the gala occasion to take prospective buyers on conducted tours through the emerging residential districts of St. Francis Wood, Forest Hill, Parkside, Ingleside Terrace, and Westwood Park."[15]

City government thus organized the creation of the transportation link that made development of the land speculators' tracts possible. This bears out the view of geographer James E. Vance that one should see "the [street]carline as primarily a device to encourage real estate development."[16] The roughly $4 million cost of the tunnel was mainly passed on to new home buyers, since about seven-eighths of this amount was assessed to those who stood to gain from the venture, the property owners in the districts west of Twin Peaks.[17] The tunnel reduced the trip downtown from more than an hour to twenty minutes. By 1923, five years after the inauguration of the Twin Peaks Tunnel, Prentice Duell could write in the *Western Architect* that "today [the subdivisions mentioned above] . . . contain the choice residences and gardens of the newer city."[18]

Three features characterized this "newer city" and made it distinctive in relation to the familiar patterns of residential construction in San Francisco. First of all, the subdivisions built southwest of Twin Peaks were conceived as commuter suburbs. As the description of the opening-day festivities for the tunnel recounts, the promotion of the district's development invoked both public streetcar transportation and private automobiles. Similar to other "streetcar suburbs," the success of this area's development depended on public transportation links;[19] most of the subdivisions' houses, however, included garages for the accommodation of autos as well. The remoteness of a district in which "hunting small game was still a major diversion" made it attractive once the barrier of distance from downtown was removed.[20]

Figure 24. This topographical map of the area south of San Francisco's Mount Davidson shows how traces of the district's racetracks were maintained by oval street patterns. The street plan of Westwood Highlands reflects a smaller site and looser design than the one seen in plans for Baldwin and Howell's unrealized Woodcrest subdivision.

Secondly, the design of curvilinear streets that followed the contours of the slopes broke with the standard "crossword puzzle effect,"[21] as one writer described the grid that covered all but San Francisco's highest peaks. These subdivisions were recognized as "among the best planned in San Francisco."[22] While sometimes developers simply adapted street plans to the preexisting pattern left by oval racetracks, they also responded to progressive opinion regarding the felicity of deliberately curved streets and their placement within the natural setting. The 1912 site plan for Saint Francis Wood, created by the Olmsted Brothers' landscape architecture firm, reflected this family's tradition of such garden-suburb design. Developers of other tracts adapted this ideal to their own needs.

Finally, many of the subdividers working in this district created lots that were larger than the parcels common in most San Francisco neighborhoods—traditionally twenty-five feet wide. Lot sizes vary both from one development to another and within individual developments, but the presence of detached, single-family houses sitting in the middle of their lots stamps the character of the area.

The Baldwin & Howell realty company was one of the early developers who shaped the "newer city" in the district west of Twin Peaks. It was a well-established firm, founded in 1885, and one of its entities, the A. S. Baldwin Residential Development Company, had made the initial purchase of acreage from Adolph Sutro's Rancho San Miguel holdings in 1911. Baldwin & Howell developed part of this land, beginning around 1917, as Westwood Park, one of the often-praised early subdivisions. It lies between Monterey Boulevard and Ocean Avenue, where flat terrain was conducive to the establishment of both a streetcar line and a shopping district. A planted strip that runs down Westwood Park's central axis, Miramar Avenue, bisects the main oval of the tract. John M. Punnett, an engineer, designed the scheme.[23] More than a dozen different builders were responsible for the construction of single-family houses on Westwood Park's seven hundred lots.[24]

By 1925, Westwood Park's lots were completely sold, but even before that Baldwin & Howell had begun to develop an adjacent tract on the north side of Monterey Boulevard.[25] The first name for this new subdivision was Woodcrest (fig. 25). According to engineer Punnett's proposed street plan from 1922, the 175-acre tract extended from Portola Drive south to Monterey Boulevard, east of the existing Saint Francis Wood development created by Mason-McDuffie. Mount Davidson, which reaches a height of 927 feet, rises just south of Portola Drive (see fig. 24). Punnett divided the steepest area of the site into large, irregular blocks bounded by roads that would have curved steeply right over the summit of the hill. This contrasts with the more stylized design of the southeastern part of the site, in which curving streets radiate concentrically, fan-like, from the intersection of Yerba Buena Avenue and Monterey Boulevard.

Two other records testify to the original conception of Woodcrest as a "villa site subdivision." These are photographs of renderings for a decorative structure to be placed at the Yerba Buena and Monterey intersection, the formal entrance to the subdivision (fig. 26, a and b). Relatively simple rectangular piers embellished with wrought-iron lanterns and grills mark the formal entrance to Westwood Park at Monterey Boulevard and Miramar Avenue; barrel vaults supporting trellises span the sidewalks (fig. 27). In contrast, the projected "features" for Woodcrest, set on a roadway island, are more elaborate and classical in style. Rams and winged horses bearing urns, Corinthian columns, and benches are envisioned within the still-sylvan setting. The classicism of these sculptural and architectural civic amenities playing against organic landscape forms harkens back to the ideals of the turn-of-the-century City Beautiful movement.[26] Architects John Galen Howard and Henry Gutterson had created more modest versions of features like these in 1912 for nearby Saint Francis Wood.

Between 1922 and 1924, Baldwin & Howell set aside the engineer's proposals for Woodcrest and created a different street plan and subdivision name. The elegant structures designed by architect John Reid Jr. were never built; instead, very simple metal signs attached to lamp-posts at the corners of Yerba Buena, Plymouth, Colon, Valdez, Hazelwood, and Ridgewood Avenues marked the boundary of the tract at Monterey Boulevard (fig. 28). These north-south streets, corresponding to the fan-shaped portion of the 1922 plan, now curve with the topography. Hazelwood Avenue bends to the west as it

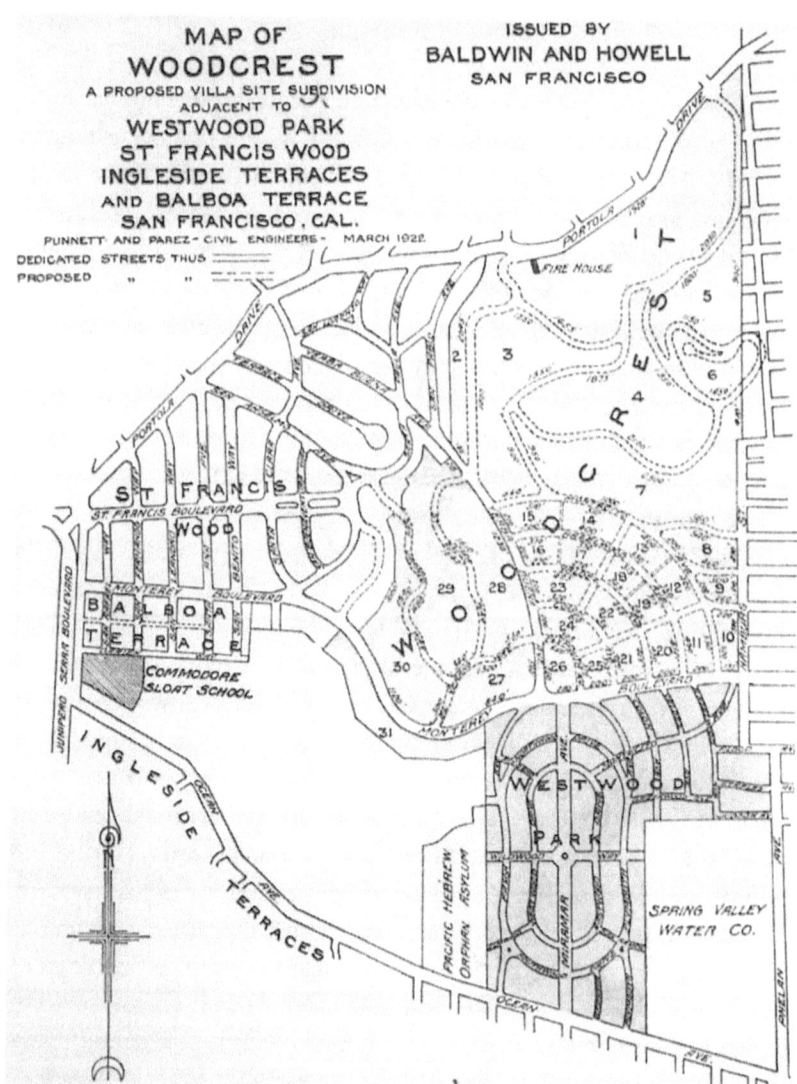

Figure 25. To take advantage of the success of their Westwood Park development, Baldwin and Howell first designed a "villa site subdivision," to be called Woodcrest. It combined a formal, fan-like configuration of rectangular blocks with curvilinear streets that meandered over the steep slopes of Mount Davidson. This map of the design and location of the proposed scheme emphasizes its proximity to recently developed subdivisions that were already bringing acclaim to the district.

climbs the slope, looping around to Yerba Buena Avenue and becoming the northern boundary of the development. The subdivision no longer includes the northern and western portions of the 1922 site, and this reduction perhaps led to the rechristening of the subdivision as Westwood Highlands.

There are no records extant that explain the transformation of Woodcrest into Westwood Highlands, but most of the changes seem to follow from a different idea of the market for housing in this subdivision. The scale and elegance of Reid's features, and the varied terrain of Punnett's "villa" site plan, suggest that Woodcrest had been modeled on a prestigious enclave such as Saint Francis Wood. At the same time that Baldwin & Howell dropped those aspects of the original scheme, they decided to work with a builder, Hans Nelson, and an architect, Charles Strothoff, from their already-sold Westwood Park development. For Westwood Park, which they characterized as a "restricted residence park," Baldwin & Howell made suggestions to buyers about the kinds of houses it would be appropriate to build, such as those illustrated in their booklet, *Attractive Bungalows of Moderate Cost for Westwood Park*.[27] In this, as in their use of restrictions to ensure the maintenance of aesthetic and socioeconomic standards, the developers conformed to practices typical of the projects in this district and elsewhere. However, when they engaged a builder and an architect for Westwood Highlands, Baldwin & Howell decided to sell lots only with houses already constructed on them. They must have assumed that they had a good sense of the middle-class market that had been attracted to Westwood Park, and that by building from 100 to 150 houses a year they could lower costs as well as continue to serve that market.[28] The tract's new name, too, suggests an extension of Westwood Park, rather than a wholly different development, to appeal to a market that would be familiar with the earlier subdivision. This continuity also took advantage of the publicity that Westwood Park's success as one of the prominent subdivisions in the "newer city" had garnered.

A typical advertisement for Westwood Highlands (fig. 29) reflects some of these appeals to prospective home owners, referring both to Westwood Park ("now all sold out") and to Westwood Highlands

Figure 26, a and b. Elaborate designs for an entrance feature attest to the conception of Woodcrest as an elite enclave. The classical vocabulary of these Beaux Arts structures, set off against the organic forms of the landscape, links them to turn-of-the-century City Beautiful ideals.

Figure 27. The features that mark the entrance to Westwood Park establish a formal boundary by using simpler elements than those conceived for Woodcrest. Instead of relying on historicist imagery, these features combine spare, geometrical piers and barrel vaults with ironwork grilles, lanterns, and trellises. They define the entrance to the main axial boulevard of the subdivision.

("Moderate Prices—much less than it would cost you to build such a home"). The ad's photograph of houses on Plymouth Avenue prominently features an auto, but the text assures the reader of easy access by streetcar as well.

In 1927, most of the Westwood Highlands houses sold for $9,500 to $12,000, with monthly payments around $70.[29] This was about twice the national average cost for a new single-family house and twice what San Francisco streetcarmen's families, for example, could afford.[30] In the area's subdivisions in general, home buyers seem to have moved from the Mission District, "where accelerating development threatened the suburban ambience."[31] They were predominantly skilled workers, lower-middle-class businessmen, and pro-

Figure 28. When Westwood Highlands supplanted the proposed Woodcrest development, plans for an elaborate entrance feature were set aside. Instead, simple metal signs attached to lampposts at street corners along Monterey Boulevard marked the boundary of the new subdivision.

Figure 29. This March 1925 advertisement for Westwood Highlands from *Home Designer and Garden Beautiful* reflects the middle-class appeal of the new subdivision. An ad for Nelson Bros., it nevertheless creates the impression that the prospective home buyer would establish a relationship with the architect and the home builder. The developer of the tract is not mentioned in the ad at all.

fessionals; their ethnic backgrounds tended to be Irish, Italian, and German Catholic.[32]

Baldwin & Howell, as the real-estate developer, seems to have played the major role in shaping Westwood Highlands. To the extent that the subdivision can be seen as a unity, however, the contributions of the builder and the architect must be considered as well, for they articulated the developer's scheme. The blurb quoted above (see fig. 29) is, in fact, an advertisement for the builder: "Built by Nelson Bros." It also mentions the architect: one of the listed features is "Pleasing Architecture—the work of Charles Strothoff." The ad does not, in fact, refer to Baldwin & Howell at all. Instead, it highlights the individuals with whom prospective home owners would interact were they themselves commissioning the construction of their houses; it deemphasizes the relationship to the corporate realty firm that purchasing a house at Westwood Highlands actually entailed. Unfortunately, few records remain concerning the working relationship among these individuals, or about this part of the builder's and architect's careers. A somewhat clearer picture emerges, however, by combining such information as does exist with an examination of built form.

Little is known of the career of Hans Nelson, the builder. According to the February 1927 article in *Building Age* that featured his work at Westwood Highlands, he arrived in the United States in 1908 from Sweden.[33] After taking up carpentry, he entered the construction business with a brother in Colorado. Nelson moved to San Francisco in 1911 and built his first houses in the Richmond District. In 1918, he began building houses in Westwood Park for Baldwin & Howell, sometimes working with his brother as Nelson Bros. He lived in Westwood Park during the first half of the 1920s, at 1375 Plymouth Avenue, and in Westwood Highlands, at 460 Yerba Buena Avenue, from 1928 to 1939. Hans Nelson died in the mid 1950s.[34]

Charles F. Strothoff, the architect for Westwood Highlands, was born in 1891 or 1892 in San Francisco.[35] He received his training at the Wilmerding School of Industrial Arts, a building-trades school established by a wealthy San Francisco merchant and administered by the regents of the University of California. The school had been created "to teach boys trades, fitting them to make their living with their hands, with little study and plenty of work."[36] When the school opened in 1900, it offered training in carpentry, bricklaying, plumbing, architectural ironwork, clay modeling and artificial stonework, wood carving, cabinetmaking, and architectural drawing. Strothoff, like Albert Wood, developed his architectural skills through a combination of vocational education and apprenticeship experiences.

For at least one year, 1912–13, Strothoff served as a draftsman in the office of architect Albert Farr.[37] Farr had established his practice in San Francisco in the early 1900s; at the time Strothoff was working for him, the house that he had designed for Jack London, Wolf House, was under construction in nearby Sonoma County.[38] Farr specialized in domestic architecture with a Tudor or Georgian character, and his designs often reached the baronial in scale. By the 1920s, he enjoyed a well-established reputation as a designer of period houses.[39]

Strothoff's early career seems to have followed Farr's in its focus on domestic projects, if on a more modest scale. Later, he worked for public institutions, serving as executive director of the Richmond Housing Authority, across the bay. The nature of Strothoff's employment reflects the trend in this period toward residential architects working for large developers and state agencies. He also worked for the San Francisco Recreation and Park Department and for Contra Costa Junior (now Community) College. Charles Strothoff died in 1963; he had been a member of the American Institute of Architects since 1944.[40]

A few photographs from a Westwood Park photo album from the 1920s illustrate the work that Nelson and Strothoff did for Baldwin & Howell in that project, separately and together.[41] The house they collaborated on, 185 Westwood, is least characteristic of the district, for it is in a colonial revival style with wooden clapboards (fig. 30).

Nelson built one of the most prominently placed houses in the subdivision, 591 Wildwood, at the intersection of Wildwood and Miramar Avenues, the center of the tract (fig. 31). At this point, a circular landscaped island in the middle of the intersection punctuates the planted mall that runs the length of Miramar Avenue. The four houses fronting the center all have their entrances at the corner, facing

THREE SUBDIVISIONS AND THEIR BUILDERS

Figure 30. 185 Westwood, Westwood Park, under construction. Hans Nelson, builder, and Charles Strothoff, architect, were among the many builders and architects working at Westwood Park. They collaborated on the construction of this house before Baldwin and Howell hired them to design and build Westwood Highlands.

the street intersection, with two wings branching off at right angles, as in the one built by Nelson illustrated here. Although each is designed according to a different style within the broad repertory of Mediterranean revival, their disposition in relation to the public space provides unity and underscores the formality of the scheme.[42]

Another house designed by Strothoff, more modest both in scale and style, is a stucco cottage (fig. 32) in which details such as window and entrance shapes, roofline, and applied decoration serve to individualize the box-like structure.[43] Nelson, too, built houses like this one.

Baldwin & Howell used their achievement at Westwood Park, and the experience gained there by Nelson and Strothoff, to plan and build their new subdivision, Westwood Highlands, in its entirety. This represented an innovation in subdivision development in the

Figure 31. 591 Wildwood, Westwood Park, under construction. Its location, facing a landscaped island at the center of the development, makes this one of the most prominent houses that Nelson built at Westwood Park. The entrance to the house is sited at the corner, in the angle between two wings, which draws attention to the formality of the intersection's public space.

district. By the mid 1920s, the ground had been well prepared for such an initiative. As already noted, the principal real-estate developers of the district had first worked with the City of San Francisco to create the infrastructure to bring the rural West of Twin Peaks District into the suburban orbit of downtown. The array of early subdivisions, shaped by a number of major developers, established a vocabulary of practices in the district that included curvilinear street plans and detached single-family dwellings set on landscaped lots. The middle-class market for housing in the district had been attracted to Baldwin & Howell's Westwood Park, which had completely sold; and this market provided the impetus for continuing development at Westwood Highlands.

In undertaking such a project, however, what features did Baldwin

Figure 32. 25 Northwood, Westwood Park, under construction—another example of architect Strothoff's work at Westwood Park. Nelson, the builder, constructed similar modest, stucco cottages. Both men contributed to the eclectic character of the subdivision's houses.

& Howell seek to recreate? One of the familiar notions they applied to Westwood Highlands was the use of a curvilinear street plan suited to the topography. Also, a sense of the identity of the new neighborhood was established by the installation of signage at the intersections along Monterey Boulevard. But a closer look at the built forms of Westwood Highlands, taking into consideration the role of stylistic elements and analyzing the organizing principles of the new subdivision, illuminates the concepts that guided the design of this project as a totality.

The Role of Style

The houses that Strothoff and Nelson designed and built for Westwood Highlands share features with the examples of their earlier work discussed above, with the exception of 185 Westwood (see fig. 30). The purchasers of this lot had been able to choose the house style they desired, in this case Dutch colonial, which was not possible for the home buyers in Westwood Highlands. This style is an anomaly in Westwood Park, where stucco and simplified Spanish colonial or English styles predominate. While it would have been possible for the developers to accommodate such diversity in Westwood Highlands, too—programming anomalies, as it were, into the design of the subdivision—in fact they did not. Instead, they chose to balance diversity of surface design with unity of materials and plan. They restricted the materials to stucco, sometimes embellished by wood or brick. Against this backdrop, Strothoff was then able to orchestrate a great variety of details drawn from Spanish colonial revival, Moorish, mission, classical revival, and other styles that fuse to form the Mediterranean revival character of the district.

There certainly were precedents for such an approach in the patterns of residential building in San Francisco. The decorative inventiveness of Victorian builders had also been spun over an underlying unity of construction materials. Although that particular fabric and its embellishment were spurned in the 1920s, the two periods share a similar logic in their attitudes toward the relationship between unity of materials and diversity of surface design. For the builders of the 1870s-90s period, of course, wood was used throughout, for framing, sheathing, and ornamentation. The horizontal bands of flat wooden siding served as a field against which contrasts of texture, shape, and light and shadow could play; they were both the protective skin over the underlying structure and the ground for eclectic ornamental figures. At Westwood Highlands, the houses are wood-framed, but stucco is used as cladding. Nevertheless, stucco serves the same role here as wood had earlier, both within each building, where it bridges structure and surface detail, and within the tract as a whole, where its consistent planar use balances the multiplicity of ornamentation.

Historicist details, then, serve to individualize each house and to create an overall sense of variety within the subdivision. Windows, entrances, porches, rooflines, and applied ornamentation are treated as expressive and pictorial features. But while they define the appearance of the tract, they do not reflect or convey its underlying organization. In earlier tracts such as Westwood Park, control over the composition of the whole was exercised by restrictions that established price, size, and setback guidelines. If the home buyer selected a period style, as was the case at Westwood Park's 185 Westwood, the builder or architect could design a house that both fit the guidelines and conformed to that style in massing, orientation, and materials as well as in details. At Westwood Highlands, in contrast, Strothoff determined the subdivision's composition, probably according to economic goals and constraints set by Baldwin & Howell. The architect did not use stylistic elements at all to generate the overall organization of the project. The detailing functions only to vary the patterns that he established through other means.

The approach that Strothoff took, then, is reminiscent of that used by Wood in the Ford Homes. As there, it is necessary to look beyond the stylistic treatment of the houses to locate the generating principles that organized the design of Westwood Highlands.

The Principles of Organization

Strothoff seems to have manipulated three significant elements to organize Westwood Highlands: the repetition of modules, the treatment of corners, and the hierarchy of streets. The abovementioned article on the subdivision in *Building Age* discusses the division of streets into price areas as one of the tract's features.[44] Restrictions, imposed by the realtor, that established a minimum price for houses on each street enforced this kind of system in a development such as Westwood Park. But in Westwood Highlands, where no lots were sold without houses already constructed on them, the developers executed their own edicts. The largest houses, on somewhat larger lots, can be found along Yerba Buena Avenue, Plymouth Avenue, and Monterey Boulevard, although the majority of houses on these streets are medium-sized (see fig. 29). Lots decrease in size as the slope increases; the views that these sites afford may have offset some of the impact of this reduction on cost. The most modest houses are located at the eastern edge of the development, on Ridgewood Avenue (fig. 33). This price-driven pattern also reflects the distance from the streetcar and shopping district on Ocean Avenue of the lots on the north and east.

Anne Bloomfield noticed this kind of hierarchy in her study of The Real Estate Associates (TREA), one of the largest developers in San Francisco in the 1870s. She observed that TREA built "a few larger and several medium-priced houses on the more important streets, slightly less expensive houses on the side streets, inexpensive houses on interior streets."[45] Although she does not pursue the connection in greater detail, Bloomfield suggests that "perhaps unconsciously, TREA was following principles of Georgian town planning by providing for a whole community."[46] The practice of organizing wealth spatially was, thus, a familiar one within the community of San Francisco developers, and the system used by Baldwin & Howell fits within this pattern.

Corner lots in Westwood Highlands are also an aspect of this hierarchical pattern, for often, though not always, they are larger than inside lots. This, too, follows earlier practice.[47] But whereas in the nineteenth century larger corner lots became the sites either of grander residences or of stores, they serve another function in this 1920s subdivision. Houses situated at corners are frequently designed so that their entrances, set diagonally, face the intersection (fig. 34). This focuses attention on the street as a public, formal space. Aside from the familiar arrangements of lawn, walkway, and porch, this is the

Figure 33. A two-module type, on Ridgewood, between Joost and Mangels, Westwood Highlands. The simplest configuration of modules that architect Strothoff orchestrated sets a narrow, recessed entrance module next to a broader module that includes shallow bow windows above a street-level garage. Variants of this type on streets that are less steep are somewhat more ample; fully detached, they are set further back from the street.

major device used to express the relationship between the houses and the street, for there are no amenities such as malls or planted islands at Westwood Highlands. This orientation also provides continuity between the two sides of a block that meet at a corner. The corner acts less to anchor or conclude a horizontal row of houses on a street than to produce a flow of movement around the corner. Perhaps this softening of the corners was intended to underscore the curvilinearity of the street plan, although it also occurs at intersections where the streets are roughly perpendicular to each other. By deemphasizing the unitary quality of a single street, it suggests continuity within a larger neighborhood scheme.

The use of a house plan that permits the entrance to face the intersection is not unique to Strothoff's designs for Westwood Highlands. One of Nelson's houses at Westwood Park, 591 Wildwood, has already been discussed as one of four that are configured in this way to contribute to the formality of the public space they define (see fig. 31). This seems to be an urbanistic application of the "bent" house that one historian has called "the single most important nineteenth-century innovation in American domestic architecture."[48] Deriving from pattern books of the 1840s, the bent house is composed of two perpendicular wings whose junction occurs at the entrance. An influential picturesque house type, the irregularity and segmentation of its parts permitted later designers such as Strothoff to pivot the wings to adjust to peculiarities of site, such as corners.

Figure 34. 250 Hazelwood, Westwood Highlands. An important strategy for organizing the design of this subdivision was to orient the entrances of corner houses toward the intersection. This adapts a nineteenth-century picturesque type, the "bent" house, to create a site plan that integrates individual houses with the street and surrounding houses. The entrance module becomes the hinge of the ell-shaped composition, the angle softened by substituting steps and a small patio for the meeting of wall surfaces.

The third important element in the organization of Westwood Highlands bears on the earlier discussion of the relationship between unity and diversity. The overlay of decorative detailing individualizes houses that are otherwise unified by their construction materials. Repeating elevational modules in a variety of combinations also achieved this balance. As in the earlier analysis of the Ford Homes, the term *module* refers to units of the public facade of the house. Here, all of the houses present on their street side an entrance, windows, and garage doors. But Strothoff orchestrated these units in a variety of configurations so that the order they confer is muted by a sense of diversity.

The smallest configuration consists of two modules, in which a narrow entrance module is juxtaposed with a broader module containing windows set above a street-level garage (see fig. 33). The largest houses encompass four modules, with a window module being repeated so that the facade reads garage module/window module/entrance module/window module (figs. 35 and 36). The widest range of variations is found among three-module types (figs. 37 and 38).

Often the garage module, and occasionally the entrance module, is recessed. Visually, variable elements such as bow windows, entrance hoods, porch parapets, and wall angles create projections and reces-

---

Figure 35. A four-module type, on Yerba Buena, between Brentwood and Hazelwood, Westwood Highlands. Repetition of the window module is the typical device used to create the four-module type. In this variant, small windows are set over the recessed garage module, the entrance is angled, the large window module follows, and the front wall plane is extended to embrace an arched gateway that leads to the back of the house.

Figure 36. A four-module type, on Hazelwood, between Yerba Buena and Brentwood, Westwood Highlands. The four-module type is also characterized by the dramatic articulation of surface planes. The examples seen here are on relatively narrow lots at the northern boundary of the subdivision. Each break in the wall surface is emphasized; the compression of tall, narrow modules, sharply defined by light and shadow, creates a syncopated visual rhythm.

sions that yield contrasts of light and shadow. These accentuate the divisions between modules and heighten the individuality of each dwelling. Organizationally, modules allow for both a range of house sizes and the sensitive adjustment of each house to its site. Their flexibility can accommodate the narrow lots along steep Ridgewood Avenue, where two-module types are found, as well as more generous lots such as those along Monterey Boulevard, where larger houses are sited (fig. 39).

Also interesting is the way in which corner houses are treated. We have already noted that they are often placed so that the entrance faces the intersection. The modular organization of these houses allowed Strothoff to pivot the units around a corner without disturbing the underlying principles of composition. The house located at the intersection of Hazelwood and Brentwood Avenues, for example, where the block ends in an acute angle, has been dramatically segmented to fit its site (fig. 40). Other solutions that make use of the bent-house form can be found at the intersection of Joost and Hazelwood Avenues, where four-module types pivot around the corner (see fig. 34).

Although it is veiled at first by the overlay of individualized detailing, the pattern of modular types and their variations emerges as Westwood Highlands is observed more closely. Further study of other neighborhoods built in the 1920s might well reveal similar configurations, even where many builders were involved. In other areas of the West of Twin Peaks District, for example, it is possible to notice both familiar modular arrangements and corners where houses are sited in

---

Figure 37. A three-module type, 325 Colon, Westwood Highlands, 1927. The typical three-module type juxtaposes the main window module with the entrance and sets smaller windows above the recessed garage. Photo taken in 1927.

Figure 38. A three-module type, on Hazelwood, between Los Palmos and Brentwood, Westwood Highlands. In this variation, the superimposition of windows set above garage doors, familiar from the two-module arrangement, projects forward from another window module. The entrance, reached by stairs, is placed like a hinge between the two.

Figure 39. 944 Monterey, Westwood Highlands. Modular design allowed the architect to accommodate houses to varying lot sizes. By adding major or minor window modules, he created stretched-out versions of the basic house types for larger lots. Here, an extended design includes another window module and the enlargement of the entrance porch to create a patio.

WESTWOOD HIGHLANDS

Figure 40. A corner house at intersection, Hazelwood and Brentwood, Westwood Highlands. Modular design allowed houses to be configured on unusual sites. This block ends in an acute angle and the house is pivoted dramatically to fit the space. The garage is located under the entrance module, but the garage doors are at a right angle to the entranceway, in the ell created by flipping the second window module so that it is perpendicular to the rest of the mass.

a similar way. It may be, as discussion of Bloomfield's study suggests, that there was among builders and designers in San Francisco by this period a common body of practice that Strothoff drew on when he was faced with the task of providing designs for an entire subdivision's houses.

Certainly, the modular framework has been useful retrospectively in allowing historians to analyze the physical elements of community design. In her study of San Francisco's Alamo Square area, Anne Vernez Moudon locates modular elements that create a stable, repetitive underpinning for the diversity of individualized decorative embellishment characterizing the Victorian houses found in this neighborhood. Influenced by both the urban rowhouse and suburban models, and evolving over time through Stick, Italianate, and Queen Anne styles of detailing, the elevations of the houses are, nevertheless, composed of vertical divisions into entry, window, and recess modules.[49] This aspect of Moudon's analysis is suggestive here, since Strothoff was manipulating similar modular elements. To what extent his self-conscious use of modular design came out of an awareness by Strothoff of specifically Victorian practices cannot be ascertained. His use of recessed modules is provocative, however. The need to maximize access to light and air within the constraints of box-like houses built close together on narrow urban lots accounts for the presence of such modules in the earlier structures.[50] Strothoff, designing predominantly detached houses on larger lots, was not working with the same constraints, but he maintained this traditional element and, in many of his compositions, enlarged it and adapted it to new uses by locating the garage within the recessed module. Strothoff also seems to have seen the possibilities inherent in modular organization as double-edged; he used modules as instruments to create both order and diversity.

The modular treatment of the facades at Westwood Highlands also reflects to a certain extent the pattern of interior planning (figs. 39 and 41). Public spaces are grouped toward the front of the house or the corner; the main window module corresponds to the living room. Bedrooms are clustered at the rear of the site; a bedroom is placed over the recessed garage module. The prominence of the garage, especially when it is set at the building line, underscores such spatial differentiation of public and private functions at a point in time when these were changing. As one scholar of the automobile's impact has observed, the garage moved to the front of the house and became attached to it when the backyard replaced the front porch in importance.[51] This reconfiguration shifted social interaction to the private sphere, while the space that formerly bridged the public and private domains, the porch, was ceded to automobile storage.

Most of the houses contain two or three bedrooms. A series of plans for the most prevalent three-module type, consisting of entrance, window, and recessed garage modules, shows the way in which variations in size could be achieved within a basic format. Rooms could be

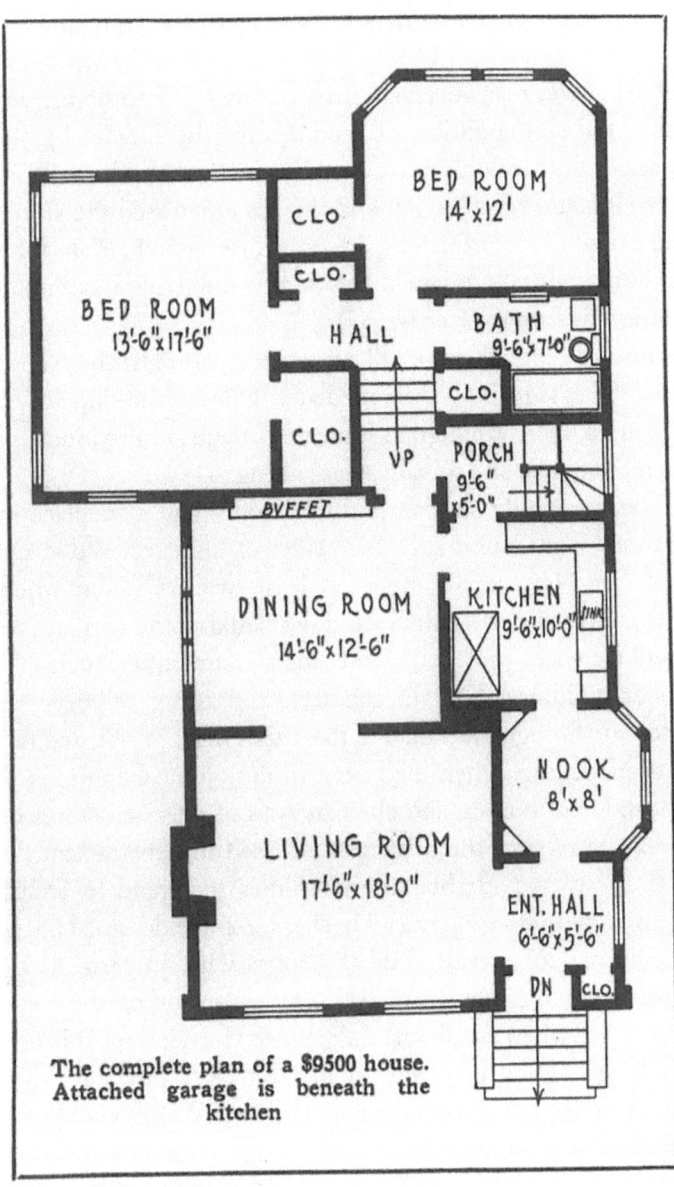

Figure 41. Two-bedroom plan, Westwood Highlands. The modular character of the facades reflects the modular arrangement of the interiors. This plan for a compact, three-module-type house (entrance/window/recessed garage) clusters the public spaces toward the front and groups the private areas at the rear.

added on at the rear, increasing the number of bedrooms, without affecting the configuration of modules on the facade; by shifting the space of the breakfast nook laterally, the kitchen, the hall, and the nook itself could be enlarged, and this also increased the size of the entrance module, transforming the stoop into a porch. Plans for larger corner houses reveal similar clusters of functional spaces, although the orientation was altered (see fig. 39).

The houses generally have full basements, part of the high base that includes the garage. This base mediates between the slope of the lot and the main floor, although in some cases there are also interior stairs between the public and private areas (see fig. 41).

All houses include a separate dining room and a fireplace in the living room. Ventilation and the quality of light received attention, for each bedroom usually enjoys at least two exposures; when the living room faced north, small windows flanking the fireplace on the west wall were also provided. Other interior amenities, such as wood or plaster moldings, built-in cabinets, and coved ceilings, can be glimpsed in photographs taken in the 1920s (figs. 39, 42, and 43).

Strothoff's charge, then, had been to design a coherent yet varied neighborhood of houses, and close analysis of these structures makes it possible to recover the principles he used to generate them. His work at Westwood Highlands exemplifies the trend in architects' involvement with housing traced in chapter 2. He designed an aggregate of houses for a real-estate developer who, in turn, had been responsible for the transformation of this sector of the city into enclaves of suburban dwellings. Baldwin & Howell were able to draw on this longstanding involvement in their city's physical evolution when they undertook the development of their Westwood Highlands subdivision.

The realty firm of Baldwin & Howell had been founded in 1885; by the time they built Westwood Highlands in the 1920s, the business of real-estate had achieved the identity of a profession. The process of professionalization of real-estate enterprises—a process to which Baldwin & Howell contributed—began in the late-nineteenth century; by the 1920s, there was a national organization, with its own publication, that had working relationships both with other profes-

A MODERN HOME IN WESTWOOD HIGHLANDS

Figure 42. 225 Valdez, Westwood Highlands. The character of interior spaces can be seen in this spread from the March 1925 issue of *Home Designer and Garden Beautiful*. As in the Nelson Bros. advertisement in figure 29, here, too, the builder and architect are acknowledged but no mention is made of the developer.

The entrance hall in the residence of Mr. G. H. Wills, at Westwood Highlands, San Francisco, Calif. On the opposite page is shown additional views of the house, together with the floor plan.

Figure 43. Interior of 944 Monterey, Westwood Highlands, 1925. The expansiveness of this entrance hall reflects a stretched-out design that incorporated a patio beyond the door at the left. The dining room and breakfast nook are off the hall to the right. The hall terminates in the living room.

sionals concerned with urban and development issues and with governmental agencies, as well as licensing and other mechanisms through which the qualifications and activities of its members could be controlled. The creation of this organizational structure took place at the same time as the redefinition of the real-estate business. Among the endeavors for which realtors began to claim a special responsibility was the development of large-scale single-family housing communities. The project built by Baldwin & Howell is, thus, emblematic of the activities of realtors in this period. It illustrates the practices of the profession at the same time that it is illuminated, in its turn, by the larger historical trends of which it is a part. The exact nature of these trends in real-estate practices emerges from consideration of the ways in which realtors molded their profession and from looking at how residential subdividing activity contributed to that project.

Realtors: The Professional Project

The history of dealings in land in the United States is primarily one of speculation in undeveloped areas, entailing high risks, the lure of extravagant profits, and the potential for abuse by "land sharks."[52] Arranging property transfers in settled communities, the real-estate agent traditionally served merely as a go-between, collecting commissions on transactions between buyers and sellers. By 1922, however, there was a transformation in the activities of such businessmen. One writer defined the new real-estate professional vividly and succinctly:

> The Realtor of today represents America's best type of citizenship. He is a thinker, a planner and a builder. His studies are those of development and his aims are those of the altruist. He believes in better habitations, better cities and more productive farms. He holds no brief for capital or labor, for class or faction, but he possesses a firm and an active faith in his community, his country and in the imperishable qualities of the commodity in which he deals.[53]

While the boosterism of Babbitt is surely one aspect of this picture, another is its representation of the realtor's appeal to community development as disinterested. The latter reflects the newly professionalized identity that had been forged over the preceding thirty years.

The mechanisms that real-estate businessmen used to construct this new identity as professionals were those employed in other professional projects, as they have been analyzed by Magali Sarfatti Larson in *The Rise of Professionalism: A Sociological Analysis*.[54] Studied retrospectively, such developments as the formation of a national association, the definition of ethical procedures, the transmission of expertise through the education of new practitioners, and the grounding of that expertise in claims to scientific theory can be seen as steps leading consistently toward a group's redefinition as a profession. Larson develops this analysis of professionalization primarily in relation to medicine, law, and engineering, but it applies to realty (and, as we have seen, architecture) as well. Like other professions that have emerged since the turn of the century, realty modeled itself on the paths that medicine and law had already trod to achieve market monopoly and social status. Nor were contemporaries unaware of this process. Economist Richard T. Ely articulated the self-conscious development of the profession in exactly these terms in his contribution to one of the early texts on real-estate practice published in 1925. There he observed that "as the real-estate business develops into a true profession, the experience which men have had formerly in law and medicine will be duplicated, for this business is following along those lines of development which have made those other occupations real professions."[55]

One instrument for realizing the professional project was organization. There were efforts to organize real-estate businessmen into local associations as early as 1847, but until the 1880s all were short-lived. The severe depression of the 1890s undermined the first attempt, in 1891, to create a national organization. As soon as the economic tide turned, however, the initiative was renewed, and in 1908 the National Association of Real Estate Boards (NAREB) was founded.[56] The need to distinguish qualified and honest brokers from unscrupulous "land sharks" had been the spur to organization, and this remained a concern of NAREB. In 1916, the new term *realtor* was adopted to signify a member of the organization; although the attempt to copyright the term failed, in several states it was registered under trademark laws.⁵⁷ An identifying emblem was adopted in 1923. All three mechanisms, the national organization, the title, and the emblem, were designed to indicate respectable practitioners to the public and to other realtors.

One of the first issues that NAREB tackled at its yearly conferences was a code of fair practice. By 1913, a draft ethical code was formulated, following the practice of other professions. As one student of the professions has observed, ethical behavior was a "prerequisite for being trusted to control the terms of work without taking advantage of such control."⁵⁸ Following the passage of the code in 1915, the public was to be assured that members of NAREB would operate in an honest manner. The ethical code underpinned the formation of "a relationship of trust and confidence between principal and agent" that the author of an early realty text saw as critical to "the elevation of the real estate business to the plane of a profession."⁵⁹ It served as an additional way of defining proper practice in contrast to unscrupulous activity, and as a mechanism to police the profession. State licensing laws were urged to enforce the code, and in 1919 California and Michigan became the first states to establish regulatory licensing systems.⁶⁰

NAREB members used their yearly meetings to discuss and resolve issues of shared concern. Between meetings, the magazine of the organization, the *National Real Estate Journal,* provided a venue for debate and information. This organ, which began publication in 1910, was an important unifying element for the profession, framing the ideas that guided its activities. The basic procedures governing modern real-estate methods were formalized through the discussions conducted in these two arenas during the decade from 1910 to 1919. These consisted of the principle of exclusive agency, the use of written agreements and multiple listings, and cooperative selling.⁶¹ Thus were established a body of practice as well as an ethics of practice that all realtors could reliably be expected to uphold.

Other practices evolved in the early decades of the century that affected the activities of those realtors specifically involved with community development. Such devices as deed restrictions, one scholar has observed, constituted a new form of "knowledge about the shaping of residential space."⁶² The construction of these new strategies differentiated developers from other actors in the housing-provision arena and helped define their professional identity.

Characteristically, professions emphasize the scientific or theoretical basis of their expertise. This reflects the value that modern society places on cognitive rationality, especially as the basis for establishing an endeavor's legitimacy.⁶³ In the first two decades of the twentieth century, realtors' practices followed this pattern, as reflected in their concern with developing a mathematical method for determining the value of property. Discussions of competing systems took place at national meetings in an effort to base valuations on objective criteria. Efforts to compile data on real-estate values in order to establish patterns to aid appraisals and the prediction of future values began in 1907. By 1913, realtors often received fees for their appraisal services, an acknowledgement of their role as consulting professionals, akin to doctors and lawyers.⁶⁴

All these strategies of the professional project—the creation of a professional association, the delineation of ethical and procedural norms, and the claim to a distinctive body of knowledge—were means by which realtors, like other groups, attempted to establish control over the market for their services. The development of ways to standardize "the production of the producers" of these services was also important for this goal. Larson uses this formulation to describe the transmission of skills and knowledge to new members.⁶⁵ As early as 1904, the Real Estate Board of Brokers in New York City presented the first series of lectures on real estate. The first university courses were offered in 1905 at the Wharton School of Finance and Commerce of the University of Pennsylvania, at the University of Pennsylvania's Evening School in Philadelphia, and at New York University's School of Commerce.⁶⁶ Educational issues were a major concern following the founding of NAREB. A 1915 study acknowledged the inadequacy of available texts bearing on real estate; a review of the forty relevant titles in the Library of Congress revealed that fewer than a dozen were worthwhile. World War I intervened before this problem could be redressed, but in 1923 NAREB sponsored the publication of nine new texts by Macmillan. In the same year, there were conferences to discuss the needs of real-estate education and construct a two-year standard course. A related development entailed the creation of the first research body in the United States for the economics of real estate, the Institute for Research in Land Economics and Public Utilities, founded in 1920 by the above-quoted economist at the University of Wisconsin, Richard Ely; from its inception, it maintained a working relationship with NAREB, and in 1924 Ely became an economic adviser to NAREB.[67]

Larson elaborates on the overall importance of the educational system as a route toward professionalization and on the flexibility of the system of higher education in the United States that enables new fields to gain credibility through university affiliation.[68] For NAREB, the relationship with the state seems to have played an equally crucial legitimizing role. We have already noted that NAREB turned to state governments for enforcement of the code of ethics through licensing agencies. The state provided "the appearance of neutrality necessary to guarantee the 'objectively' superior competence of a category of professionals."[69] This may have been deceptive for, as Weiss notes, NAREB members often administered the state agencies that enforced licensing laws.[70] Nevertheless, by accepting NAREB's criteria for competence, the state affirmed the organization's definition of real-estate practice.

During World War I, the profession also received recognition from the federal government, when realtors served in the Real Estate and Commandeering Division of the United States Housing Corporation, the Office of the Alien Property Custodian, the Shipping Board, the Bureau of Industrial Housing and Transportation of the Department of Labor, and the Real Estate Division of the War Department. Realtors within these bureaucracies contributed to the war effort by performing appraisals, providing data on housing supply and costs, managing real estate and mortgages, acquiring land and buildings, and organizing the construction of housing. Whereas direct government construction of much-needed housing for war workers was urged by some planners, architects, and engineers, realtors promoted government aid for the "private financing of private builders."[71] The United States Housing Corporation's Real Estate Division "established a special federal mortgage loan program to stimulate private construction of moderate-cost housing for war workers, supplementing the government housing construction program of the USHC directed by city planner F. L. Olmsted, Jr."[72] When the federal government did build housing projects, it attempted to turn them over to private developers as quickly as possible at the conclusion of the war. The war-housing effort was considered "an experiment that it was hoped would become a model for private builders after the war. In particular, the hope was that big construction concerns would emerge that could tackle vast projects in their entirety, as opposed to developers who merely put in the infrastructure before selling the land plot by plot."[73] Realtors also exerted their influence in the extensive "Own Your Home" campaign that was launched after the war and was widely publicized as having the support of the Secretary of Labor. The involvement of NAREB members in government service in this period resulted in the relocation of its headquarters from Minneapolis to Washington, D.C., in 1918. The organization also briefly established a research bureau there, in 1920, to conduct fact-finding for the support of legislative work and lobbying.

By 1922, NAREB had consolidated its constituency through the establishment of norms of practice and had successfully provided expertise during the war mobilization. Based on these early experiences, the association reorganized its constitution in 1922 to tighten its administrative structure and to create seven specialized divisions. These divisions articulated the diversity of emphases that had developed within the profession. One of them was the Home Builders and Subdividers Division, which eventually broke off from its parent organization and became the National Association of Home Builders. However, housing and the creation of residential subdivisions were important concerns for realtors throughout the process of professionalization; this history and its implications require a closer look.

Realtors as Community Builders

One of the significant features of the 1922 description of realtors quoted earlier is the writer's emphasis on the disinterested role of the realtor as a community developer. Among the developers encountered in this study, Taylor explicitly referred to his work as community building; Baldwin & Howell contributed to the transformation of a formerly rural district by means of, among other devices, the firm's support for the construction of new municipal infrastructure. To the extent that realtors identified themselves with the city-building activities of the late-nineteenth and early-twentieth centuries, this further enhanced their professional project.

During this period in which corporate capitalism and the state reached new accommodations, the concepts of rationality, efficiency, and the public interest were forged into a single dominant ideological construct that was used to define new political, social, and civic institutions.[74] Both established and emerging professions embraced this construct since the concepts of rationality, efficiency, and the public interest allowed social practices to be conceived as scientific data that could be manipulated by disinterested experts who commanded all of the force of objective truth for which modern society reveres the activities of natural scientists. On the one hand, this ideology transformed complex and potentially divisive social issues into seemingly objective realities that could be quantified according to scientific procedures. On the other hand, it presented those who used these procedures as neutral facilitators of objective processes.

The city embodied many of the conflicting interests that had to be reconciled, not only politically but also physically, in order for the corporate economy to continue to grow. Many of the professions that emerged in this period, including city managers, planners, engineers, and social workers, saw their role as contributing, within the framework of their particular expertise, to this process of reconciliation that would lead, they felt, to greater social progress. The city, in other words, was a focus for the energies of many kinds of professionals who were striving to create a more efficient environment for general social and economic development by applying rational solutions to its problems.[75]

We have already noted that one of the bases of the realtors' professional project was their claim to cognitive rationality in their role as appraisers, developing scientific methods for the determination of property values. By embracing the task of city building, becoming "architects of the fortune of cities," as one 1892 editorialist expressed it,[76] realtors also laid claim to professional status by virtue of their promotion of rational and efficient means for civic improvement in the public interest.

By the 1880s, local real-estate boards supported infrastructural development, such as the laying of streetcar and railroad tracks, and the civic encouragement of new industries and population growth that would promote the expansion of their cities.[77] The Twin Peaks Property Owners Association in San Francisco (encountered in the discussion of the development of Westwood Highlands), formed in the second decade of the twentieth century, is an instance of an ad hoc organization of realtors created to support municipal construction of public transportation. Once the national realtors' association was formed, it, too, spoke out in favor of efforts that were instrumental for urban expansion. For example, a resolution at the 1911 NAREB meeting urged all levels of government—federal, state, and county—to undertake the paving of roads to meet the needs of autos and, by extension, of suburban growth.[78] Although individual real-estate ventures would profit by improvements such as these, the profession voiced its support for them in terms that embraced the well-being of the entire community. But what is of particular concern here is the way in which realtors addressed issues of housing and subdivisions.

In *The Rise of the Community Builders,* Marc Weiss notes the range of subdividing activity that real-estate men engaged in. At the disreputable end of the scale were the "curbstoners," speculators in "vacant, unimproved lots heavily encumbered with private debt and public tax and special assessment obligations."[79] Often these were not licensed realtors, and the drive toward professionalization was in part an effort to eliminate such individuals from the field. Established realtors who did not engage in such fraudulent practices could be involved with subdivisions either as brokers, who sold lots on behalf of the subdivider, or as subdividers themselves. The general practice was to sell unimproved lots.

In the course of the 1920s, the trend toward realtors taking responsiblity for the entire development of subdivisions, from infrastructural improvements through house building, deepened. Realtors who had pioneered community development had found "that combination lot-house sales were more stable, profitable, and marketable than just pure lot sales."[80] B. E. Taylor's discussion of his sales of houses in order to sell lots reflects this trend. By the time such experiences became more generally influential, a body of discussion and practices had evolved that the wider community of realtors could draw upon.

At its 1892 meeting, the first, short-lived national association, the National Real Estate Association, discussed the importance of encouraging home ownership and the development of planned communities as a way to lower costs for buyers as well as to improve living conditions through amenities such as parks and playgrounds.[81] Such topics were of interest to NAREB as well, and its 1910 meeting "centered on practical methods for laying out new home areas."[82] By this date, subdividers were urging each other to develop plans that included modern improvements, that used contoured streets to take advantage of local topography, and that made use of trees and park spaces.

Realtors' discussions of subdivision design and standards in these early years were lent weight by their ability to point to models that could be emulated. Edward H. Bouton's Roland Park in Baltimore, begun in 1891, was the first community singled out as setting a standard.[83] Another influential subdivision was J. C. Nichols's Country Club District in Kansas City; Nichols himself addressed NAREB's 1912 meeting and gave a report on his work. For realtors, Hugh Potter's River Oaks in Houston was "the country's third nationally noted planned residential community."[84]

These model subdivisions are significant for three reasons. First, it is noteworthy that realtors created these developments; they served as models just as much for the way their processes of development had been organized as they did for the design principles put into practice there. Other professionals involved in suburban development, including architects and landscape architects, championed designers who introduced such principles as contoured streets, landscaping, and park spaces. Realtors, on the other hand, pointed to the developers who harnessed these principles in works on the ground. Bouton, for example, had worked with landscape architect Frederick Law Olmsted Jr. at Roland Park and at Forest Hills Gardens, for which Bouton was also the developer. Design professionals saw Olmsted's work as the key shaping force for these projects. But within the realtors' community, Olmsted's ideas were viewed through the process of development organized by Bouton as the developer. For the realty profession as a whole, such concepts as garden-suburb design and neighborhood unit planning became accepted as standards of the period, incorporated into the general body of notions that were identified as modern and progressive, because of their successful implementation in realtors' model developments.

Second, through such built form and in the writings and reports of the projects' developers, these model subdivisions yielded a set of principles for community building. This extended the body of knowledge on the basis of which realtors as a profession could claim expertise. Roland Park developer Bouton organized informal discussions during the 1920s at his home, to which he invited Nichols and Potter, among others, to exchange information and new ideas.[85] In more public arenas, articles and discussions about residential subdivision development proliferated during the 1920s at annual NAREB meetings and in the pages of the *National Real Estate Journal*, especially following the creation of the Home Builders and Subdividers Division in 1922. Drawing on these sources for his 1930 study, *Financial Aspects of Subdivision Development*, published by the Institute for Economic Research (formerly the Institute for Research in Land Economics and Public Utilities, founded by economist Ely), A. D. Theobald noted the stabilizing potential of this set of practices.[86] Within the profession itself, these practices functioned to regulate the behavior of members, providing alternatives to the risky speculative activities associated with curbstoners. Theobald also claimed that, over time, the body of research amassed through the study of successful practices and the analysis of built examples served to strengthen professionalism. The role of subdivision development in stabilizing property values was perhaps most important for the process of professionalization. Instead of being subject to the always tricky business of assessing and predicting values, realtors had the opportunity to shape values in their residential subdivision developments. And economic value, of course, was the measure of their success. To the extent that the community-building project, when weighed in the scale of value, showed stable or increased property valuations, realtors could point to what they saw as an objective basis for their claim to professional status. This is what Nichols was referring to when he wrote, in 1925, that "[realtors] have realized that they cannot regard their business as a profession if they simply transmit values as they find them and fail to apply scientific principles in building cities."[87]

The third significant aspect of these subdivisions as models for realtors is their scope. In all of them, the realtor maintained control over the entire process of development, from land acquisition through street design, building, landscaping, marketing, financing, and the location of community and commercial services. In other words, through these projects, realtors asserted an ideal of their activities that emphasized large-scale and multidimensional planning and organizational skills. They presented themselves as assuming responsibility for the shape that the physical growth of suburban residential areas would take, in terms of tree-lined enclaves of predominantly single-family houses; for the economic stability of these developments, in terms of the maintenance of property values through use, building, and design controls; and for the definition of social well-being, in terms of residential areas that provided safe play areas for children, access to shops, schools, community facilities, and churches, separation from industry and commerce, and a controlled mixture of socioeconomic groups. In short, such commitments demonstrated that realtors were not interested merely in short-term gain through the buying and selling of a commodity. A 1908 editorial in the *Chicago Tribune* reflected this when it stated, "The real estate dealer is no longer a mere speculator in land or buildings. His activities have increased until he is recognized among the influential forces of the community."[88] The realtor claimed to address the needs of the community as a whole and to provide both tangible and intangible patterns for physical and social development.

Another manifestation of realtors' identification with large-scale planning is their early and sustained organizational relationship with city planners. The 1909 NAREB meeting took place one month after the first National Conference on City Planning (NCCP) and included a speaker on city planning who relayed information about this conference to the realtors. NAREB leaders increasingly were involved in the NCCP: in 1913, Nichols joined its general committee and several realtors were featured speakers at its annual conference in 1915. In 1917, Nichols, Bouton, and two other developers were among the founding members of the American City Planning Institute, which later became the American Institute of Planners.[89]

Within NAREB, interest in planning issues first took organizational form in 1914, when Bouton, Nichols, and Duncan McDuffie, among others, established the City Planning Committee.[90] This committee drew together realtors who were concerned with land development, residential subdividing, and house building. When NAREB was restructured in 1922 to accommodate the growth of professional specializations, these realtors became the leaders of the Home Builders and Subdividers Division.

The close relationship between realtors and planners that characterized these early years culminated in 1925, when the Home Builders and Subdividers Division worked with the American City Planning Institute to develop guidelines for subdivision controls. The document that the two groups jointly formulated in 1927 became the foundation for *A Standard City Planning Enabling Act,* the model for land-use planning and regulation that the United States Department of Commerce issued to state governments beginning in 1928.[91]

Thus, realtors' professionalization and their focus on issues of community development enabled them to join with other professionals who were shaping physical and social patterns of urban decentralization. One emblem of the way in which realtors' concerns meshed with those of others can be seen in a 1923 advertisement in the *National Real Estate Journal.* The ad offered to developers the services of a landscape architect and engineer whose credentials included not only a sample site plan incorporating curvilinear, tree-lined streets and a riverfront park, but memberships in NAREB, the American [*sic*] Conference on City Planning, and the American Association of Engineers (fig. 44).

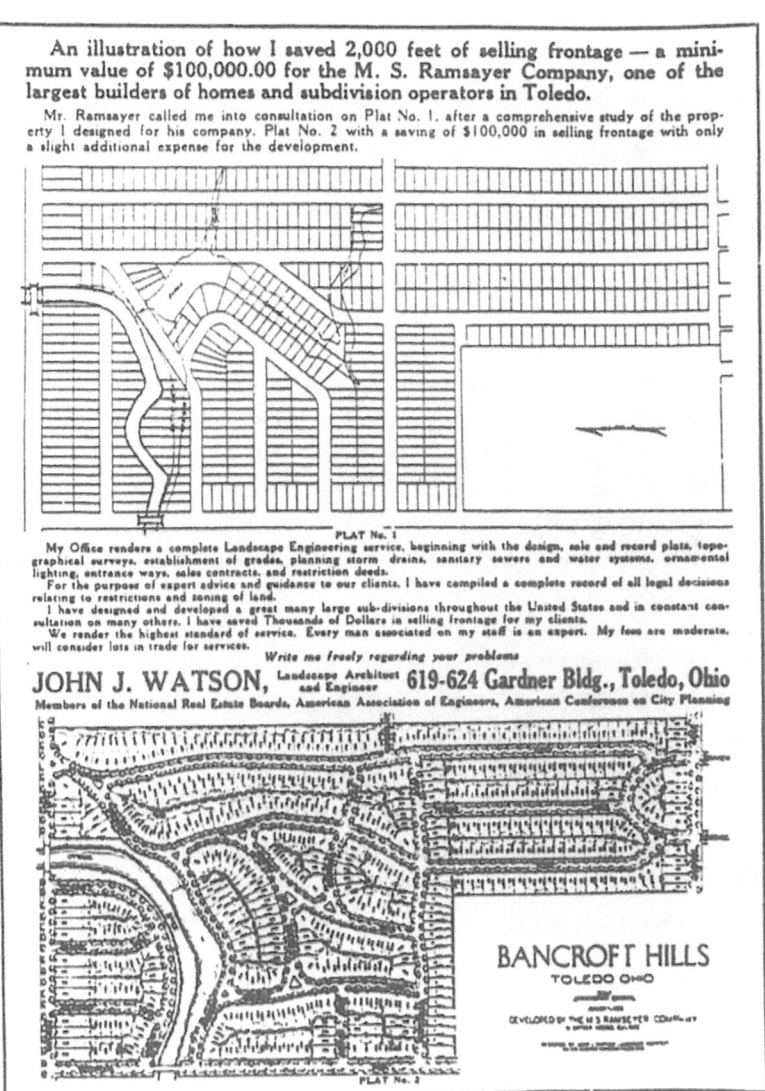

Figure 44. This 1923 advertisement from the *National Real Estate Journal* indicates the close working relationship that had been forged among professionals involved in housing development. Here, a landscape architect and engineer offers his services as a subdivision site planner to realtors. He notes that he is a member of the National Association of Real Estate Boards, the American Association of Engineers, and an organization of city planners.

A 1924 address by Nichols, who was one of the most vocal spokesmen for the leadership of realtors as city builders, provides another token of the forms that professional interaction took. He began by asking, "What man in any city is better fitted to serve as mayor than the Realtor?" and he continued,

> In Kansas City we have several Realtors members [*sic*] of our city council; an ex-president of the real estate board as president of the board of park commissioners; an ex-president is chairman of the city plan and zoning commission with four other Realtors on the board; a Realtor a member [*sic*] of the board of education; a Realtor on the fire and water board commission; our county commissioners, law enforcement league, building code commission, board of public works and health board. Your splendid president of the National Association has long been active in our welfare work; a Realtor is president of our Art Institute, vice president of the Symphony Orchestra Association and Liberty Memorial Association, and so on throughout all the activities of our city.[92]

Just as his Country Club District served as a model subdivision for developers in the 1920s, Nichols's incantation of realtors penetrating all levels of civic administration provided a model of a network of experts leading urban development. This contrasts with Albert Wood's vision of suburban residential development nurturing popular, broad-based civic involvement. The next chapter will look at how it was that Nichols's model prevailed.

Rationalizing Development

The realtors' professional project provided a solid basis for the public leadership role that Nichols urged upon his colleagues. The creation of a national organization with a clear identity and codified procedures meant that clients and fellow practitioners could rely on set standards of service by realtors. It also consolidated and transmitted realtors' collective expertise. By systematizing knowledge, increasing the predictability of transactions, and improving efficiency, the professionalization process rationalized realty practices.

The three subdivisions we have examined also reflect the use of rationalized practices. Assembly-line production procedures, standardized materials, and modular plans contributed to the greater efficiency of these projects through speed and lower costs of construction, as well as to the predictability of the end product.

The principle of rationalized organization links the histories of realtor-developers and large-scale suburban residential subdivisions. Both emerged at the same moment and responded to an interlocking set of needs and possibilities in building practices, house design, planning models, city expansion, and professional capacities, all of which promoted rationalized development. The entrepreneurial skills that their professionalization reinforced—the abilities required to organize and manage multifaceted projects—put realtors in the best position to pursue subdivision development.

Building-craftsmen's work was also rationalized, but in a direction that narrowed their sphere of activity. Just as the need for planning and logistical coordination of the construction process increased, building-craftsmen's tasks became simplified, specialized, and routinized. Their dependence on construction continued to make them vulnerable, too, to the impact of wider economic forces on their industry. As the value of housing in relation to the gross national product slid, beginning at the turn of the century, building-craftsmen had few alternative uses for their skills.[93] By 1930, however, realtors who engaged in speculative building were deriving their profits not from construction but from the combined sale of land and structures.[94] Taylor's experience at Brightmoor exemplifies this; as he described it to his fellow realtors in 1923, "I build the houses to sell the lots."[95] Both the nature of building-craftsmen's work and the value of their labor embedded in their product were shrinking. Realtors who organized the entire development process, on the other hand, were in a position to absorb a shift in value and continue to make a profit.

Architects' skills in manipulating standardized, modular elements contributed to realtors' large-scale projects. Since "what the average consumer was now purchasing . . . was a new dwelling in a new district of completed dwellings, rather than a vacant lot in an undeveloped area with an uncertain future,"[96] developers needed an array of houses that balanced individuality with unity and that presented a satisfying and familiar image of stability right from the outset.[97] A rationalized system of design permitted architects to generate such plans.

It seems that architects were somewhat less successful as designers of overall planning strategies for entire subdivision developments. On the one hand, they did not offer a special competency in this regard; engineers (such as Westwood Park's Punnett and the Toledo advertiser in fig. 44), landscape architects, and planners were among those acknowledged as capable of designing new residential sites. On the other hand, architects' planning contributions did not always meet the criteria for economy and efficiency that dominated developers' concerns. The fate of Albert Wood's innovative proposal is instructive here; his idea to cluster houses and services was rejected for the Ford Homes in favor of a more conventional alignment of houses with the street.

Realtors needed to control the volatility of real estate if they were to ensure its dependability as an investment. This meant rationalizing the physical environment, securing a predictable order so that residential developments would maintain their value. It was in pursuit of this goal that realtors employed individual deed restrictions, which Weiss describes as the initial "very significant abridgement of private property rights."[98] More sweeping devices for ensuring stable, use-restricted development, such as subdivision controls and zoning, followed, sometimes forged through collaboration between realtors and planners. To these must be added, however, the physical patterns that realtors imposed on subdivision development. In all of these ways, developers succeeded in shaping land use in the 1920s and later, justifying the 1925 comment by a past president of the National Conference on City Planning to NAREB's Home Builders and Subdividers Division: "It is the Realtor subdivider who is really planning our cities today, who is the actual city planner in practice."[99] Realtor Nichols saw his colleagues' role as formative, declaring, "I believe that the work the subdivision men have done in this country has been, in a certain degree, the foster mother of the city planning movement."[100]

Of the three developers we have considered here, the firm of Baldwin & Howell best bears out Nichols's claim and comes closest to the model of the emerging community builder. They were indeed realtors engaged in subdividing and house building, among other brokerage activities.[101] The success of their association with other realtors in guiding development of the West of Twin Peaks District toward protected residential use exemplifies the kind of dependable community of realtors that NAREB had been organized to achieve. Baldwin & Howell's promotion of the construction of the Twin Peaks Tunnel demonstrates realtors' collaboration with local government to bring about infrastructural improvements that made further residential development feasible. Westwood Highlands itself was developed in relation to other new residential tracts in the district, and extended the patterns that had already evolved there, in terms of both site design and housing. The innovative aspect of this subdivision within its district was the developer's confidence in market acceptance of these patterns. This confidence enabled them to build the houses on speculation and as part of a single, unified scheme, rather than selling the lots alone.

By developing such speculative subdivisions, realtors stamped the physical environment with a predictable order that derived from built form itself. The decisions this entailed depended upon responses to trends in suburbanization and home ownership that were worked out by a larger network of housing professionals of which realtors made up only one part. To continue to explore the success achieved by rationalized residential development it is necessary to look more closely at this network and its activities.

PART II

AGENCY, FORM, AND MEANING

CHAPTER 4

THE HOME-OWNERSHIP NETWORK

Constructing Community

How did a consensus in favor of suburban single-family subdivision development emerge that led to the dominance of this housing solution? Spokesmen from a number of different but reinforcing sectors repeatedly articulated the benefits of this particular pattern of housing. The same themes were broached again and again, inflected by the concerns of disparate spheres of activity. These reiterations melded the voices of those making them into a unified, activist bloc that achieved widespread acceptance for subdivision development.

In short, the developers of the Ford Homes, Brightmoor, Westwood Highlands, and others like them were not alone responsible for the pattern of development found in these subdivisions. Realtor-developers lent their voices to a larger chorus of housing professionals that included engineers, social reformers, bankers, university professors, building-materials suppliers, heads of government agencies, and others. The resulting network provided, on a larger stage, the kind of organizational leadership on housing issues that the National Association of Real Estate Boards performed for just one sector of this network, the realtors. The interlocking pyramids of professional organizations that comprised the housing network—in which local members were guided by their national leaders as well as by the combined expertise shared by these leaders across professions—reflected a style of management that was rooted in the Progressive Era's claims for experts' objectivity and that reached maturity during Herbert Hoover's tenure as secretary of commerce.

The housing network that was established in this way was concerned especially with promoting home ownership. While the single-family house was the dominant type of dwelling in this period and suburban development was growing, home ownership itself was limited. The campaign to increase home ownership enrolled numerous strategies, but central to these was the notion of community. The home-ownership network promulgated a schematic, minimal idea of community, one that Clarence A. Perry crystallized in his neighborhood unit plan. This reduced form of community was sufficient to stamp the residential character of a tract and to ensure its perpetuation, thus minimizing home owners' investment risks.

The pattern of suburban subdivision development responded, then, to a broad range of concerns. Before tracing these and the network that addressed them, it is necessary to consider the housing trends that provided their basis.

The Prevalence of the Single-family Detached Suburban House

On any graph that describes housing trends in the United States, the decade of the 1920s stands out like an exclamation point, punctuating periodic rises and falls with its steady climb toward record-breaking heights—and then its rapid decline from them (see fig. 1). The average number of nonfarm housing starts per year during the 1920s was 703,000, almost double that for the first decade of the twentieth century, which had previously held the record.[1] Between 1922 and 1929, from recovery following the post–World War I depression to the stock-market crash, the average number of housing starts per year climbed to 833,000, more than twice that of any previous seven-year period.[2] While this surge was in part stimulated by the all-time building low during World War I that intensified housing shortages, it also continued the trend toward increased residential construction evident since 1880. Analyzing housing statistics from the late-nineteenth century, one historian noted that "by all previous standards, the extent of residential construction in all American cities in the 1880s and 1890s was staggering."[3] Each succeeding decade through the 1920s amplified this growth.

The majority of this residential construction, moreover, consisted of single-family units. There were local anomalies, such as the prevalence of multifamily dwellings in New York City, but in twenty-one out of twenty-five selected cities, more than 50 percent of the houses were single-family units in both 1890 and 1930; in fifteen of these the figure was 75 percent or more.[4] Although the construction of multifamily housing increased dramatically during the decade of the 1920s, single-family units never accounted for less than 56 percent of new housing starts.[5] Construction statistics from the late-nineteenth and early-twentieth centuries, then, substantiate the dominance of the single-family house as a residential form in the United States.

Pattern-book writers, journalists, social reformers, architects, and others helped to promote this housing form during the nineteenth and early-twentieth centuries.[6] But even individuals who had little or no contact with one or another type of this persuasive literature often chose to live in detached single-family houses. A study of housing patterns in Detroit, for example, found that there was a higher incidence of such dwellings among recently arrived immigrant groups than among native-born, middle-class residents, those most likely to have been the target of promotional efforts in popular magazines and other literature.[7] Instead, a higher proportion of the native-born middle class lived in apartment buildings.

On the national level, indeed, increased apartment-building construction during the 1920s seemed to challenge the tradition of detached single-family housing. Other successfully implemented alternatives offered models for contesting that tradition, such as the medley of fourteen hundred rowhouse, duplex, triplex, single-family, and apartment units constructed at Yorkship Garden Village in Camden, New Jersey, in 1918 for the United States Shipping Board's Emergency Fleet Corporation.[8] As early as 1913, some proponents of detached housing had not been above designing strategies to subvert such alternatives, as when housing reformer Lawrence Veiller suggested that his colleagues

> do everything possible in our laws to encourage the construction of private dwellings ... and penalize ... the multiple dwelling of any kind ... if we require fire escapes and a host of other things, all dealing with fire protection, we are on safe grounds, because that can be

justified as a legitimate exercise of the police power.... In our laws let most of the fire provisions relate solely to multiple dwellings, and allow our private houses and two-family houses to be built with no fire protection whatever.[9]

The fine-grained study of Detroit housing suggests that these concerns were relevant for particular localities or the preferences of a particular class. The norm throughout the United States, however, remained the single-family house, encouraged by popular media but not entirely dependent on them for its acceptance.

Home ownership, however, was not as widespread. Even in upper-middle-class suburbs, house rental was sometimes preferred to ownership.[10] In 1890, 36.9 percent of nonfarm dwellings were owner-occupied. Thirty years later, a gain of only 4 percent had been made, reflecting at least in part the effects of economic depressions and war. During the single decade of the 1920s, the increase in home ownership surpassed that of the entire preceding period, raising the total to 46 percent; in only five of the twenty-five selected cities mentioned above were 50 percent or more of the homes owned by their residents in 1930.[11]

Wider availability of financing contributed to this increase in home ownership. Savings and other time deposits had swollen to $52 billion in 1929, from about $5.2 billion in 1900, growing at a rate three times that of the overall economy.[12] This provided a source of investment funds for developers and it also underwrote the increase in home ownership.[13]

The single most important institution to widen access to financing was the local building and loan association (more frequently after the 1920s referred to as a savings and loan association). First established in 1831, these were "the only financial institutions created to specialize in lending on homes and very little else."[14] They suffered virtual destruction during the long depression of the 1890s. Afterwards they were reorganized and began slowly to recover public confidence. By the 1920s, they had succeeded in reestablishing their soundness: building and loan associations had financed fewer than 700,000 houses during the first decade of the century, but they underwrote construction of 4,350,000 houses during the 1920s.[15] By offering mortgages for longer terms (up to fifteen years) and for a greater portion of the value of property (up to 75%), and by calculating amortization so that repayment of principal and interest was divided into manageable monthly installments, building and loan associations became more attractive than other sources of financing despite their somewhat higher interest rates.[16] By 1929, home owners owed $20 billion on their houses; building and loan associations held about $8 billion, or 40 percent, of these loans.[17]

Encouraged by these financing arrangements, the percentage of owned houses that were mortgaged increased. As one recent analyst has concluded, "more people were borrowing more money to buy homes, particularly smaller-sized, modest-priced homes."[18] If the gap between single-family residence and home ownership were to be narrowed, this would be achieved by addressing the market for the small house. As early as 1914, Kansas City realtor J. C. Nichols was publicly urging his colleagues to pay attention to working-class dwellings, for he doubted that "the housing problem [would] ever be successfully solved until more consideration is given to the creation and permanent safeguarding of neighborhoods of considerable area for the man who earns $2 a day, or less."[19] Indeed, it was widely recognized in the 1920s that the housing needs of people with modest means, "the wage earner and small-salaried man," in the words of leading realtor Irenaeus Shuler, should be taken into consideration. "It is the duty of the subdivider and home builder to provide for all classes of people," he wrote in a professional textbook.[20]

The impetus for this sentiment derived in part from an awareness of existing tensions created by the steep rise in rental costs burdening both working- and middle-class tenants; rents rose an average of more than 50 percent between 1914 and 1920. "Class antagonism between landlords and tenants as such is becoming very intense," observed a reporter for the United States Department of Labor.[21] Such conflict seemed menacing in a world shaken by recent revolutions in Russia and Mexico, especially when postwar recession resulted in unemployment peaking at about 12 percent in 1921.[22] Many saw home ownership as a bulwark against class tension and threats of political turmoil in the United States. "A contented home owner is the best insurance in the world against social unrest," is just one especially succinct formulation of a viewpoint that recurs throughout the 1920s in discussions of housing solutions.[23] This was seen as another reason to bring home ownership in line with the already-high incidence of single-family residency.

In terms of the wider economy, as one student of the industry wrote, residential construction served as a "pulmotor," a machine that pumps oxygen into ailing lungs until they recover the strength to function on their own.[24] This image stands as something of a warning, for the pulmotor cannot substitute indefinitely for the body's mechanisms. In the decade of the 1920s, "the average index of residential construction was forty-five percent above that of industrial production";[25] without a strong general economy, the strength of residential construction alone could not avert the depression that ended the period. In fact, for many analysts this imbalance between investment in production and investment in fixed capital represents the root of the crisis that culminated in the crash of 1929 and the Great Depression.[26] One of its first expressions was the steady decline in housing construction that followed the extraordinary peak in 1925.

The image of the pulmotor also expressed the extensive impact of residential construction on the body economic, from building-materials producers to wholesalers, distributors, and retailers, as well as the stimulation of household-equipment production and nonresidential construction. The exceptional boom in the 1920s resulted in new residential construction that alone accounted for 6 percent of the gross national product in the peak year of 1924, a dramatic climb from the low of barely more than 1 percent during the war.[27]

The site of this new construction, increasingly, was the suburbs. Land became available as a result of the steady fall in the prices of farm commodities in the three decades following the Civil War; as their acreage lost its value for agricultural uses, farmers sold land to be developed for other purposes.[28] Lower prices of land at the periphery, combined with the introduction of new transportation technologies, made such parcels attractive for residential construction; the three subdivisions examined earlier exemplify this pattern. Then, beginning in 1914, a war-induced recession in urban land values further stimulated the market for suburban real estate.[29] In 1900, 10.7 percent of the population of the United States lived in suburbs; by 1930, the proportion had grown to 18 percent. During the decade of the 1920s, the increase in suburbanization accelerated over that of previous years, growing 39.2 percent. This was more than twice the growth of central cities.[30]

Thus, the pervasive trend in the early-twentieth century was toward single-family housing in a suburban setting. The maintenance of a trend toward home ownership, however, seemed less secure. Many of the housing initiatives of this period were made expressly to bolster this weak link.

The Home-Ownership Network

A major concern in an industry such as construction, one that is extremely sensitive to the periodic recessions and depressions of the economy, is to protect investments. Although urban housing reformers such as Edith Elmer Wood urged government planning and financing as an alternative to reliance on undependable market forces, the prevailing mood in the 1920s was to encourage private enterprise.[31] As one critic later wrote, "During the 1920s period of peak identification between governmental agencies and business welfare, it was unnecessary for the federal government to do more than give its warm approval to the home ownership movements sponsored by the building interests."[32]

Spurning government planning, this period relied on another route to extend and deepen the trends of the preceding decades toward the ownership of detached, suburban, single-family homes. Described by one scholar as "non-statist social and economic planning,"[33] this route entailed the forging of a network of increasingly organized, well-defined, and mutually-supportive groups, including realtors, building-materials producers, contractors, housing reformers, financiers, architects, engineers, and planners, who gathered and shared information and engaged in promotional activities. The federal government, too, performed a role in this network, fostering the initiatives undertaken by these groups and increasingly providing opportunities for them to meet.

By the end of World War I, most of the groups with roles to play in residential construction were organized at the national level. Building-craftsmen belonged to the United Brotherhood of Carpenters and Joiners and were represented in the Building Trades Department of the American Federation of Labor. The National Association of Real Estate Boards spoke for realtors; in the 1922 restructuring of the organization, the Home Builders and Subdividers Division was created, in recognition of the distinct interests of this group within the profession. Building-materials manufacturers and suppliers were organized as well, by individual trade groupings (the National Lumber Manufacturers Association, for example, was founded in 1902) as well as across the sector (the National Federation of Construction Industries was founded in 1918). The embryonic planning community had established the National Conference on City Planning in 1909, which brought together people with diverse backgrounds who shared an interest in planning issues; as planners developed a professional identity, they formed the more specialized American City Planning Institute (later called the American Institute of Planners) in 1917. Contractors had first organized in 1886 when they founded the National Association of Builders; this dissolved during the 1890s recession but was reestablished in 1919 as the National Association of Building Trades Employers. Contractors also broke away from the National Federation of Construction Industries to create, in 1918, the Associated General Contractors of America. Individuals at local levels who were interested in housing and planning had begun, by the turn of the century, to organize local improvement societies; these united nationally in 1900 in the American League for Civic Improvement, which became the American Civic Association in 1904. The architects' professional association, the American Institute of Architects, had some interaction with these groups, but interested architects also tended to function as individuals within this network, as did engineers; the 1921 founding of the Architects' Small House Service Bureau provided another kind of organizational presence, however.[34]

Gathering information was a major impetus for organization, first within each of these fields and then among them. We have already seen the role it played in bringing realtors into association. Among materials suppliers, to consider another example, the exchange of information stimulated regional organization as early as the 1870s. The Chicago Lumberman's Exchange began to compile statistics on lumber deliveries in 1874; although ostensibly these became the basis for grading standards, they also allowed for controlling production during periods of oversupply.[35] On the one hand, "these supplier organizations provided a mere taste of the collusive, restrictive and oligopolistic arrangements for which the building-materials industry would become notorious."[36] But these organizations also provided an institutional framework for contact with other groups in the arena of residential construction, and the data they collected began to lay the groundwork for more comprehensive statistical studies of the industry. When the National Lumber Manufacturers Association was organized in 1902, this tradition continued, for "the maintenance of industrial statistics was recognized as one of the vital economic problems of the lumber industry."[37] This concern led to the compilation of production and delivery reports on a monthly basis in 1912; these reports were issued weekly beginning in 1916.

Gathering information also seems to have constituted the federal government's main involvement with residential construction prior to World War I.[38] The United States Census Bureau compiled varying sorts of data relating to housing; in 1890, for example, census reports began to include home-ownership statistics.[39] The Bureau of Labor Statistics started to collect data on construction volume and building permits in 1921; these statistics laid the basis for studies of the industry by economists and others.[40]

Under Secretary of Commerce Herbert Hoover, this trend became more widespread as he shaped this agency into "a clearing house [for the] helpful dissemination of ideas."[41] Data collection and reports proliferated. The use of voluntary associations to form and enforce policy recommendations was characteristic of Hoover's administration of the Department of Commerce, too. This had been an element of Hoover's style of management since he embarked upon public service in 1912 as an international organizer for the Panama-Pacific

Exposition. Later, as head of the Food Administration, he explained to a Senate committee in 1917, "Our theory of administration is that we should centralize ideas and decentralize execution."[42] He aimed to avoid legislation. Instead, he wanted to bring networks of representative experts together to formulate recommendations that would then be distributed to the wider memberships of their organizations through reports, publicity, press and journal articles, and personal contact. The associations that had been formed by groups connected to the residential construction industry were exactly the sorts of voluntary organizations that Hoover looked to "to resolve the great social problems of the day without scrapping such 'national instincts' as individual initiative, equal opportunity, and local responsibility, and without resorting to the 'dangers of centralized and federally imposed control.'"[43]

The residential construction industry was significant to Hoover not only for its developed structure of interconnected voluntary professional organizations that matched his conception of efficient administration; he also considered this industry essential to the maintenance of a stable economy. Looking for ways to use the industry to help manage the business cycle, he sought to design a type of economic planning by means of which cooperation would temper laissez-faire capitalism.[44] Both goals are evident in the 1921–22 Conference on Unemployment and the subsequent report issued by the committee responsible for assessing the economic impact of seasonal operations in the construction industry. Composed of the presidents of the National Lumber Manufacturers Association, the American Federation of Labor's Building Trades Department, NAREB, and the International Brotherhood of Electrical Workers, as well as the heads of a construction company and a bank, and the vice president of the AIA, the committee proposed cooperation and voluntary action within the industry to smooth periodic economic disruptions.[45]

As we observed in connection with realtors' activities, professional organizations maintained contact through attendance at each others' national meetings. Sporadic interchange also occurred over specific concerns as when, for example, the American Institute of Architects and the National Association of Builders' Exchanges, a contractors' organization, jointly published standard contract forms in 1915. Similar interaction, independent of government sponsorship, continued to take place, but increasingly federal resources and support were provided, especially when discussion led to policy formulations. In marshaling the expertise of all participants in the residential construction industry, Hoover helped strengthen a network of organizations whose leaders were in a position to shape the course of housing. The promotion of both standardization and home ownership became guiding themes for this network.

Standardization was the leitmotif of Hoover's program to rebuild the postwar economy. Inspired by the work of the Conservation Division of the War Industries Board during World War I, whose functions were transferred to the Commerce Department's Division of Simplified Practice after the war, Hoover saw in "simplification the best means to lower production costs and thus broaden markets."[46] In 1920, as president of the Federated American Engineering Societies, Hoover had initiated the study *Waste in Industry*.[47] The conclusions reached by this study also served to guide his program of standardization. The concept was applied to every level of activity within the housing arena. In 1921, for example, the Bureau of Standards established Simplified Practice Recommendations for all industries, including manufacturers of building materials and equipment. The National Lumber Manufacturers Association worked very closely with the Department of Commerce to establish lumber standards.[48] In 1922, the Building Code Committee, organized by Hoover and consisting of architects and engineers, recommended standard regulations for the construction of single-family and duplex houses, based on information gathered from architectural and engineering societies, builders' exchanges, organizations of building-materials suppliers, and building officials.[49] Similarly, in 1921 Hoover appointed realtors, planners, engineers, and housing specialists, among others, to the Advisory Committee on Zoning. This group produced *A Standard State Zoning Enabling Act* in 1924. A similar body developed *A Standard City Planning Enabling Act* in 1928.[50] Each of these groups established a model that was intended to guide general practices within each field.

Many of the activities of the Department of Commerce that related to residential development became centralized when Hoover established the Division of Building and Housing in 1921. In 1923, this unit published *How to Own Your Home: A Handbook for Prospective Home Owners*, by John M. Gries and James S. Taylor, each of whom in turn headed the new Commerce Department unit. Consisting of advice on evaluating and financing lots and houses, the book included a foreword by Secretary Hoover that seems to have been directed as much toward the business community as it was toward prospective home buyers. After extolling the virtues and rewards that home ownership yields in terms of health, family happiness, material wealth, and civic responsibility, Hoover added: "[Businessmen] see that taking a neighborly interest in developing sound financing and other machinery for the use of home seekers, and insisting on the observance of honest, straightforward methods by those who deal with home seekers is not paternalism but good business and good citizenship. It is the 'square deal'—and it is not only right but essential that the cards should not be stacked against the home seeker."[51] If read by such a home seeker, this book provided advice and reassurance. But its intended audience also seems to have been home builders and realtors, for whom its outlook would provide a model for desirable business practices.

This book complemented a promotional effort that the real-estate community initiated just before the United States entered World War I and that flourished in the postwar building climate. Under the slogan "Own Your Home," local realtors organized expositions to demonstrate "how modern real estate developments, modern building conditions and modern financing are making home ownership possible."[52] In 1918–19, the Labor Department's Division of Public Works and Construction Development coordinated this effort; posters advertising expositions were signed by the secretary of labor. A 1920 ad for the campaign in *Building Age* referred to the slogan itself as "A New Declaration of Independence," supported by Uncle Sam (fig. 45). Realtors sought the collaboration of "representatives called from forty-seven national organizations covering financial groups, architectural bodies and building equipment and furnishing interests with home purchase and home building [sic]" to launch Own Your Home drives.[53] Local real-estate boards promoted them in their communities, often tying them in with other local organizations and activities. An account of the activities of the Toledo Real Estate Board, for example, described the involvement of schoolchildren, and without embarrassment breathlessly claimed that "this plan constitutes a general campaign directed principally to the children of the city to instill in their minds a comprehension of the responsibilities of citizenship and the Own Your Own Home thought is interwoven with numerous lessons pertaining to the duties and privileges inherent to citizenship and the obligation of the individual in governmental, political and social matters."[54] Apparently it was not unusual for realtors to target schoolchildren for their home-ownership campaigns; in 1919, Nichols, the Kansas City developer, sponsored an essay contest in the schools on the theme "Why Father and Mother Should Own Their Own Home."[55]

Another promotional effort that grew in strength throughout the decade and that received government support was the Better Homes in America movement.[56] This was established in 1922 by Marie Meloney, an editor of the *Delineator*, a Butterick publication with a circulation that exceeded one million. The focus of the organization was to designate annual Better Homes weeks, for which local committees then developed model demonstration houses; its National Advisory Council selected winners nationwide. The movement grew rapidly: in 1922, more than 500 committees exhibited houses; participation doubled the following year and, by 1930, there were at least 7,279 committees.

The construction of a National Better Home on the Mall in Washington, D.C., by the General Federation of Women's Clubs launched the Better Homes campaign in 1922.[57] President Harding led the opening ceremony at the site. Secretary Hoover was aware of the organization from its inception, when it was brought to his attention by an aide whose job it was to monitor and develop contacts with the periodical press. In a memo to Hoover, the aide noted that the Better Homes campaign was "exactly the thing needed to shove over the whole housing and better homes ideas [sic] of the Department."[58]

Figure 45. The federal government helped coordinate the real-estate industry's Own Your Home campaign. This advertisement from the June 1920 issue of *Building Age* shows Uncle Sam's support for home ownership and celebrates the campaign's slogan as "A new Declaration of Independence."

Hoover contacted Meloney, joined the Better Homes advisory council, "and before long had become the organization's most prominent booster, assisting in its 'Demonstration Home' exhibits and securing, in his words, 'advance blasts . . . of propaganda' for them by persuading the president to sign endorsements and by writing material for presidential speeches."[59] When the *Delineator* could no longer fund the project, Hoover reorganized it as a national educational corporation, secured private funding for it through a grant from the Laura Spelman Rockefeller Foundation, and made it "a sort of collateral arm to the Housing Division of the Department of Commerce," as he described it.[60] Hoover served as its president, Gries as its treasurer. As he did on numerous occasions, Hoover asked his friend A. L. Lowell, the president of Harvard University, to "lend" him a faculty member to serve the government; James Ford, a professor of social ethics, became executive director of Better Homes in America, Inc.[61] Ford, brother of city planner George B. Ford, had taught at Harvard since 1909 and in 1918–19 had managed the Homes Registration and Information Division of the U.S. Housing Corporation.[62] He had written on housing issues, including critiques of apartment construction that retailed the negative effects of this type of dwelling. These included noise, the easy spread of disease, and lack of control over the type of neighbors one would encounter. All of these were summed up in Ford's conclusion that "in general the atmosphere of the tenement or apartment house is one destined to create a race of adults that is unhealthful, puny and socially highly artificialized."[63] He would be a strong advocate for the Better Homes movement.

The culmination of the strategy of using the network of organizations with a stake in residential construction to pool information and resources to promote single-family home ownership was the President's Conference on Home Building and Home Ownership. Established by President Hoover, the conference was held in December 1931; more than thirty-seven hundred people concerned with diverse aspects of housing attended. More than five hundred specialists from all relevant organizations and professions participated in thirty-one committees that issued reports that the following year were published in eleven volumes. The reports dealt with financing and taxation, types of dwellings, the relationship of income to home ownership, house design and construction, household management and homemaking, methods of subdividing, and planning and community concerns, as well as urban housing problems, the housing of African Americans, and rural housing. One of the co-editors of the reports was Gries (coauthor of *How to Own Your Home*), who served as executive secretary of the conference.[64] The other editor was Ford, executive director of the reorganized Better Homes in America movement.

The planning committee for the conference reflected the reliance on networks of organized experts that characterized Hoover's leadership. Headed by Gries and Secretary of Commerce Lamont, the committee was composed of representatives from nineteen associations; the list of these underscores the commitment to bringing together a broad, if mainstream, range of groups whose interests related to issues of housing and home ownership:

American Civic Association
American Farm Bureau Federation
American Federation of Labor
American Home Economics Association
American Institute of Architects
Association of General Contractors
Association of Life Insurance Presidents
Better Homes in America
Chamber of Commerce of the United States
General Federation of Women's Clubs
National Association of Builders' Exchanges
National Association of Real Estate Boards
National Congress of Parents and Teachers
National Farmers' Union
National Grange
Russell Sage Foundation
Savings Bank Division of the American Bankers' Association
United States League of Building and Loan Associations
Women's National Farm and Garden Association.

As in other projects backed by Hoover, such as Better Homes, private funding was sought to pay the expenses of the conference.[65]

The conference reports established federal policy in relation to residential construction, which is to say that they ratified the approach laid out by Hoover a decade earlier: promotion of single-family home ownership by fostering the organized elements within the industry, compiling information, and establishing standards. One reviewer wrote, "The Conference, on the whole, appeared to endorse the policy of leaving the field to private enterprise, contenting itself with appeals to existing organizations, threats of government action, and recommendations for further research."[66] The conference editors acknowledged such a point of view when they wrote that "since the World War there has been a significant change. Today it is possible, as it was not in the past, for a community to guide and regulate its house building. Today public interest and private interest, sound social policy and sound economic policy more evidently run together."[67] Written during a period of deepening depression, this statement seems especially blind to realities, yet it continued to represent the dominant view of the relationship between government and the private residential construction sector.

The conference took positions that reiterated the justifications for single-family home ownership that were leitmotifs throughout the literature of the residential construction industry and its allies in the 1920s. In one of the most succinct statements of this rationale, Gries and Ford wrote:

> In designating the Conference as one on Home Building and Home Ownership, the President was profoundly aware of the importance of the ownership of homes in safe-guarding the traditions and developing the ideals of our Nation. Responsible citizenship is largely dependent upon individuals having a stake in the community, which is the major source of civic pride and judicious participation in the affairs of local government. Through the relation of his home to its neighborhood and to the city government, the home owner acquires a keener civic interest and a greater sense of civic responsibility. In addition, home ownership means high standards and better control of the en-

vironment by the occupant. It helps also in the development of thrift and self-respect, facilitates wholesome living, and promotes character development in that it gives the family a fresh incentive for sacrifice and a new and high ideal.[68]

The question of the kind of home to be owned was not in doubt. The editors noted that "it is unnecessary to argue for the detached single-family house or for the suburban community suitable for homes for those who have moderate incomes. A family usually has a natural desire to own such a home and live in such surroundings."[69] The task of the conference, then, was to affirm and encourage these established trends by specifying the best means to achieve them.

The reports consisted of discussions and analyses of current practices as well as recommendations. Committee members represented organizations or professions involved in that aspect of the housing question under consideration. For example, the committee on construction was chaired by the president of the Associated General Contractors of America. Three other contractors joined him, along with the director of the National Association of Real Estate Boards, five representatives of building-materials producers, two architects, one developer, an engineer, and one representative of a finance agency. A representative of the Division of Building and Housing of the Department of Commerce served as secretary. The sole note of dissent was struck by the one representative of labor, the president of the Building Trades Department of the American Federation of Labor, whose remarks were included in the final publication. Whereas the report supported efforts to standardize construction, the representative of the building trades stated:

> I am opposed to too much standardization in home building, as it takes the individuality out of the construction of homes, and is a means of adding to our already large number of unemployed building tradesmen.... I am not in favor of erecting homes in the same manner as automobiles are built. The report savors too much of a machine-made home and, as a practical building trades mechanic, I know that the reforms as advocated in this report are not practical; hence, I am opposed to the report in full.[70]

The report of the construction committee ratified the progressive standardization of construction practices that had been occurring over the preceding decades and that had received support from the Department of Commerce during the 1920s. The spokesperson for the builders indicated by his dissent from the report how out of step with such developments the representatives of labor were.

Standardization was also endorsed by the committee on design, chaired by the president of the Architects' Small House Service Bureau. Twenty other architects, drawn from across the United States, served on the committee, along with E. H. Bouton, who had developed Roland Park in Baltimore, the executive secretary of the National Association of Real Estate Boards, and the head of the Division of Economics of the United States Department of Agriculture. The committee's research secretary was Henry Wright, co-designer of Radburn, New Jersey. Their report on house design observed that "the committee noted a marked similarity in the building product of each type [of dwelling] in many cities, extending often to details.... There is thus a certain standardization followed by builders all over the country, indicating that it is practicable to establish standards."[71] The object under consideration was, of course, the small house, whose design had traditionally been left in building-craftsmen's hands; they were not represented on this committee, however. Instead, architects embraced standardization on their behalf, and elsewhere in the report they urged cooperation between architects and developers. Both positions are understandable in light of the dynamics among architects, building-craftsmen, and developers that we traced in previous chapters. By the time of the conference, architects were familiar with the needs of large-scale residential construction. It is significant in this regard that a representative of the Architects' Small House Service Bureau led this committee, for its report also endorsed architects' production of stock plans.[72]

By the 1920s, standardization had advanced to a level that suggested that the rationalization of the single-family house had reached its limit. This is acknowledged in the report by the correlating committee on technological developments, whose charge was to define directions for future research aimed at further reducing the cost of single-family houses. Composed mainly of engineers and directors of research and development from corporations such as General Motors and General Electric, the committee's recommendations stressed the development of shop fabrication.[73] Short of prefabrication, further simplification of the shell elements and their assembly did not seem possible.

Recommendations concerning financing complemented the reports' emphases on standardization and simplification of design and construction. The committee on finance supported the establishment of a Federal Home Loan Bank System to enable prospective home owners to acquire mortgages with lower down payments and at reduced interest rates. This was one of only two resolutions—and the only substantive resolution—to be passed unanimously by the thousands attending the conference.[74] Hoover had been a long-time supporter of such a plan, which was originally inspired by the 1916 Farm Loan Act that provided reasonable long-term mortgages to farmers. In 1919, Frederick Olmsted Jr. cited this precedent as a model for governmental promotion of home ownership in his final report on the lessons gained from the efforts to provide wartime housing.[75] The mortgage-loan program established by the Real Estate Division of the United States Housing Corporation during the war served as another precedent.[76] Two of the business leaders of the Own Your Home campaign, the chairman of a construction-industry information-services bureau and an executive of a building and loan association, formulated a proposal based on these earlier initiatives; in 1919, it was presented to Congress, where it failed.[77] Revived in a statement issued by Hoover on November 13, 1931, and published in the final report of the President's Conference, the Federal Home Loan Bank Act was passed by Congress in July 1932.

The conference, then, summarizes and illustrates both the method for creating policy and the content of policy as these had evolved during the 1920s. Addressing the graduating class of William Penn College in Oskaloosa, Iowa, in June 1925, Secretary Hoover defined the aim of progressive government as "a 'partnership' of responsible and interdependent social groups acting together to stretch 'an enlarged vision of neighborly relations' over 'the nation as a whole.'"[78]

This describes the 1931 assembly of experts who represented the network of professionals concerned with housing issues.

Although Hoover spoke figuratively of "neighborly relations" in his commencement address, his support for detached, single-family, suburban home ownership emphasized the literal cultivation of a form of neighborliness. Developers addressed this theme, too, when they searched for subdivision strategies that would reduce their expenditures on land, utilities, and site improvements.[79] The home-ownership network embraced the idea of neighborhood to describe a number of contemporary subdivision practices. What did the notion of neighborhood mean, and how did it encourage home ownership?

The Neighborhood Unit Plan

By 1921, when an editorial in the *National Real Estate Journal* described the Garden of Eden as the first subdivision, it was clear that developers saw themselves as the primary shapers and lawgivers of new communities.[80] This contrasts with the pattern of development that Sam Bass Warner reconstructed for late-nineteenth-century Boston suburbs. He called this "regulation without laws" to express the order that was achieved despite "extreme individualization of agency" as "nine thousand different people made separate decisions to build houses."[81] This kind of subdivision activity persisted, but contemporaneously there were some developers who also built houses on a speculative basis in their subdivided tracts; The Real Estate Associates, in San Francisco, is one we have already noted, and another often-cited example is the much larger-scale work of Samuel Eberly Gross in Chicago in the 1880s.[82] As this form of residential development became more widespread, the issue of how to design such subdivisions grew in importance. What shape should these latter-day gardens of Eden be given?

The associational network of experts—whose interactions led to the forging of housing policy and its dissemination to practitioners working at the local level—provided broad parameters to guide developers toward the solution of this question. This diverse array of realtors, architects, planners, engineers, financiers, and others involved with housing issues reached a consensus on the necessity and urgency of promoting home ownership; the campaigns and organizations traced above make this clear.

In the course of the 1920s, mechanisms to ease the achievement of home ownership were improved: financing, for example, was more widely accessible and, through building and subdivision codes, standardization, and professionalization, a sounder, more predictable product was increasingly available. As the report of the correlating committee on technological developments for the President's Conference on Home Building and Home Ownership indicated, the cost of the individual house was not viewed as likely to change. Although this was regarded as limiting the possibilities for home ownership for those with smaller incomes, it did not discourage developers, since the dwelling itself was not their source of greatest profit. It did seem, however, that home ownership had reached a plateau and that if greater heights were to be achieved, as the network of housing professionals desired, another route would have to be taken.

Indeed, there was another route, one that both promoted home ownership and guided the design of residential development. This was not a network of human actors but an idea that was reinforced through its reappearance in diverse forms. The idea was to create neighborhood identity. Frequently referred to as "community-building" by developers, or as the designation of a "residential district" by planners, the creation of neighborhood identity entailed a set of flexible and fluid practices that had evolved by the 1920s. These practices both framed and addressed the question of the organization of large-scale housing development.

It is also necessary to differentiate this idea of neighborhood identity from developers' or planners' related ideas. To the extent that a "residential district" is the product of regulated land use achieved through deed restrictions and zoning mechanisms, the term *residential district* entails a narrower conception of how to shape the physical, social, and economic features of a development. These were certainly important devices for 1920s developers, but they represent only one set of tactics. Developers marshaled a broader array of practices, including spatial and architectural means, to physically stamp the character of a housing tract.

We must also distinguish the concept of neighborhood identity from the idea of community used by period developers. While the notion of community played an important part in the formulation of practices designed to create neighborhood identity, often the term *community* was also a part of the self-description of realtor-developers. It would be a mistake to accept unquestioningly developers' appropriation of the term, as when they invoked their role as "community builders." Indeed, as William S. Worley has noted in his study of J. C. Nichols, what this leading realtor referred to as "community features," far from signifying devices to encourage genuine human solidarity, meant ones that we would generally categorize today as public-relations gambits.[83] Only if we maintain a critical distance from realtors' uses of the term can we locate the meanings of the idea of community that enabled it to function effectively in subdivision development.

One way to achieve a sense of neighborhood identity was to manipulate the physical design of the setting for a large development of houses. A distinctive feature of developers' subdivisions was the emphasis placed on nature, from planning the layout to providing for ongoing maintenance. Ideally, the natural topography of a site would guide the pattern of a subdivision's streets, creating curvilinear arrangements where possible. Landscape features would grace roadways, and some portion of the tract would be dedicated to development as a shared park and recreation area. In addition, of course, each house would be nestled within its own natural environment of trees, shrubs, and flowers.

This notion of "rus in urbe," as one report from the President's Conference described it—"The benefits of country life along with the advantages and conveniences of urban living"[84]—stemmed from the ideals of suburban residence formulated by Andrew Jackson Downing in the 1840s. Concretized in early romantic suburbs such as Alexander Jackson Davis's Llewellyn Park (1852) and Frederick Law Olmsted's Riverside (1868), and promoted from pulpits and press as the healthiest physical and moral environment for the family, these ideals were influential throughout the nineteenth century.[85] Around the turn of the century, they were infused with English garden-suburb planning ideas and began to be incorporated into developers' subdivision designs.[86] In the vivid terms of one 1920s writer, these took "the cream of the country and the cream of the city, leaving the skim-milk for those who like that sort of thing."[87]

Among realtors, one of the most visible promoters of "garden-like" suburban development in the second and third decades of the twentieth century was Jesse Clyde Nichols, developer of Kansas City's Country Club District. Nichols had been impressed with the physical design of villages he had seen while on a bicycle tour of England during his college years at the University of Kansas.[88] His interest in attempting to construct developments himself began to take shape following a year's study of law and real estate at Harvard University. He related his experiences and argued for the strategies he worked out for successful subdivisions in speeches, articles, and interviews. For example, in an address entitled "Real Estate Subdivisions: The Best Manner of Handling Them," given at the fifth annual convention of the National Association of Real Estate Boards in 1912 and later published by the American Civic Association, he argued that the City Beautiful movement, which had focused on civic centers, must extend to residential development as well. After describing the curvilinear streets, parks, and plantings that enhanced his own project, he concluded, "It really does pay to spend more money upon the beautiful things."[89]

By 1925, when he contributed the chapter on town planning to a textbook on real-estate practices, Nichols had a very clear vision of the aspects of physical design that could shape a subdivision scheme as a totality. He described, for example, how residential streets, in contrast to through-traffic arteries,

> should be so planned as to eliminate alleys, follow the contour of the land, be fitted to the lots and blocks, afford sites of interesting shapes, and permit individual landscape treatment. They should preserve and reveal vistas, creating street pictures.... Closed street views, so inter-

esting in the medieval towns, should be frequent. . . . Building lines should not be uniform, but should be varied according to site and view; blocks should be treated as a unit; and, wherever possible, harmonious group planning and collective building should be carried out. Residence streets should have a cozy, domestic character, be quiet, self-contained, garden-like.[90]

The picturesque aesthetic that Nichols describes is clearly indebted to garden-suburb precedents and it serves both to design the form and to define the character of a residential enclave.

Even in less-ambitious schemes, it was widely recognized that both streets and landscaping were important devices for linking new subdivisions to existing development through the extension of thoroughfares and park systems; both were useful to maintain separation as well. Boundaries could be defined by traffic arteries and landscape buffers, and the interior of subdivisions distinguished by independent street patterns and park areas. When Olmsted introduced, at Riverside, the planting strip between the street and the pedestrian walkway, a "physical and visual separator," he demonstrated how planning devices could function both practically and as distinctive visual features.[91] Streets and landscape features could contribute, in other words, to the creation of a neighborhood identity, but so could other devices.

The leitmotif of the early romantic suburb was nature, and a pure example of it was often used as the focus of the community's design. Downing conceived a park as the centerpiece of his ideal community; the public space at Llewellyn Park was The Ramble. In his plans for Riverside, however, Olmsted included facilities for schools and recreational activities, and by the 1920s it was common to find these, too, as important elements in subdivision designs.

Over the intervening decades, a broad network of Progressive Era reformers argued that such anchors for neighborhood identity were increasingly crucial in residential environments. Clarence A. Perry provided the most succinct formulation of this argument in his proposal for the "neighborhood unit plan" in 1925 (fig. 46). Perry's concept became one of the central themes of the reports from the

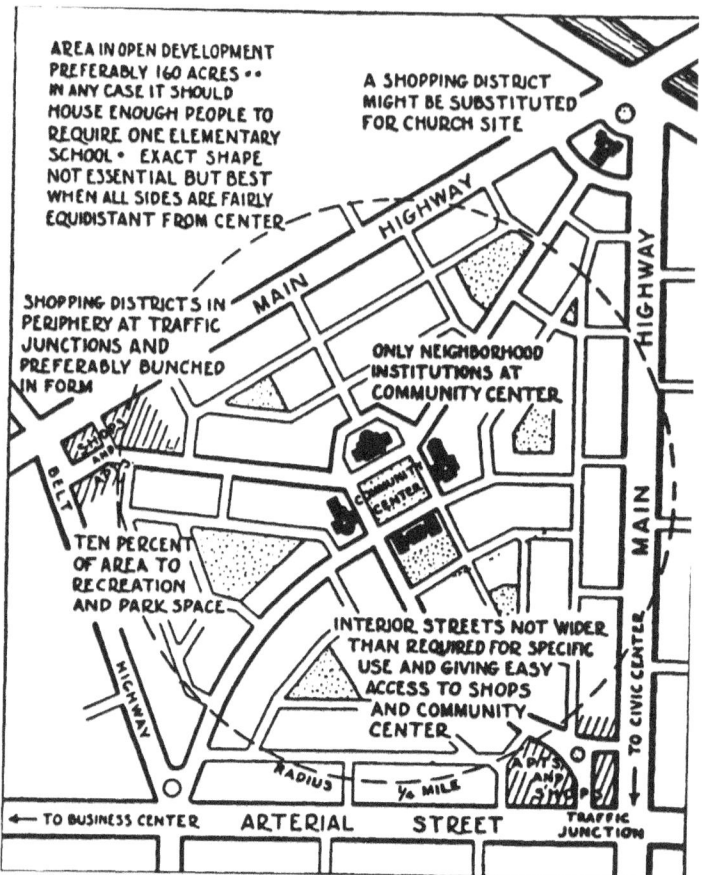

Figure 46. Clarence A. Perry's presentation of the neighborhood unit plan. His use of an abstract diagram emphasized the applicability of its principles to any residential environment. The scheme, generated by the capacity and location of the elementary school, is based on the separation of functions. Perry's thinking about neighborhood design was influenced by his experiences in the community-center movement and as a resident of Forest Hills Gardens.

President's Conference on Home Building and Home Ownership. Although there were other rationales for including schools and recreational facilities in subdivisions, the notions of neighborhood and community provided the language developers used to describe their projects.

The generative element in Perry's scheme for neighborhood units was the elementary school. The number of families necessary to provide the enrollment for one school would determine the size of a community demographically. Spatially, it would extend for a radius of half a mile from the school, the maximum distance schoolchildren should have to walk. The school would serve as a center for community activities, possibly supplemented by other neighborhood institutions. Concerned with a safe environment for children, Perry located main traffic arteries at the boundaries of the neighborhood and limited the size of streets within it. Scattered parks and open spaces were included throughout the neighborhood; shops were grouped at its edges.

Perry made his first public presentation of the neighborhood unit plan in a lecture entitled "A Community Unit in City Planning and Development" in December 1923 at a joint meeting of the National Community Center Association and the American Sociological Society.[92] The first published account of the neighborhood unit plan appeared in a volume of selected papers from the proceedings of the 1925 American Sociological Society annual meeting.[93] It received wider attention as part of the multivolume *Regional Plan of New York and Its Environs*, sponsored by the Russell Sage Foundation and published in 1929.[94]

The ideas presented in the concept of the neighborhood unit plan were not novel. Rather, in a simplified form, they represented a synthesis of proposals that had evolved in the context of planning and design theory, on the one hand, and through social reform movements, on the other. Perry's personal experience placed him at a junction of these two worlds; since he drew on his experiences for the formulation of the neighborhood unit plan, it is useful to look briefly at his background and, through it, to the network of influences that helped shape his scheme.

In 1909, Perry began working for the Department of Recreation of the Russell Sage Foundation, a philanthropic organization that had been founded two years earlier.[95] He was hired "to find out to what extent school buildings and grounds were used outside of school hours, or might advantageously be used for recreation and for other social and civic purposes."[96] His study of this question resulted in *Wider Use of the School Plant*, a 1910 publication that became very influential and inaugurated Perry's activities in the movement to develop neighborhood centers.[97] His exhaustive examination of the uses served by school facilities after day-class hours, both existing and potential, was based on the conviction that "the school is the natural focal point of the community's social life since it centers the universal interest in children and cuts through social, religious and even racial lines."[98] By using the school building for evening and summer-vacation classes, public lectures and entertainments, meetings and recreational activities, the school could serve as a center for neighborhood social and civic life.

The idea of using the local school as a community center had been proposed as early as the 1890s by Jacob Riis and, in 1902, by John Dewey.[99] Its roots were in the emphasis placed on neighborhood self-development by the social settlement movement. Inspired by the founding of Toynbee Hall in East London in 1884, the first settlement house in the United States, Neighborhood Guild, was established in New York City in 1886. By 1910, there were more than four hundred settlement houses throughout the United States.[100]

The settlement program tended to focus on poor and working-class urban immigrant communities, in which assimilation to a new culture as well as issues of health, nutrition, and education were primary concerns. Sociologist Charles Horton Cooley's influential writings in the first decade of the century laid a theoretical foundation for extending the emphasis on community development to all sectors of society.[101] Cooley's work stressed the role of human relationships in the development of personality and social organization, especially through what he called primary associations with family and community groups. He targeted these face-to-face interactions as a counterweight to the dislocating and disintegrating forces of industrialization and urbanization that affected all social groups. The community-center movement, as it came to be known, encouraged the reconstruction of a sense of neighborhood—a site that would nurture Cooley's primary associations—through the use of the local school. Such a neighborhood center was also seen as "a possible cure for the evils of the political machine," since it offered an independent site for political discussions and voluntary associations.[102]

Edward J. Ward, a leader of the community-center movement, initiated the first citywide program for the use of school buildings for social and civic activities in Rochester, New York, in 1907. In 1909, Ward established the Wisconsin Bureau of Civic and Social Center Development, where he developed a framework for extending school centers statewide. Two years later, Ward moved to the national level, organizing the first National Conference on Civic and Social Center Development, which Perry attended as an active delegate. Perry was one of the organizers of the National Community Center Association, an outgrowth of the conference, in 1916.[103] This body was short-lived, however; in 1924 it was absorbed by the National Education Association. Nevertheless, Perry continued to work with the idea of the school as the focus of community life while he turned his attention to other aspects of residential design affecting the definition of neighborhood identity.

While Perry's work at the Russell Sage Foundation led him to become involved with the community-center movement and to incorporate its emphasis on the school into his neighborhood unit plan, his choice of residence was also connected to the work of the foundation and this provided inspiration for his plan as well: in 1912, Perry was one of the first to move into Forest Hills Gardens, the model suburb designed by Frederick Law Olmsted Jr. and Grosvenor Atterbury, developed by realtor Edward H. Bouton and funded by the foundation.[104] As Perry noted in his chapter on the history of the neighborhood unit plan in *Housing for the Machine Age*, his later book, "When the writer analyzed the Gardens development into its essential elements, he found that they constituted the main principles of an ideal neighborhood."[105] Incorporating some of the concepts of English garden-suburb design, Forest Hills Gardens presented Perry with a model for his own schematic neighborhood plan. Perry found his own community exemplary—in size, in its inclusion of open space, and in its provision of special structures to serve neighborhood institutions. He thought that its street system was admirable to the extent that it broke away from the uniformity of the grid, but it also had shortcomings: it neither made adequate provision for the automobile nor separated through-traffic from the internal circulation system of the community. As a model, however, Perry found that "even its unsatisfactory features were helpful" in solving the problems of neighborhood design.[106]

Thus, in the neighborhood unit plan Perry wed the Progressive goal of creating opportunities for community organization and face-to-face interactions with the garden-suburb aesthetic of curvilinear streets, landscaping, and distinctive internal architectural features. Lewis Mumford, writing about Perry's work, pointed out that

> what Perry did was to take the fact of the neighborhood; and show how, through deliberate design, it could be transformed into what he called a neighborhood unit, the modern equivalent of the medieval quarter or parish: a unit that would now exist, not merely on a spontaneous or instinctual basis, but through the deliberate decentralisation of institutions that had, in their over-centralisation, ceased to serve efficiently the city as a whole.[107]

Such ideas were basic to the social thought of the Progressive Era and were so widespread that, as Mumford acknowledged, Perry had "crystallis[ed] many diffuse efforts." These included such earlier initiatives as the plan created in 1907 by the Committee on Civic Centers in Saint Louis to establish neighborhood centers; this appears not to have been known to Perry.[108] He probably was aware, however, of another significant example of interest in community development, the 1913 competition organized by the City Club of Chicago "for Subdividing a Typical Quarter Section of Land in the Outskirts of Chicago."[109] The program of the competition included providing for social and recreational centers; one of the entries specifically described its design as a neighborhood unit plan.[110] Perry's scheme, in contrast, was not tied to a particular locale and was much more simplified and abstract than the plans submitted to the Chicago City Club. In the spirit of the times, which, we have seen, emphasized standard models, Perry produced a distillation of elements to be applied in varied forms in situations ranging from new suburban developments to the renewal of decayed urban areas.[111]

Furthermore, the confluence of experiences and ideas that Perry channeled into the neighborhood unit plan is an example of how physical design and social transformation were often linked during the early decades of the century. In his history and analysis of Ebenezer Howard's garden city scheme, Stanley Buder situates the evolution of Howard's concept within the context of his involvement in social, spiritual, and political movements for social change. The garden-city idea, Buder shows, was nurtured within "the small fervid world of late-nineteenth-century communitarianism."[112] When Howard's idea was realized in the form of early-twentieth-century garden suburbs, however, it shed its challenge to private property relationships and to the fragmentation of the industrial city. Yet the sense of order represented by garden suburbs was attractive, in the United States, to "reformers gathered around the settlement-house movement, who welcomed the message of the Garden City movement as an extension of their own interests in environmental and social innovation."[113] By synthesizing garden-suburb ideas with the reform spirit of the community-center movement, Perry's neighborhood unit plan embodied Buder's argument that Howard's "search for a new environmental ideal provided the passageway for ideas and individuals to cross over from" the social radicalism of the late-nineteenth century "to the twentieth-century profession of town planning."[114] Perry's scheme did not claim to effect profound social transformation but rather offered a seemingly objective planning instrument to add to Progressives' strategies for rationalizing urban development.

By the time Clarence Stein and Henry Wright designed Radburn in 1928, they had discussed the neighborhood unit plan with Perry; this testifies to the awareness of his ideas within the progressive planning community.[115] The publication of his contribution to the *Re-*

gional Plan of New York and Its Environs the following year extended his audience. In 1931, he participated in the President's Conference on Home Building and Home Ownership, serving on the committee on housing and the community, which considered issues of health, crime, and safety. His ideas had a much wider impact, however; they appear in the reports on city planning, subdivision layout, and house design, as well. Each of these embraced neighborhood unit planning as the best way to create physical, economic, and social stability within a healthy, safe, and moral environment.

The neighborhood unit plan represented a diagrammatic, replicable model that, by the time of the 1931 conference, paralleled the practices of many large-scale suburban residential developers. As we have seen, realtors who engaged in large-scale development adopted the language of Progressive community building as part of their professional project. They scorned identification with the facet of real-estate practice that concentrated on buying and selling commodities to achieve short-term gain. Instead, realtor-developers emphasized their disinterested commitment to civic improvement through rational and efficient means. However, their communitywide focus also provided a way to accomplish financial ends—the protection of investments—by stabilizing property values. This was developers' recurring concern. The value of land and property was always subject to the play of market forces, as Carl O. Sauer, a professor at the University of Michigan at the time and a land-use specialist, noted at a realtors' convention in 1921. How could these complex and seemingly elemental agents be controlled? The next convention speaker, lawyer and planner Edward M. Bassett, offered a solution: Bassett gave an address on zoning ordinances, of which he was a well-known proponent.[116] This juxtaposition of speakers—one posing the question, the other providing an answer—reflects the fact that increasingly realtors were looking to planning instruments and public regulations, including master plans, subdivision controls, and zoning, in addition to deed restrictions, in their search for greater economic predictability and stability.[117]

Within the subdivision, physical design and construction played the same role as these instruments. Contoured streets, the diversion of through-traffic, landscaping, and schools and recreational facilities contributed to the definition of the neighborhood as a predictable and self-perpetuating community. In his many addresses to conventions of the National Association of Real Estate Boards and to other bodies, developer J. C. Nichols increasingly stressed the interconnections among subdivision design, community planning, and profitability. The report in the *National Real Estate Journal* on a talk he gave in 1924 entitled "Suburban Subdivisions with Community Features" noted that the topic was "one Mr. Nichols is especially well qualified to discuss because of the thorough manner in which he has carried out the development of the community idea in his own subdivisions."[118] The social and recreational facilities of the Country Club District, including its four golf clubs, were well-known features of the project. In another address to the same year's convention, Nichols emphasized the economic goals of development: "The Realtor can and should stabilize our property values, not only as a national economic saving insuring permanency of investment, but to justify the security for larger loans." After listing various types of zoning and design considerations that would serve these goals, Nichols noted, "There is a growing consciousness of the subdivider that he is not alone concerned in the values and prices at which he may sell lots in his subdivision, but that he has a professional responsibility for the maintenance of the value of the wares he sells his client."[119] The kinds of planning and design decisions that developers made would preserve the investments of individual home owners as well as those of the realtors.

If home ownership was to become more widespread, it seemed, it would have to be through the reduction of risk provided by the kinds of large-scale developments that shared the features of neighborhood unit planning, for which Nichols argued and with which he was identified. With land-use regulations, design controls, independent street patterns, landscaping, schools, and other facilities, the character of the neighborhood as a residential enclave could reasonably be assured for the indefinite future.

Communities on the Ground

This web of social concerns and solutions—settlements, Cooley's theory of community, the school-center movement, garden-suburb design, the neighborhood unit plan, assurance of the security of property investments—mirrors, in its multiplicity, the network of interactions among diverse groups within the arena of residential design and construction that shaped suburban subdivision development. There was no single line of influence, but an intersection of varied and overlapping proposals that met within the fluid framework of "associational progressivism."[120] *Associational progressivism* is the term introduced by historian Ellis Hawley to describe the organization that Herbert Hoover established as secretary of commerce. Hoover used his governmental base to project "an extensive net of promotional activities, cooperating committees, and other ad hoc structures, all tied to private groupings and associations and all designed to energize private or local collectivities and guide them toward constructive solutions to national problems."[121] By the time Hoover forged this theory of administration, the idea that expertise from diverse fields could be pooled to resolve public issues was widespread. The loose network of realtors, architects, planners, engineers, financiers, reformers, materials suppliers, and others concerned with housing was already in place and prepared to develop both regulative and physical model structures to shape the built environment.

Whereas earlier chapters pointed to evident tensions among some of these groups (building-craftsmen, architects, and realtors) as they struggled for professional recognition, this chapter focuses on collaboration among some of these same groups (realtors, architects, and planners) as professional equals. The establishment of professional competence, including an organizational framework with ethical and procedural standards, was necessary in order to achieve recognition within the world of expertise. Once competence was established, the ethos of managing social development through gathering information and marshaling experts meant that cooperation was necessary. A succinct statement of this spirit can be found in an article from 1912, "Model Towns in America," by architect Grosvenor Atterbury, written while the development of Forest Hills Gardens was under way. He noted that "cooperative design and development make possible the employment of experts in all departments by distributing the greater part of the first cost of their services over a large area of development."[122] Similar encouragement of cooperation among experts in the development of residential projects can be found in writings by realtors such as Nichols and in the reports from the President's Conference. It is worth noting, however, that building-craftsmen remained peripheral to this network, as the history of the transformation in the nature and level of their skills might suggest.

The experts that are necessarily the focus here are the ones who were active at the national level and in interaction with each other. But it is important to remember that they represent organizations that functioned pyramidally to disseminate information and ideas to their grassroots memberships. Through reprints of speeches, reports on meetings, and news of publications printed in professional journals such as the *National Real Estate Journal,* as well as through regional and local meetings, the models established by the national network filtered through each professional group. This was the process of education and enforcement encouraged by associational progressivism.

It is possible to see the impact of this process, especially in regard to the notion of neighborhood, by returning to the three subdivisions investigated earlier and reconsidering them in the light of the present discussion. Although each subdivision manifested the neighborhood idea in a different way, it was significant in all of them and to a significant extent guided the overall conception of each scheme.

Taylor self-consciously referred to himself as a "community-builder," and although the design elements that defined Brightmoor were minimal, he did anchor the subdivision with commercial and community facilities. In this connection, the Brightmoor settlement house can be seen as a literal transposition of a late-nineteenth-century solution to urban problems into a twentieth-century suburban context. By the 1920s, the community facilities available in most suburban subdivisions were not as obviously rooted in institutions of social reform. It is likely that Taylor felt that since the inhabitants he was soliciting for his community were new to the urban industrial environment, they would benefit from the same kind of neighborhood center that had been created to foster the assimilation of earlier newcomers. In later subdivisions that he built for residents with somewhat higher incomes, Taylor followed Nichols's precedent and substituted golf courses to serve as the centerpieces of his projects.

In the Ford Homes, a neighborhood anchor was created by the construction of the elementary school, the only community facility that was actually built, although a park had also been projected. It is possible to see this now as exemplifying a broader theory of neighborhood development current in this period, distilled in Perry's neighborhood unit plan. And perhaps Ford Homes architect Albert Wood regarded this as providing an adequate site for the development of the civic activism he wrote about in "Community Homes."

Westwood Highlands, in contrast, embodies the aspects of this approach to neighborhood development that emphasize physical layout and design. Baldwin & Howell substituted contoured streets that follow their site's topography for the grid that Taylor merely extended in Brightmoor and that had already been platted in Dearborn. The boundaries of the San Francisco subdivision were clear, especially to the south, where the major traffic artery skirted the project. Design features such as the subdivision signage along this main boundary defined the community, as did the treatment of corner houses within the tract to acknowledge public space and suggest a larger whole of which each house and street was a part.

On the other hand, Westwood Highlands was less of a self-sufficient neighborhood than the other two subdivisions, since it shared its community facilities with contiguous developments in the West of Twin Peaks District, including an earlier tract developed by Baldwin & Howell. The district as a whole, however, includes significant features of neighborhood design, such as the location of shopping areas along the periphery on a main thoroughfare that was served by a streetcar line. Taylor, too, at Brightmoor, used the commercial area to define the neighborhood, but he located it closer to the center of the community rather than at its edge.

In different ways, then, a sense of neighborhood was integral to the development strategies used in these subdivisions. This contrasts with

THE HOME-OWNERSHIP NETWORK

the streetcar suburbs that Sam Bass Warner studied, where he found that "there was nothing in the process of late nineteenth century suburban construction that built communities or neighborhoods." Rather, development there was geared to "an economically efficient geometry [the grid] which divided large parcels of land as they came on the market," and thus "the result was not integrated communities arranged about common centers, but a historical and accidental traffic pattern."[123] The subdivisions studied here exemplify, instead, new neighborhood environments that were designed deliberately, as Mumford noted in his description of Perry's work.

By the 1920s, the awareness of neighborhoods as significant arenas for socialization and the integrated-design precedent found in garden-suburb schemes had merged with realtors' needs for secure investments to provide a new model for subdivision development. Landscaping, street pattern, schools, and community facilities were devices to create physical and social coherence that could be self-perpetuating. The potentially long-term stability that this offered protected the realtor's original investment as well as those of the neighborhood's home owners. By controlling the character of the community, the developer was better able to control otherwise unpredictable market forces. The Federal Housing Administration and the structure of the federal income tax code, both dating from the New Deal, provided additional assurances to encourage home ownership. But short of these final building blocks, Dolores Hayden's observation that "the development of suburban home ownership as the national housing policy in the United States offered a post–World War I idea to a post–World War II society" is borne out by the history traced here.[124]

One other unifying element of these projects is the houses themselves. We next look at how these contributed to the form that suburban subdivision development took in the 1920s.

CHAPTER 5

ARCHITECTURAL STYLE
The Charm of Continuity

No single approach to architectural style was taken in the three subdivisions examined in part I, nor was architectural design used to generate the spatial organization of those projects. Instead, the variety of stylistic approaches found there suggests that a broad array of forms were equally useful and meaningful for entrepreneurial vernacular schemes. What determined the choice of forms, and how did they contribute to subdivision development?

The home-ownership network does not provide answers to these questions, for the housing experts involved in subdivision development were not particularly concerned with visual form. Architectural design issues received no emphasis in the reports of the President's Conference on Home Building and Home Ownership, nor was there substantial discussion of this topic in realtors' literature. Not even Albert Wood, the architect of the Ford Homes, addressed this subject when he wrote his proposals for new housing schemes in his booklet "Community Homes." Clarence Perry's neighborhood unit plan took the form of a disembodied, abstract diagram, without specifying how this might be realized in any particular project. The consistency with which design issues were avoided prompts us to ask why visual form received so little attention from the home-ownership network and what this signifies for the architectural forms that were selected for constructed subdivisions.

Part of the answer lies in the concern of the national network of housing professionals to create model solutions rather than blueprints for residential development. They couched their proposals in diagrammatic and schematic terms; this allowed their easy transmission to developers working at the local level who would adapt and apply subdivision concepts to the diverse circumstances they faced.

ARCHITECTURAL STYLE

The silence of the home-ownership network about architectural design issues suggests that housing experts considered visual form to be an aspect of the variable local conditions that each developer addressed individually. We must, then, revisit the three subdivisions, for it is through analysis of their design features that significant architectural elements and the principles that shaped design decisions emerge. The designers of entrepreneurial vernacular tracts did not invent a new architectural language for these projects. Instead, they adapted existing vocabularies in ways that reinforced distinctive characteristics of subdivision developments.

This means that developers reconfigured conventional design elements to support the new meanings that stemmed from this housing solution. Identifying these meanings requires taking a larger view of architectural style that encompasses more than visual forms alone. For in 1920s suburban residential tracts, architectural style needed to perform in ways that were not limited to the orchestration of visual elements. Architectural style did more than construct the scenery of the tract; it addressed some of the contemporary trends in social and construction practices, many of which we have noted in earlier chapters. The architectural envelope had to reconcile the process of production of the house, its internal arrangements, and the public face that the house presented both to the prospective home buyer and to its neighbors. Furthermore, the individual house was only part of the suite of dwellings that made up the subdivision; architectural style also had to negotiate the relationship of singularity and multiplicity, of unity and diversity, that was one of the tensions underlying such housing developments.

Ultimately, design aided the risk-management mission that we have identified as the focus for so many features of entrepreneurial vernacular construction. The burden placed on style was to resolve tensions arising from new patterns of household arrangements, building practices, and neighborhood creation. By manipulating images of past and future, design devices conveyed an assurance of continuity and stability that represents one of the distinguishing motifs of entrepreneurial vernacular subdivision developments. Consideration of wider cultural frameworks that had an impact on housing provides

AGENCY, FORM, AND MEANING

the context for this complex set of meanings, but first it is necessary to locate the specific architectural features of entrepreneurial vernacular developments that grounded these broader ideas.

The Ford Homes

The Ford Homes were conceived as a unified visual composition. It is not known to what extent the architect's ideas as expressed in "Community Homes" influenced his colleagues in the Dearborn Realty & Construction Company, but a number of design decisions contributed to the visual definition of the subdivision. The simple and straightforward devices that Albert Wood employed enabled him to balance elements that unify the whole project with others that differentiate individual dwellings and create a sense of variety. To achieve this goal, Wood coordinated the project on three levels: the tract as an entirety, an intermediate level of smaller groupings of houses, and the individual house.

In addition to their similarity in scale and massing, it is the style of the houses that unifies the subdivision. Wood evoked the image of an eclectic colonial style by deploying a few telling features, including rooflines, dormer windows, shutters, fanlights, columns, and trim. Analytically, it is possible to see that Wood marshaled both "formal" elements (those referring to "plan, volumetric organization, and general compositional massing") and "figural" motifs ("the particular appearance of elements, ornamentation, and decoration") to shape the subdivision's identity in architectural terms.[1] The repetition of these formal and figural features still serves to distinguish the neighborhood from surrounding houses.

Since the grid of streets and lots had already been platted when the land was purchased, the only original planning device used for the project was the setback of houses in staggered groups of three or four. This was intended to provide visual variety along the streetscape and was also an attempt to define intermediate clusters of houses. There was substantial interest during this period in grouping houses to avoid the monotony of dwellings spaced evenly along the perimeter of blocks and to create subgroups of neighbors in the spirit of turn-of-the-century sociologist Charles Horton Cooley's notions of primary group associations. Wood's proposal for houses grouped around cul-de-sacs in "Community Homes" reflects such ideas, and a multitude of examples using similar devices appeared in period journals.[2] However, the staggered setbacks used in the Ford Homes represent a timid, limited contribution to this trend; since they did not alter the uniformly frontal siting of the houses, they created little real sense of distinct groups within the project as a whole.

While the attempt to define a more intimate scale between the subdivision and the individual house was not entirely successful, the designer did achieve a balance between the unity of the total scheme and variety at the level of the single dwelling. Although the devices that define the style of the tract are standardized and repeated, the configurations of the masses within which they appear change according to the modular formal scheme analyzed in chapter 1. Assured that the six models would be scattered by their assignment to specific lots, the designer used a limited range of detailing to simultaneously link and differentiate the houses. When the few decisions that were left to home buyers were made, affecting the type of exterior cladding and the color of the roofing shingles, the function of the details as unifying accents became more apparent. Massing in combination with color and texture variations then created the individualizing features.

The colonial revival style certainly lent itself to this kind of manipulation of details within related configurations of mass. One promoter of this style explained in *House and Garden* in 1917 that "it is perfectly feasible to build endless varieties of this type by following certain fixed precedents, and creating a building which is consistent."[3] Its rectangular shape and gabled roof were readily adapted to balloon-frame construction, and its decorative wood details were easily standardized and mass-produced.

In addition to conforming to the production process that the Ford Homes were created, in part, to demonstrate, the colonial revival style was also appropriate to the design needs of the sort of project represented by the Ford Homes. By the 1920s, this style had become very familiar in the United States. Beginning with the centennial in 1876, interest in colonial architecture and artifacts grew during the succeeding decades. The vocabulary and image of colonial styles came to be immediately recognizable through the rehabilitation of colonial structures, as well as their reconstruction, reproduction, or reinvention in contemporary forms.[4] This made it possible to conjure the whole through its parts—to successfully suggest a colonial village through the selective use of figural details.

Documents on the history of the Ford Homes do not record whose decision it was to use elements of colonial revival style. In "Community Homes," Wood did not present architectural elevations or discuss style. But considering Henry Ford's architectural and historical predilections as these were revealed in later projects, it is very likely that the choice of this style was his. In 1923, Ford bought the Wayside Inn in Sudbury, Massachusetts, a colonial structure celebrated by Henry Wadsworth Longfellow in his 1863 *Tales of a Wayside Inn*. Ford had it restored and operated it as a museum and restaurant. Stimulated by this purchase, in 1927 he began his acquisition and reconstruction of colonial buildings at Greenfield Village, virtually next door to the Ford Homes.[5] In this highly eclectic, idiosyncratic, and idealized environment, relocated colonial structures from Pennsylvania, Massachusetts, and other states occupy sites next to Ford's own mid-nineteenth-century boyhood home, the Wright brothers' bicycle shop, and virtually the entire Menlo Park laboratory of Thomas Edison from New Jersey. This juxtaposition merged the forms, meaning, and history of the colonial past with those of more recent periods. It equated the clarity and harmony of diverse colonial buildings with the inventiveness that Ford both admired and embodied; it grounded this inventiveness in the simple and direct forms of the nation's origins. Transplanting individual buildings to Greenfield Village isolated each from the specific architectural and social traditions that had shaped it and made all of them equally emblematic of national virtues. At Greenfield Village it is possible to see that colonial architecture symbolized for Ford the perseverance, creativity, and ingenuity that he identified with the history of technology and its impact on daily life in the United States. Furthermore, as Karal Ann Marling has suggested, it linked the dynamism and profusion of ongoing technological developments with a view of the past as similarly ambitious and productive, yet known, contained, and stable: "The past was just like the present: clean, prosperous, busy, mobile, and stocked with every imaginable consumer durable."[6]

Students of the colonial revival seem to agree that by the 1920s the style was linked with a sense of national identity.[7] For Ford and others concerned with the Americanization of immigrants, it served a didactic role.[8] Discomfort with increases in the numbers of immigrants may have stimulated enthusiasm for the colonial revival as an expression of nativist sentiment.

Within architectural circles, there was an interest in the historical record, conveyed through measured drawings and renderings of extant buildings, but no need was felt to imitate this heritage slavishly. Talbot Hamlin's comments in *The American Spirit in Architecture,* published in 1926, reflect this flexible and diffuse attitude toward the style: "In recent years at least, the most prolific source of inspiration in house design has been the Georgian and colonial of our own country's youth. It has proved to 'belong'; its own closeness to us has made it seem at home... throughout the country." An illustrated example, supplied in the book, Hamlin said "shows how beautifully a modern adaptation of colonial precedent can suit a small house. Like most modern colonial, this is a free adaptation; it is in no sense archaeological."[9]

As a range of forms that suggested links with the nation's past, colonial became the stylistic currency for the wider public as well. In 1929, the editors of *Popular Mechanics* advised, "Styles in houses come and go like styles in cars...It pays to build in a style as liquid in public approval as a Liberty bond at a bank. Colonial is such a style."[10] And, indeed, in their survey of popular magazines appearing in 1925, Jean Gordon and Jan McArthur found that this was "the hands-down favorite" among published house styles. They also noted that these magazines ignored that year's International Exposition of Modern Industrial and Decorative Arts, held in Paris, which showcased the style that became known as Art Deco, but provided extensive coverage of the inauguration of the Metropolitan Museum's American Wing, another source for colonial imagery.[11]

Thus, while Henry Ford seems to have held a special brief for the colonial style, the style itself was sufficiently widespread at the time to bear at least a general significance for many people—designer and prospective home owner alike. But one of the most important reasons for its successful use in the Ford Homes was the fact that its details could suggest the style in its more elaborate versions. Features such as the configuration of rooflines and dormer windows and the inclusion of fanlights, shutters, and columns were sufficient to establish the character of the style, without resorting to an archaeological reproduction of specific models. Through a sensitive selection of such figural elements, Wood was able to create a unified subdivision composition that preserved a sense of individuality in its parts. Also, because these telling elements could be simplified and standardized, thus fitting into the industrialized process of construction, the colonial style remained a flexible conveyor of meaning in the context of large-scale residential design.

Brightmoor

Unlike the Ford Homes or the dwellings in Westwood Highlands, the houses that B. E. Taylor built at Brightmoor were not designed within the framework of a revival style. Rather, the simplicity of their massing and their lack of ornamentation tend to emphasize their clear shapes and standardized, machined elements. Nevertheless, if the links that were noted between the Brightmoor houses and owner-builder traditions in Appalachia are justified, this simplicity and absence of detail does not mean that these structures lacked architectural associations or the ability to convey meaning. On the contrary, one of the aspects of Brightmoor that emerges from this analysis, in contrast to the other subdivisions, is that this community seems to have been conceived in relation to a particular group of prospective home owners. The houses at Brightmoor were designed to seem familiar to families from the rural upland South newly arrived in Detroit to work in the city's factories. Although constructed according to industrialized building practices and processes, Brightmoor houses maintained continuity in design with traditional housing forms. Using a term offered by scholars of vernacular building, the Brightmoor houses are related to the southern cabin form of homestead.[12]

To point out this continuity in design is not to overlook the impoverishment of the community that Taylor abetted by omitting bathrooms, basements, and other amenities. The absence of these features may also have been familiar to Brightmoor home owners, but the cost reductions achieved in this way risked residents' health and became social costs when private, municipal, and state agencies were called upon to redress the problems they created. Taylor calculated not only the ways in which he could bring his clientele into the formal, urban realty market by selling houses in order to sell lots, but also how he could skimp on amenities that they might not expect anyway.

Size, ornamentation, and range of amenities are all features of housing that can vary depending on the projected cost of the structure—and therefore, in the case of speculative subdivisions of the sort studied here, on the class of the home owners whom the developer intends to attract. Brightmoor is readily legible, in these terms, as a community built for the working poor, whereas the Ford Homes and Westwood Highlands were conceived for a broader range of working-class and middle-class home owners. Beyond class, however, the language of forms used in the latter projects does not convey any other sense of the residents' backgrounds. At Brightmoor, in contrast, the choice of forms may have reflected the home owners' residential roots.

It is important to note, too, that the simplicity of Brightmoor's houses also derives from Taylor's ability to preserve in a general way traditional, craft-based, owner-builder patterns while using standardized elements and industrialized building processes.

Westwood Highlands

The analysis of Westwood Highlands indicated that manipulation of modular elements generated the overall organization of the subdivision. The configurations of plan and elevational modules designed by architect Charles Strothoff allowed him to take into account different siting problems and house sizes and to create a sense of variety while maintaining an underlying unity. Although stylistic elements were not central to this fundamental level of planning the neighborhood as a whole, they were used to achieve a complementary balance in visual terms. Materials and textures—primarily stucco wall surfaces, Spanish tile, and carved wood trim—were consistent, but their shapes and detailing varied a good deal.

It is instructive to note how this methodology contrasts with the one Wood used to generate the Ford Homes. In Dearborn, details were uniform, whereas both a certain variety of materials and textures and their distribution were programmatically left unplanned and allowed to achieve irregularity, since these were the features that prospective home owners could determine. In the Ford Homes, details were chosen for their ability to evoke colonial style, and hence played a major role in the visual and associational unity of the project. At Westwood Highlands, however, specific materials and textures were necessary to convey the sense of the Mediterranean revival style that dominates the subdivision. Since this is a more diffuse stylistic category, however, it was possible to draw upon a wider range of details, all of which would contribute to its evocation. This diversity in appropriate details allowed for the appearance of greater figural individuality within the overarching associational totality.

Another feature of Westwood Highlands that it is useful to recall is the provocative echo of past planning and design strategies found there. Although a complete exploration of the nature of the links between residential construction in the 1920s and that of the nineteenth century in the Bay Area is beyond the scope of this study, the latter serves as a helpful background against which to consider the meanings expressed through 1920s design. We have already noted a similar contrast in Victorian design between the uniformity of the sheathing, that served as a visual ground, and the multiplicity of ornamentation, through which variety within a structure, and from building to building, was created. This suggests that the ornamental elaboration and diversity that characterizes the houses at Westwood Highlands might owe as much to local traditions regarding the relationship between surface and decorative detail as it does to the particular stylistic language used there. Or, to put this another way, one of the aspects of Mediterranean revival that made it attractive in the early decades of the twentieth century may have been this conceptual similarity with the tradition of Victorian design in the area, despite the obvious differences in materials, massing, and vocabulary of forms.

These differences were certainly important, however, for the explicit references to the past that Mediterranean revival was understood to suggest were to an earlier period than that represented by Victorian structures. Not long after the centennial celebrations and the explorations of New England colonial architecture that they stimulated, a similar interest in colonial building in the West arose within architectural and wider intellectual circles in California.[13] Studies were made of the missions and of colonial and indigenous domestic structures, although the architecture inspired by them, as with eastern colonial revival designs, tended to be selective and picturesque rather than archaeological in spirit. Stucco walls, tile roofs, arched openings, and parapets were sufficient to suggest the Spanish colonial past of the region. More ambitious designs included quatrefoil windows, cusped Moorish arches, and towers. These features functioned, thus, much the same as the dormer windows, fanlights, columns, and other details had in the Ford Homes, evoking through simplified and schematic forms the aura of a more complex stylistic totality.

Colonial and colonial revival architecture in the West did not, of course, have the overtones of nation building that were part of the range of associations of East Coast colonial. Instead, Western revival styles evolved to include references that were based on geographic and climatic considerations. Influences from Spain, North Africa, and Mexico were joined by design inspiration from Italy to produce a regional visual identity that emphasized the appearance of cooling, solid masonry walls and the possibility of contact with the outdoors. By the time the Panama-Pacific Exposition of 1915 popularized the Spanish colonial revival, architects in California had already moved toward the eclectic synthesis of elements from these diverse sources generally referred to as the Mediterranean revival style, which characterized the architecture of the region through the 1920s.

Use of the Mediterranean revival vocabulary of forms and materials at Westwood Highlands reflects the fact that the style had become the contemporary vernacular. Although houses built in earlier subdivisions in the district west of Twin Peaks were designed in a number of styles, stucco and tile increasingly came to define the character of the "newer city." In addition to the claims of fashion and the desire to construct a regional identity, another reason for the adoption of this style was the attempt to minimize the appearance of wood in the aftermath of the 1906 earthquake and fire.[14] The materials used in Mediterranean revival designs were visually reassuring, despite their undergirding frame structures. Breaking with the appearance of local traditions of wood building, Mediterranean revival houses seemed safer as well as more up-to-date. Thus, eclectic as Mediterranean revival was, it was also synthetic, in the sense that it fused images of the past with those of contemporary living.

That each of these subdivisions can be characterized in their distinct ways as drawing from the stylistic reserves of the past is not surprising, for historicism has long been recognized as the hallmark of the period. By considering the specific applications analyzed here, however, it is possible to see that their use functioned in a number of different ways simultaneously. First, in each example the selection of house design was a response to associational motivations. Second, the design forms that were chosen admitted of a high degree of simplification and standardization that fit them to current construction practices, while at the same time enabling them to preserve their stylistic character. And third, these designs provided solutions to the compositional requirements of large-scale developments by achieving a balance between unity and variety, between multiplicity and the individual dwelling.

This suggests that while the selection of the particular style may have been flexible in the 1920s, whatever was chosen had to be capable of performing in diverse ways. The range of historicist styles certainly provided many options that would function adequately to meet these needs. It remains to consider, however, whether such contemporary adaptations of past forms may not have answered other needs as well.

ARCHITECTURAL STYLE

Stylistic Pluralism

Each of the subdivisions considered in this study, then, marshaled selected details, materials, shapes, or textures from past architectural styles to evoke a range of associations. The Ford Homes suggested the roots of the national past in the colonial experience in New England. The use of Mediterranean revival styles at Westwood Highlands fused allusions to colonial experiences in the West with a sense of place; by drawing on styles from related geographic and climatic sources, these designs suggested an organic as well as a historic rootedness. At Brightmoor, where a historicist style was not used, the particular tradition of the anticipated residents was adapted, if our analysis is justified, to provide a familiar image of home.

Whichever style or model the design of subdivision houses emulated, the stylistic precedent was treated very loosely, as Talbot Hamlin observed of colonial revival designs in the passage quoted earlier. That is to say, there was no attempt to recreate the past faithfully. In all cases, the contemporary character of the design was given visual, if muted expression through the simplicity or selectivity of forms, the free play of details or materials, or the appearance of standardized and machined elements. This interplay between associations to the past and acknowledgment of the present emerges as a recurring and distinguishing aspect of entrepreneurial vernacular design.

The capacity of an architectural style to evoke simply the idea of the past also seems to have been more significant than the particular connotations of any given visual vocabulary. Some contemporary writers stressed the romantic qualities of Spanish colonial revival, for example, while others celebrated the durability or the simplicity of New England colonial.[15] Some writers became identified with their promotion of individual styles: Rexford Newcomb, for one, was especially enthusiastic about Mediterranean styles.[16] There was some concern for geographical appropriateness, as in the censure expressed by the *House and Garden* writer in 1923 toward "building a Spanish Mission villa in a New England village";[17] this reflected the fact that the "wrong" styles were used, as we noted in the anomalous colonial revival house at 185 Westwood in San Francisco's Westwood Park.

What we do not encounter, however, is competition for stylistic supremacy. Rather, as Alan Gowans notes, it was a period of pluralism regarding stylistic selection, in which many styles coexisted.[18] The lack of emphasis on this subject in the reports from the President's Conference on Home Building and Home Ownership, including the report of the committee on house design, reflected the availability of a range of equally suitable styles.

To many in the field in the 1920s, this stylistic pluralism represented a major achievement of modern architecture. Designer William Delano expressed this when he wrote, "I wish people would accept the present method of construction for what it is, and be satisfied to call the result 'modern.' A modern style . . . takes sound traditions wherever they can be found and adapts them to present day conditions."[19] According to this position, because of the inherent flexibility and cost reductions of new building practices, modern architecture mined the riches of the past and effectively put them to the service of contemporary requirements. This was an evolutionary view that saw modern construction practices, including mechanization, standardization, and simplification, as enhancing the ability of architects to reinterpret the imagery of history to meet present needs. From this standpoint, new technologies produced time-and-cost-saving advantages that allowed resources to be applied to the preservation, continuation, and wider dissemination of the cultural tradition. Modern architecture, accordingly, "draws its inspiration liberally from the past and adds the ingenuity of modern craftsmanship and modern machinery, together with all that modern designing has learned from the Golden Past."[20]

Another view of modern architecture, one that Delano seems to be contesting with some exasperation, looked to the new methods of construction and their industrial associations for the creation of a new language of forms. Expressed increasingly in the architectural press from the middle of the 1920s, this position received strong support from those most aware of contemporary European developments.[21]

The subdivisions analyzed in this book all depended upon rationalized construction practices involving mechanized mass-production and standardization for their development. But while these methods are evident to a certain extent in the repetition of forms and in the relative simplicity and tendency toward clean lines found in each of these tracts, the design vocabulary does not emphasize the construction methods. The modern system of building that had evolved and that made the construction of these large-scale residential developments feasible is not represented in a new figural language.

The observations of two scholars of southern California architecture are applicable to this prevailing nationwide pattern when they note that "the ubiquitous mode of building, balloon-frame construction, produced few, if any, stylistic consequences on the surface. Inner architectural structure became a mere prop onto which builder or owner might project any surface."[22] Even as this structural system evolved, there were efforts to ensure that the appearance of a house would not express its construction technology. Indeed, as Peter Rowe has noted, "technical changes occurred in the construction of the single-family house in order for it to appear to stay the same. Technical advancements were made within the industry to maintain affordable prices and to meet rising consumer expectations with regard to performance; however, considerable care was taken to suppress and disguise these changes so that they would not intrude on matters of appearance."[23] Walter Lippmann put the matter pithily in 1923 when he wrote, in connection with the rustic Vermont setting for Calvin Coolidge's swearing-in ceremony as president, that Americans "praise the classic virtues, while continuing to enjoy all the modern conveniences."[24] Stylistic pluralism clearly abetted this program, providing an array of historical costumes for the same underlying structure. It remains to consider what encouraged this suppression of the present as represented by modern building practices in favor of stylistic pluralism's allusions to the past.

Gowans, who rejects a radical, utopian interpretation of European modernism, contrasts the attitudes of post–Victorian American builders with those of European modernists and claims that Americans inherently treated technology as "their servant, not their master."[25] But four other features of housing development in the United States account perhaps more fully and plausibly for the reliance on stylistic pluralism instead of the creation of a style that articulated modern building practices, at least in subdivisions of the sort we are concerned with here. These features can be summarized as: (1) the distancing of building-craftsmen and the architectural elite from a conceptual role in the design of housing; (2) the evolution of the open plan and of simplified design schemes that derived from the confluence of progressive aesthetic and social ideas: (3) the occurrence of dynamic social and technological changes within the household itself; and (4) the need to represent in visual and physical form the security of realtors' and home-owners' investments in subdivision developments. How did these contribute to the dominance of stylistic pluralism?

THE IMPACT OF CHANGES IN THE DIVISION OF LABOR

Examination of the histories of building-craftsmen, the architectural elite, and realtors in part I led to the conclusion that the first two of these groups were not centrally involved in subdivision house design. The new system of building that produced 1920s dwellings evolved over several decades and involved technological changes as well as changes in the structure of work that were sometimes bitterly contested. This occurred within a context of industrial development that affected the shaping of all material wealth. Building-craftsmen, who were traditionally in the best position to see the implications of processes of change in construction were, during this period, in the most conflictual relationship to these processes. Whereas in the past they had championed new technologies when these increased the efficiency and flexibility of their work, by the 1920s they were experiencing further routinization and specialization, a deskilling and displacement that diminished their ability to contribute to the overall design of structures.

At the same time, during most of this period members of the architectural elite were uninterested in the problems of small-house design and thus took no leadership role in its advancement. Individual architects involved in small-house design increasingly worked for developers, whose requirements defined the limits on their creativity. Additionally, architects could not be relied upon to support new technologies.[26] Without claiming that had things been different either builders or architects would have developed a new style of housing to articulate modern building practices, it is possible to note that the two groups who would have been capable of achieving this were not engaged in the conceptualization of subdivision house design in this period.

A corollary of this process of differentiating conceptual and technical tasks was the instrumentalization of construction. That is to say, just as building-workers were increasingly relegated to routine and specialized operations, so their activities were seen as having solely a technical or functional impact on housing, with no bearing on design issues. In short, the separation of the conceptual and physical aspects of building that has been observed—the division of mental and manual labor—diminished the role of building-craftsmen and the significance of their activities in shaping subdivision design.

THE IMPACT OF THE MINIMAL HOUSE

The second observation that sheds light on the prevalence of stylistic pluralism concerns the process and direction of change in house design during the decades flanking the turn of the century. By the 1920s, new housing typically included simplified and informal design elements, fewer specialized rooms, outdoor living areas, and an open plan. The end product of these and related changes was a house that was as schematic in its basic features as Perry's neighborhood unit plan was diagrammatic for community planning. Architectural historian Gwendolyn Wright refers to the result of this process as the minimal house.[27] She traces its formulation to the circle of architects, social reformers, journalists, and others interested in progressive social and aesthetic issues who were contesting Victorian patterns of domestic arrangements and design at the turn of the century. Concerned about health, family relationships, and the interconnections between the family and the larger society that could be established at the neighborhood level, this circle looked, in part, to design for solutions to social and political problems.

A recent design scholar has argued that the ideals of these progressive reformers found their expression in the aesthetic of the colonial revival, which was characterized by simplicity, efficiency, rationality, naturalness, and organic unity.[28] However, by the 1920s it would be truer to say that these qualities could be achieved using any of the aesthetic envelopes that were offered by the range of designs represented by stylistic pluralism. For example, a contemporary description of a design for a small, starkly unornamented "Italian villa" celebrates "the decorative quality which the house possesses [as] one of its finest features. Decoration has been obtained not by adding ornament, but through the happy arrangement of the parts, the use of color in the exterior, and the fine massing of walls and openings."[29] The simplification and standardization evident in both the Mediterranean and colonial revival styles at Westwood Highlands and the Ford subdivision ensured adaptability to several plans, all of which embraced the principles of the minimal house. The abstractness of the minimal house meant that it could serve as a model that the housing network could easily promote.

Indeed, by the 1920s, the rationalization that characterized the design of forms and spaces extended to a functionalist relationship between plan and elevation. As one contemporary popularizer of the colonial revival style explained to his readers, "any exterior, or elevation, is governed by its floor plan, and the most successful designs express on their exteriors the general arrangement of the interior."[30] This goal could be met using any of the pluralist styles; Strothoff's and Wood's modular systems exemplify the manipulation of such a relationship between elevational units and interior space. The simplified figural vocabularies that they employed were well suited to the evolution of spatial design, enabling the architects to embody the modernity of the house while simultaneously clothing it in reassuring references to the past.

THE IMPACT OF HOUSEHOLD CHANGES

Another feature of housing in the United States that contributed to the value of stylistic pluralism for subdivision design was the degree to which technological and social changes permeated life within the house. The impact of new technologies can be seen in the decline in real capital invested in the envelope of the house itself during the decades after 1890. Instead, equipment within the house assumed greater importance and accounted for a larger, though more dispersed, share of capital, as the efficient house absorbed new technologies such as plumbing and electricity.[31] This occurred for domestic electrification, for example, in the second decade of the century, once the distribution system for commercial and industrial electrical uses was in place; as the electrical base load peaked during the day, the fulfillment of residential nighttime demands for power became more attractive to utility companies.[32]

Such new technologies encouraged the evolution of the minimal house. Gas lighting, for example, had required separation of spaces to contain odors and reduce drafts. Electrification, in contrast, allowed for greater flexibility and openness of interiors. Thus, when model "homes electric" were constructed to sell this new technology's possibilities and products, beginning around 1908, they also sold "the idea of the modern house itself."[33]

By the 1920s, major corporations were introducing new products for individual home use and, with them, the dilemmas of consumer choice that have since become familiar. Appliances such as vacuum cleaners and washing machines that were first developed as large units, and used in collective or institutional settings, were redesigned for privatized, domestic use in the 1920s. Companies that are identified today with the manufacture of consumer durables (e.g., Bendix, Maytag) entered the consumer market in this period with resources gained from other endeavors (the cited examples produced airplane parts and farm machinery, respectively).[34]

The press of the period unequivocally promoted these new technologies. A newspaper article on the national spread of electricity by 1924, for example, was accompanied by four smaller pieces on the needs for various electrical appliances. One of them, typical of the others, proclaims that "the kitchen today is not properly equipped if it does not have an electric vacuum cleaner, dishwasher, clothes washer, irons [sic] and range. No woman can without these helps keep her youth and vitality and remain attractive."[35] Indeed, by 1926, of the 16 million homes wired for electricity, 37 percent contained a vacuum cleaner, 25 percent employed a clothes washer, and 80 percent used an electric iron.[36] As new commodities increasingly appeared in print advertisements and on store shelves, the household became one of the major sites for renegotiating definitions of what goods were necessities, as opposed to being luxury items.[37]

Technological change abetted social change. New technologies introduced within the home did not necessarily reduce labor but they did transform it. They altered the experiences of the household's inhabitants, especially women. A new image of the woman as caretaker replaced the cult of domesticity's emphasis on her responsibility for moral and educational development within the home; this highlighted her involvement in the hands-on, behind-the-scenes activities of running the household. Her relationship to the processes and objects of household management assumed greater importance.[38] Home economist Benjamin R. Andrews's 1929 observation that "the typical family lived in a world 'built for it by the woman who spends'" also represents an increasingly common view.[39] As the primary household consumer, she became the mediator between her family and the new commodity culture.

Furthermore, as the nineteenth-century, woman-centered ideology of domesticity merged with the male-defined ideology of the suburban ideal, by the 1920s a new family-centered image of suburban living was forged. This reshaped household and familial roles as well as the gender implications of architectural spaces.[40] Family relationships were also changing, as peer groups and other external agencies of socialization began to pull the generations further apart.[41] Fewer opportunities were available for extrafamilial, intergenerational socializing. New approaches to child development resulted in the creation of specialized products, spaces, and activities that separated children's experiences from those of adults. Public education took schooling out of the home, while literature aimed directly at children replaced traditional shared classics.[42] The home, in short, was a site of dynamic—and sometimes contradictory or conflictual—changes in identities, roles, and interpersonal relationships.

In contrast, the architectural styles of subdivisions carry associations of tradition, rootedness, and continuity. The image of home that is conveyed through stylistic pluralism is not one of transformation but one of familiarity, stability, and longevity. For stylistic pluralism, the goal was any image of home that would suggest continuity, a sense of the present as rooted in the past and extending into a knowable future. In short, stylistic pluralism offered reassurance about the meanings and function of home. It did not embrace modernity in the form of technological or social change, but masked these in the guises of tradition.

This was also the case in subdivisions in which houses were individually commissioned rather than built on speculation by the developer. The Van Sweringens's Shaker Heights outside Cleveland is an example of this type of development. Here, too, it was the common thread of association, whereby each of various styles suggested traditional homelike qualities, that unified these subdivisions. It is also worth noting that many of these same styles—colonial, Mediterranean, Tudor, and so on—were adapted to other building types, such as road architecture and small commercial structures. Not only was there no single style identified with the idea of home, but this idea was itself diffuse enough to migrate with diverse styles to imbue a range of building types, many of them new, with images of reassuring familiarity and rootedness.[43]

THE IMPACT OF SECURING INVESTMENT

The final aspect of housing in the 1920s that accounts for the presence of stylistic pluralism is one that grounds this image of continuity in requirements of the entrepreneurial vernacular. One of the early students of subdivision development observed in 1930 that "after a subdivision has been largely brought into actual use and its future seems assured," the values, or prices, of properties stabilize. "What has happened," he explained, "is that the expectations of an ever increasing number of people in regard to the future income possibilities of the community have coincided and have been brought to focus on this area."[44] Stability, in the final analysis, means fiscal reliability; the image of continuity implies the future return on one's investment.

Deed and zoning restrictions were among the instruments available to developers in the 1920s to control the financial future of subdivisions. But in addition to such legal mechanisms, not only complementing but embodying them, there was the built environment itself. To assure the perpetuation of these residential neighborhoods, and hence minimize investment risk, developers used architectural forms that reached back to the past to posit continuity. One contemporary designer concluded his description of plans for a small house with this object explicitly in view: "Due to its excellent plan, and the careful adaptation of colonial details, this is a house that will not go out of style. Its resale value is therefore stabilized, an important consideration."[45]

The use of traditional or historicist styles served as a visual buttress to the continuity of the subdivision as a whole. The actual modernity of each house, in its technologies, plan, and simplifications and standardizations of forms, reflected a necessary responsiveness to dynamic construction and household changes. But the reassuring aura of stability and longevity created by enveloping these changes in one of the designs offered by stylistic pluralism claimed that the future would be a familiar and predictable extension of the known past. These styles provided security that the home owner was joining what realtor J. C. Nichols described as an "immutably established residential district."[46]

The Charm of Continuity

Thus, stylistic pluralism negotiated a complex set of circumstances. On the one hand, by the 1920s a number of changes had occurred in house design that were absorbed into the pluralist vocabulary. This was the case with the rationalized open plan and simplification of forms that characterized the minimal house; the simplification and standardization that marked the design of pluralist styles complemented these trends. Combined with attention to the technological infrastructure of the house—its plumbing and electrical systems and the equipment and layout of bathrooms and kitchens—these features do reflect the modernity of contemporary design for which many architects and others argued. On the other hand, the rationalization of space and forms and the changing patterns of life in the home and of housework to which these and other new technologies contributed were articulated in a design language that emphasized continuity over transformation. Pluralist styles admitted of simplification and standardization, and yet they remained legible, familiar, and rooted in the past. Finally, this image of continuity was especially appropriate as a visual claim on the future; it functioned as a way of designing into the project its longevity and the stability of its property values.

The past, then, in the form of recognizable if reduced and diverse imagery, was a crucial aspect of residential developments. Gowans compares the pluralism of architectural styles in this period to the rotation of baseball teams going up to bat and to the liberal political process in which "one side may gain an ascendancy and make some laws to promote its interests for a few years, then the other takes over and promotes its interests for a while, but both have common goals in view."[47] And, indeed, as this suggests, the choice of which style to use was more or less arbitrary; stylistic pluralism reflects what Karal Ann Marling, in her discussion of the historical buildings that Henry Ford uprooted and situated within a new context at Greenfield Village, has referred to as "plasticity of character."[48] For stylistic pluralism, it is important that there be some traditional character to the visual forms, but there is no moral weight associated with the selection of one particular style. Furthermore, as standardization made inroads on design and construction, it could be seen as a virtue that such an eclectic range of stylistic possibilities were equally available. This is one of the points made in a guide to small-house design published in 1929:

> People have been building homes for no one knows how many tens of thousands of years. Architects have been doing it for several thousand. By this time, it seems, we ought to know just exactly what to do to get the best effect, the most accommodation at the least cost. But happily we do not know. There isn't any best. If we knew which one was the very best there probable would be so many houses built just alike that we would feel that the modern urge for standardization had gone too far. The best piece of architecture, like the best tune and the best piece of sculpture, is relative. All depends on the point of view.[49]

This is Babbitt's "corking standard": Every style is the best style from some point of view; all of them convey a sense of tradition and continuity, and all of them mask their underlying structural and technological uniformity. What distinguished them amounted to what was seen as their individual self-expression. In a description of "A Brick and Half Timber House," one of the more elaborately detailed examples from the same 1929 plan book, the writer states this explicitly in contemporary language: "There are certain delightful people in this world possessed of an indefinable quality that enables them to capture all hearts. Formerly we said of them that they had personality, or charm. Today we content ourselves by saying they have 'It'— and everyone knows what is meant. And so we say of this house that it has 'It.'"[50] This house is not described in terms of evocative associations that will guide or express the moral character of its owners; instead, it has an engaging personality. Emily Post, arbiter of manners and mores, emphasized this quality when she titled her 1930 book *The Personality of a House*.[51] The attribution to the range of pluralist styles of notions of "lively personal identity"[52] parallels the rise in the early decades of the twentieth century of what historian Warren Susman has called "the culture of personality."[53] By this he means the construction of a new sense of self that emphasized "both the unique qualities of an individual and the performing self that attracts others." A recent study of interior design has linked the evolution of decoration and spatial planning to this development of a new ideal of personal self-expression, illuminating an architectural site in which the culture of personality was shaped.[54] Stylistic pluralism contributed to this as well.

Applying the notion of personality to architectural design masked the rationalization and simplification of plan, construction, and forms that were found increasingly in this period. The anthropomorphic projection of personality onto the house itself served both as an emblem of the owner's individuality and as another reassuring sign of the existential reality of the house and of the appeal it would hold for future purchasers.

Thus, the very plasticity of stylistic pluralism reinforced the variety of roles it played in residential schemes of the 1920s. Historical allusions both maintained some sense of the past (one that could nevertheless project a reassuring vision of the future) and, in their simplified states, spoke the modern language of individual identity. In other words, stylistic pluralism conferred charm: it bestowed on each house its lively personal character and at the same time served as a talisman, protecting the future by identifying it with the past. Both of these features contributed to the logic of stylistic pluralism, a logic that is no less compelling because it is embedded within a dense web of evolutionary design developments and social change.

CONCLUSION

ARCHITECTURE AS SOCIAL PROCESS

Entering George Babbitt's world leads us far beyond Floral Heights and Zenith: Sinclair Lewis realized this, of course, when he chose this character as his protagonist. Babbitt's experiences as a realtor echo those of his colleagues across the nation who, in association with others involved in housing provision, shaped the residential landscape in the 1920s. This book examines the pattern of that suburban landscape, how it emerged, and how it became widespread.

The most significant features of the pattern of suburban subdivision development become evident when we consider three representative speculative subdivisions, the Ford Homes, Brightmoor, and Westwood Highlands. These features include the single-family house sited amid lawn and shrubbery; the use of landscape, street pattern, signage, and other elements to define the tract physically; the balance between unity generated by mass-production design and construction systems and the individuality of the single house; and the presence of local services or institutions that, along with planning and landscape forms, provide a sense of neighborhood. Since these features respond to the particular history and requirements of each subdivision, how did such commonalities emerge?

Pursuit of the answer to this question takes us into the wider orbit of realtor-developers, the bases for their professional project, and their interactions within the home-ownership network. Here we find both the array of conceptual tools and historical influences that guided the shaping of subdivision development and the structural and institutional frameworks for implementing these ideas. Garden-suburb planning traditions, the evolution of small-house design, urban reform experiences: these are some of the diverse strands from the tapestry of late-nineteenth and early-twentieth-century social and architectural history that were woven into the fabric of 1920s subdivisions. In the process of their adaptation for such projects, however, these strands became schematic and abstract, distilled into forms whose flexibility replaced whatever idealistic intentions their original inspirations may have possessed.

A shared interest in promoting home ownership forged the varied ranks of housing experts into a functional network that disseminated these conceptions. Realtors, architects, financiers, materials producers, engineers, planners, reformers, and others were linked through organizational interactions that ensured the transmission of ideas and standards from national leaders to grassroots practitioners. Through the exchange of information, definition and discussion of problems, and delineation of models, this network ratified and broadcast the pattern of subdivision development.

The juxtaposition of these two levels of investigation illuminates the processes used to propose and communicate this housing solution. Tracing broader, national historical and social trends provides a context for the focus on neighborhood in the subdivisions studied here and for the roles of the developers, building-craftsmen, and architects who were involved in their design. At the same time, studying the individual schemes indicates how the home-ownership network's proposals were carried out in practice as well as how they were modified by local needs and conditions. Exploration of other subdivisions would reveal additional individual variations, but examination of these three examples suggests that all would embody fundamental features of the nationally generated pattern located here. Working at these two levels of analysis involves maintaining the kind of dialogue between the local and particular and the historical and structural that created the housing solutions on which this book focuses.

Distilling a New Vernacular

Locating the figures who established this dialogue and the language they used exposes the underlying systematic approach to the fulfillment of housing needs that had evolved by the 1920s. Instead of emanating from a unified or centralized plan, the pattern for speculative suburban subdivision design was the product of an assemblage of guidelines for development that were promoted in a variety of ways by a diffuse network of housing professionals. Nevertheless, this network's organizational fluidity, its inclusive range of fields of expertise, and its reliance on models and standards rather than blueprints were deliberate consequences of the ideal of decentralized administration that grew out of the Progressive Era and that was identified with Herbert Hoover's theory of bureaucratic management. The appearance of looseness in organization or of lack of coordination in built form was not accidental but, indeed, cultivated. It stemmed from the same system of associational progressivism that animated Hoover's Commerce Department, which he had shaped to function "as an economic 'general staff,' business 'correspondence school,' and national coordinator, all rolled into one, yet [preserving] the essentials of American individualism by avoiding bureaucratic dictation and legal coercion, implementing its plans through nearly four hundred cooperating committees and scores of private associations, and relying upon appeals to science, community, and morality to bridge the gap between the public interest and private ones."[1] Within their sphere, realtors and the home-ownership network of which they were a part operated in just this way: voluntary interactions among experts at the national level led to the framing of standards; institutional structures were designed to educate and advise professionals at the local level; initiatives were justified by appealing "to science, community, and morality"; and individual developers interpreted the proposed standards and models to fit the needs of their own situations. The planlessness that appears to characterize the geography of suburban subdivision development was, in this sense, the plan.

The process that cultivated this planlessness was incremental and decentralized; initiatives such as the Better Homes campaign were seized upon whenever they arose. This process both stemmed from and encouraged the involvement of the home-ownership network, and what it achieved was the creation of a new vernacular. This was not a vernacular based on an evolution of localized housing solutions by indigenous owner-builders relying on craft traditions. Instead, this new vernacular emerged as a distillation of the array of social concerns and new practices in construction, design, and organization that were expressed and represented by the home-ownership network. Just as Lewis Mumford noted that Clarence Perry's neighborhood unit plan "crystallized many diffuse efforts"[2]—the community-center movement, the social theories of Charles Horton Cooley, garden-suburb design ideas, and the built forms of Forest Hills Gardens—so this book indicates that suburban subdivisions of the 1920s represented an equally complex and far-reaching synthesis. The home-ownership network, and the framework of associational progressivism within which it operated, provided the means by which national expertise from diverse fields was integrated with local production needs and abilities. Mediating national trends and local requirements and capacities, the home-ownership network promoted the translation of a broad range of ideas and experiences into new built forms. These encompassed Perry's neighborhood unit plan and the concerns about community and neighborhood design that it embodied, changes in building technology and in the roles of builders, architects, and realtors, conceptions of urban planning, and both formal and social transformations in the spaces of housing and their uses. The unified but flexible pattern of subdivision development that emerged from this synthesis seemed so successfully to resolve its complex origins that it appeared at once as ordinary and familiar, the expected and natural embodiment of the fulfillment of housing needs.

To refer to the outcome of this complicated and diffuse process as a new vernacular is to acknowledge that what this concept describes consists of more than stylistic elements, structural solutions, or the manipulation of particular materials. Rather, the value of the notion of the vernacular derives from its recognition of the connections between architectural forms and a broader web of social, historical, and cultural developments. Dell Upton has described vernacular buildings as the visual embodiment of a social process, in which available architectural ideas from many sources, local and international, traditional and novel, are shaped into buildings answering the special requirements of a social class, an economic group or a local or ethnic community.... It is this quality of complex response to indigenous demands, rather than to abstract intellectual or aesthetic concepts, that makes vernacular building ordinary building: It is architecture in the service of large groups of people.[3]

In the case of suburban subdivisions, it is not a single building but a pattern of residential development that emerged as a response to such broad processes. Individual tracts have their unique histories; indeed, the capacity to address local circumstances is an important feature of this housing solution. However, by stepping back to consider their shared histories and common design elements, the pattern of subdivision development that underlies each instance and ties it to broader social realities emerges.

Entrepreneurial Vernacular and the Landscape of Exchange

The social processes that this new, entrepreneurial vernacular embodied were not entirely retrospective. While suburban subdivisions of the 1920s synthesized developments in design and social theory, construction and real-estate practices, and organization that had evolved over several decades, and while they often alluded to the past visually, this is not the only tense in which they spoke. The visual language of past architectural styles addressed the future as well, since it provided assurance of stability and continuity; design elements employed allusions to the past in order to convey a sense both of historical rootedness and of persistence into the future. The notion of community with which developers operated was also a mechanism to control the future: the neighborhood, defined through landscaping, street patterns, and community amenities, embraced each dwelling and anchored its residential character. Realtor J. C. Nichols, to whom this study has often turned for his forthright and highly self-conscious statements on the mission of realtors as community builders, was referring to ensuring the future in this way when he wrote in 1929, "The goal of every subdivider and developer should be to sell not only land but to sell and deliver protection." To achieve this, he advocated "planning for permanence."[4]

That subdivision developments used the past and a sense of neighborhood to speak to the future suggests how entrepreneurial vernacular embodied another social process that it also helped to shape. For the developers whom we have met in the course of this book, the future is understood in terms of the safety of one's investment, the ability to sell a house for what had been paid for it, if not for more. Frederick Lewis Allen made this observation in 1925 when he recounted his conclusions about a drive through new suburbs with a realtor. He wrote, "A home, to me, is a place where you intend to stay. . . . To my real estate friend, a home was an investment (with incidental shelter value) to be turned over [by its owner], when the market permitted."[5] This draws our attention to the dual nature of housing within a market context, serving both as a fulfillment of needs (represented by its "shelter value" or use value) and as an object that is bought and sold (represented by its exchange value). To the extent that developers' residential subdivisions of the 1920s were designed to ensure the dwelling's exchange value, they intensified the process by which, in the United States, housing was treated as a privatized commodity, rather than as a social good.[6]

The attempt to gain physical control over the future by means of built form and neighborhood planning, as well as other devices, is an attempt to control the market value of a property investment. This is experienced by the individual, for "homeowners residing in a place are also preparing to leave it," as one scholar has succinctly observed.[7] Future market expectations for a house guide its use and maintenance. Indeed, in the course of the later 1920s, realtors and bankers developed new financing strategies that depended upon the individual home owner mortgaging his or her own future.[8] Their willingness to accept a home buyer's earnings potential as security for a loan meant that mortgages became accessible to greater numbers of people, but it also implicated wider areas of the individual's life in the future marketability of the house. The home owner's employment, decisions about the appearance, functions, and running order of the house—in all of these ways the individual became subject to the discipline of the commodity form of the dwelling, or its exchange value. The need to preserve and maximize its exchange value would shape the owner's decisions and actions.

The deepening trend toward treating houses as commodities in the 1920s took place amid the mushrooming creation of new commodities of all kinds. The outpouring of new products, such as electric household equipment, inaugurated the media-driven consumer culture that grew in intensity in later decades. At its inception, however, it provoked confusion and much discussion and forced reconsideration of individuals' understandings of which goods to consider necessities and which to see as luxuries. Thrift became questionable; that was one peculiar lesson taken from the appearance of malnutrition among World War I military recruits: savings must not be allowed to subvert the standard of living. In the face of warnings against "sordid economizing,"[9] the purchase of a house increasingly fell into the category of a necessity.

Another aspect of the process of transforming houses into commodities that subdivision development embodies is suggested by some of Constance Perin's insights in her anthropological study of the symbolic meaning of home ownership. She concludes that the status our culture grants to this form of housing tenure derives from "the achievement of a social relationship with the banker."[10] The social recognition that qualifying for a mortgage confers, and the network of sanctions that entering into this relationship can bring to bear on the home buyer—"foreclosure, the loss of property, lifesavings, and social worth"—are, she argues, badges of citizenship, criteria for "social personhood."[11] On the basis of this book's analysis of developers' subdivisions it is possible to add that it is first the developer and then the banker who embody the community of which the home buyer becomes a member. For as we have seen, the notion of building a community played a large role in the pattern of subdivision development, but one that was schematic and capable of realization in diverse forms. It functioned as a strategy to help perpetuate market values; in this regard, the future unknown buyer appears as just as important a figure to the home owner as the neighbors who presently live next door. Phantom home owners of the future compose the community that the purchaser joins when he establishes his relationship with the developer. What contributes to the abstractness of the notion of community, then, is its spectral character; the subdivision community is based on exchange relationships that it will secure only in the future. Each home owner is oriented toward the hoped-for marketability of the house; it is only the developer, and after him the banker, who encompasses and represents the collectivity.

To characterize this vernacular housing form as entrepreneurial signals the central role that realtor-developers played in its realization. As subdivision developers, realtors assumed organizational control of construction processes, managed the activities of building-craftsmen and architects, and risked their financial investments until properties sold. But the desire to attenuate risk shaped subdivision planning and design and guided the form given to neighborhood development. The flexible vocabularies of stylistic pluralism and the use of landscaping, signage, local services, and other devices to create at least a minimal form of neighborhood identity were strategies to "protect," as Nichols noted, the home buyer and his investment. Thus, the term *entrepreneurial* describes fundamental qualities of built form as well as the role of those who managed its creation.

The concept of entrepreneurial vernacular offers a prism, then, that refracts the familiar speculative suburban subdivision into its complex and diffuse constituents. It enables us to reconstruct the process through which this housing solution was forged and to describe the distinguishing features of this housing pattern. The seeming planlessness of the process was the deliberate reflection of Progressivism's ideal of decentralized administration, an ideal embodied in the operations of the housing network. A web of relationships, rather than a single person or institution, yielded the framework that guided subdivision development. The pattern of built form itself was just as abstract as this process. The schematic model of community and its shaping through architectural and planning devices parlayed references to an idealized past into claims on the future. By emphasizing the continuity and stability of the development in order to mitigate investment risk, future exchange relationships became at least as important as present interactions.

The idea of entrepreneurial vernacular also focuses the barbs of critics such as Henry Wright, whose observation that, for developers, housing was merely "a side-line to land merchandising and the mortgage business" we encountered at the outset of this study. The concept of entrepreneurial vernacular unmasks the deceptively accidental character of subdivision development and indicates how market relationships provided the armature on which such housing schemes were built.

Were there alternative models of housing provision that the promotion of entrepreneurial vernacular implicitly rejected? Albert Wood, the architect for the Ford Homes, proposed that prospective home owners establish stock companies that would allow them to develop affordable housing by pooling their financial resources. The configuration of houses that he sketched in his booklet also offered a different conception of community development. By grouping houses and providing shared service areas, his scheme introduced opportunities for neighborhood interaction and mutual support that, he hoped, would foster broader civic activism.

Few were privy to Wood's neglected proposals, but the ideas of Henry Wright, Lewis Mumford, Catherine Bauer, and other housing activists reached a national audience. They argued for a wider spectrum of options and were inspired by European models of development, many of which assumed housing provision to be a social responsibility. Few accepted their ideas; this book tells the story of how the consensus that emerged in the United States reflected a different attitude. By indicating the network of experts and ideas that forged entrepreneurial vernacular into the dominant housing pattern, this study locates the seemingly shapeless array of actors and institutions that effectively marginalized these critics' perspectives.

The basis for suburban subdivision design lies in eighteenth- and nineteenth-century patterns of organizing land-use for consumption, for the appropriation of space, time, and nature by the privileged.[12] In the twentieth century, entrepreneurial vernacular subdivisions such as the Ford Homes, Brightmoor, and Westwood Highlands made forms of this landscape of consumption accessible to wider groups of inhabitants by cultivating a landscape of exchange.

NOTES

Introduction

1. For further discussion of similar methodologies, see Deryck W. Holdsworth, "Landscape and Archives as Texts," and Dolores Hayden, "Urban Landscape History: The Sense of Place and the Politics of Space," in Paul Groth and Todd W. Bressi, eds., *Understanding Ordinary Landscapes* (New Haven: Yale University Press, 1997), pp. 44–55 and 111–33, respectively.

2. The major works on suburban housing are David P. Handlin, *The American Home: Architecture and Society, 1815–1915* (Boston: Little, Brown, 1979); Gwendolyn Wright, *Moralism and the Model Home: Domestic Architecture and Cultural Conflict in Chicago, 1873–1913* (Chicago: University of Chicago Press, 1980) and *Building the Dream: A Social History of Housing in America* (New York: Pantheon, 1981); Kenneth T. Jackson, *Crabgrass Frontier: The Suburbanization of the United States* (New York: Oxford University Press, 1985); Clifford Edward Clark Jr., *The American Family Home* (Chapel Hill: University of North Carolina Press, 1986); Alan Gowans, *The Comfortable House: North American Suburban Architecture, 1890–1930* (Cambridge: MIT Press, 1986); Robert Fishman, *Bourgeois Utopias: The Rise and Fall of Suburbia* (New York: Basic Books, 1987); John R. Stilgoe, *Borderland: Origins of the American Suburb, 1820–1939* (New Haven: Yale University Press, 1988); Margaret Marsh, *Suburban Lives* (New Brunswick, N.J.: Rutgers University Press, 1988); and Mary Corbin Sies, "'God's Very Kingdom on the Earth': The Design Program for the American Suburban Home, 1877–1917," in Richard Guy Wilson and Sidney K. Robinson, eds., *Modern Architecture in America: Visions and Revisions* (Ames: Iowa State University Press, 1991).

3. Marc A. Weiss, *The Rise of the Community Builders: The American Real Estate Industry and Urban Land Planning* (New York: Columbia

University Press, 1987) also focuses on realtors, especially in their role as planners.

4. Ibid.; Patricia Burgess, *Planning for the Private Interest: Land Use Controls and Residential Patterns in Columbus, Ohio, 1900–1970* (Columbus: Ohio State University Press, 1994).

5. On the relative mix of these housing forms, see Robert G. Barrows, "Beyond the Tenement: Patterns of American Urban Housing, 1870–1930," *Journal of Urban History* 9 (August 1983): 395–420.

6. Edith Elmer Wood, *The Housing of the Unskilled Wage Earner* (New York: Macmillan, 1919); *Housing Progress in Western Europe* (New York: Dutton, 1923); *Recent Trends in American Housing* (New York: Macmillan, 1931). See also John J. Murphy, Edith Elmer Wood, and Frederick L. Ackerman, *The Housing Famine: How to End It* (New York: Dutton, 1920); Catherine Bauer, *Modern Housing* (Boston: Houghton Mifflin, 1934); Lewis Mumford, *Sticks and Stones: Architecture and Civilization* (New York: Boni & Liveright, 1924; reprint, New York: Dover, 1955). For examples of model developments, see Henry Wright, *Rehousing Urban America* (New York: Columbia University Press, 1935), and Clarence Stein, *Toward New Towns for America* (New York: Town Planning Review, 1957), which includes an introduction by Mumford.

7. Henry Wright, "The Sad Story of American Housing," *Architecture* 67 (March 1933), reprinted in Lewis Mumford, ed., *Roots of Contemporary American Architecture* (New York: Dover, 1972), 330; this collection was originally published in 1952.

8. The concept that is most useful here is Gramsci's idea of hegemony; see Antonio Gramsci, *Selections from the Prison Notebooks* (London: Lawrence & Wishart, 1971). For a brief and very lucid discussion of the term *hegemony*, see Raymond Williams, *Keywords: A Vocabulary of Culture and Society* (New York: Oxford University Press, 1976), 117–18.

9. Ellis Hawley develops the concept of associational progressivism in his studies of Herbert Hoover's administrations. See citations in chap. 4, notes 120 and 121.

Chapter 1. The Ford Homes

1. Olivier Zunz, *The Changing Face of Inequality: Urbanization, Industrial Development, and Immigrants in Detroit, 1880–1920* (Chicago: University of Chicago Press, 1982), 16.

2. David Allan Levine vividly sketches the physical transformation of Detroit in the opening pages of *Internal Combustion: The Races in Detroit 1915–1926* (Westport, Conn.: Greenwood Press, 1976). The phrase *walking city* derives from Sam Bass Warner, *Streetcar Suburbs: The Process of Growth in Boston, 1870–1900,* 2nd ed. (Cambridge: Harvard University Press, 1978).

3. Zunz, *The Changing Face of Inequality.* 287.

4. The five-dollar wage was conditional on workers' adoption of middle-class values, which was determined by the investigators of the Ford Sociological Department, who visited every eligible worker's home to interview relatives and neighbors. Stable family life, home ownership, and a savings account were the key criteria. Allan Nevins, *Ford: The Times, the Man, the Company* (New York: Scribner's, 1954), chaps. 20 and 21; Stephen Meyer III, *The Five-Dollar Day: Labor, Management, and Social Control in the Ford Motor Company, 1908–1921* (Albany: State University of New York Press, 1981), chap. 6.

5. David L. Good, "The Ford Homes," 1975, typescript in the library of the Dearborn Historical Society.

6. Ibid.

7. Marge Colborn, "At Home with History," *Detroit News*, 28 July 1990: 2D. My thanks to Nedra Frodge for this reference.

8. Allan Nevins and Frank Ernest Hill, *Ford: Expansion and Challenge, 1915–1933* (New York: Scribner's, 1957), 254–55, 348.

9. Thomas W. Brunk, *Leonard B. Willeke, Excellence in Architecture and Design* (Detroit: University of Detroit Press, 1986), 137–47.

10. H. Ward Jandl, *Yesterday's Houses of Tomorrow: Innovative American Homes, 1850–1950* (Washington, D.C.: Preservation Press, 1991), 70.

11. Ibid., 78.

12. Ibid., 81; Ford R. Bryan, "Concrete Homes for Dearborn," *Dearborn Historian* 24 (summer 1984): 87–89; Peter Collins, *Concrete: The Vision of a New Architecture* (New York: Horizon Press, 1959), 90; David Handlin, *The American Home: Architecture and Society, 1815–1915* (Boston: Little, Brown, 1979), 293–94.

13. Nevins and Hill, *Ford*, 200.

14. E. G. Liebold, *Reminiscences*, 3:239, in the oral history section of the Ford Archives.

15. Albert G. Wood Jr., "Community Homes," 1918, in the possession of his family.

16. Ibid., 9.

17. Ibid., 21.

18. Ibid., 16. Wood refers to the success of such ventures in England, but does not provide specific examples. Letchworth Garden City was funded through a joint stock company, but this form of financing in fact limited the ability of its developers to construct houses and other facilities. See Walter L. Creese, *The Search for Environment: The Garden City, Before and After* (New Haven: Yale University Press, 1966), 215–16; Stanley Buder, *Visionaries and Planners: The Garden City Movement and the Modern Community* (New York: Oxford University Press, 1990). Contemporary accounts of cooperative development companies can be found, for example, in Arthur Coleman Comey, "Copartnership for Housing in America," *Annals of the American Academy of Political and Social Science* 51 (January 1914): 140–47; John T. Kleber, "The Garden City of Hellerav [*sic*]: A German Housing Development," *Architectural Record* 35 (February 1914): 151–61. For discussions of group ownership that arose in the wake of World War I and the end of federal housing projects, see Roy Lubove, "Homes and 'A Few Well Placed Fruit Trees': An Object Lesson in Federal Housing," *Social Research* 27 (winter 1960): 483. For an example of 1920s joint stock development, see the discussion of Garden Homes, Milwaukee, in David Barry Cady, "The Influence of the Garden City Ideal on American Housing and Planning Reform, 1900–1940," Ph.D. diss., University of Wisconsin, 1970, chap. 4.

19. Ibid., 18.

20. Ibid., 23.

21. Letter from Wood to Ajax Rubber Co., 11 December 1919, in the Ford Archives, accession 47, box 2. Although company towns continued to be built, many employers rejected the idea as authoritarian or at least potentially troublesome in the wake of the experience at Pullman, Illinois. See Stanley Buder, *Pullman: An Experiment in Industrial Order and Community Planning, 1880–1930* (New York: Oxford University Press, 1967); Carl Smith, *Urban Disorder and the Shape of Belief: The Great Chicago Fire, the Haymarket Bomb, and the Model Town of Pullman* (Chicago: University of Chicago Press, 1994).

22. Personal communication from the family of Albert Wood, June 1987; *Reminiscences of Harry C. Vicary*, and Gary Dymski, "Ford Homes," both typescripts in the library of the Dearborn Historical Society.

23. Colborn, "At Home with History," 2D.

24. Dearborn Realty & Construction Company files, Ford Archives; Joseph Oldenburg, "Ford Homes Historic District," *Dearborn Historian* 20 (spring 1980): 41.

25. International Labour Office (ILO), *The Housing Situation in the United States* (Geneva: ILO, 1925), 18; Blanche Halbert, ed., *The Better Homes Manual* (Chicago: University of Chicago Press, 1931), 53, citing the April 1931 *Monthly Labor Review* analysis of building permits in 257 cities.

26. Jay Hicks, "Houses by General Motors: The Flint Housing Crisis and GMC," *Michigan History* 71 (March/April 1987): 38.

27. See Liebold, *Reminiscences*. Nevins and Hill suggest that no more than 2 percent profit was made by the company over twenty years, 349.

28. E. G. Liebold, "Ford Tractor Company to Build Homes at Cost," *Detroit Journal*, 11 April 1919, 1, 29.

29. Liebold, in his *Reminiscences*, recalled only one case in which this clause had been used, provoked by complaints about one resident's home wine-making activities. Although the term *undesirable* was vague, it undoubtedly was intended to cover those buyers whose activities were regarded as socially and morally suspect. Such surveillance echoes that of the Ford Sociological Department—see note 4.

30. Tara B. Gnau, "School Sketches," part 3: "DuVall School," *Dearborn Historian* 17 (August 1977): 126; Oldenburg, "Ford Homes Historic District," 43.

31. Unless otherwise noted, the facts of this account were conveyed by personal communication from the family of Albert Wood, June 1987.

32. Dennis A. Andersen, "Augustus Warren Gould," in Jeffrey Karl Ochsner, ed., *Shaping Seattle Architecture: A Historical Guide to the Architects* (Seattle: University of Washington Press, 1994), 108–13.

33. See, for example, *Western Architect* 34 (April 1925): plates 10–13, for photographs.

34. George S. Koyl, *American Architects Directory*, 2nd ed. (New York: Bowker, 1962).

35. Liebold, *Reminiscences*, 239.

36. Liebold, "Ford Tractor Company."

37. For the fullest discussion of this evolution, see Gwendolyn Wright, *Moralism and the Model Home: Domestic Architecture and Cultural Conflict in Chicago, 1873–1913* (Chicago: University of Chicago Press, 1980). A convenient source for examples of contemporary houses with similar plans

and dimensions is Robert T. Jones, ed., *Authentic Small Houses of the Twenties: Illustrations and Floor Plans of 254 Characteristic Homes* (New York: Dover, 1987; reprint of *Small Homes of Architectural Distinction: A Book of Suggested Plans Designed by the Architects' Small House Service Bureau, Inc.* New York: Harper & Bros., 1929).

38. Bekka Lindstrom, "Post–Victorian Interiors: Bathrooms," *Old-House Journal* 15 (November/December 1987): 56–61; Stephen Del Sordo, "Bathtubs: An Architectural History," *Old-House Journal* 18 (September/October 1990): 38–42.

39. Benjamin R. Andrews, *Economics of the Household: Its Administration and Finance* (New York: Macmillan, 1923), 183. The author was an associate professor of household economics at Teachers College, Columbia University.

40. Liebold, *Reminiscences,* 240. Other discussions of plans appear in Liebold, "Ford Tractor Company;" "Builders with Brains Plus Courage Create an Ideal Colony for Workers," *Dearborn Independent,* 6 December 1919, 8–9.

41. Oldenburg, "Ford Homes Historic District," 31.

42. Ibid., 36.

43. "Fords Build Model Homes to House Workers in Dearborn," *Detroit Journal,* 21 July 1919, 2; "Builders with Brains."

44. Liebold, "Ford Tractor Company;" Henry Ford, *Ford Ideals: Being a Selection from "Mr. Ford's Page" in the Dearborn Independent* (Dearborn, Mich.: Dearborn Publishing, 1926), 159.

45. Descriptions of the construction process can be found in Liebold, *Reminiscences* and "Ford Tractor Company," and in *Reminiscences of Harry C. Vicary.*

46. Liebold, "Ford Tractor Company."

47. Ibid.

48. Liebold, *Reminiscences,* 241.

49. "Local Materials and Local Labor," *House and Garden* 43 (April 1923): 90.

50. Accounts of the invention and elaboration of balloon framing can be found in Paul Sprague, "Chicago Balloon Frame," in H. Ward Jandl, ed., *The Technology of Historic American Buildings* (Washington, D. C.: Foundation for Preservation Technology, 1983), 35–61, and in idem, "The Origin of Balloon Framing," *Journal of the Society of Architectural*

Historians 40 (December 1981): 311–19; Bob Reckman, "Carpentry: The Craft and Trade," in Andrew Zimbalist, ed., *Case Studies on the Labor Process* (New York: Monthly Review Press, 1979), 73–102; Amos J. Loveday Jr., *The Rise and Decline of the American Cut Nail Industry: A Study of the Interrelationship of Technology, Business Organization, and Management Techniques* (Westport, Conn.: Greenwood Press, 1983), 8–20; James E. Ambrose, *Construction Revisited: An Illustrated Guide to Construction Details of the Early Twentieth Century* (New York: Wiley, 1993); Robert Schweitzer and Michael W. R. Davis, *America's Favorite Homes: Mail-Order Catalogues as a Guide to Popular Early Twentieth-Century Houses* (Detroit: Wayne State University Press, 1990), 47–56.

51. Sprague, "Chicago Balloon Frame," 45.

52. Dell Upton, "Traditional Timber Framing," in Brooke Hindle, ed., *The Material Culture of the Wooden Age* (Tarrytown, N.Y.: Sleepy Hollow Press, 1981), 88.

53. Ibid., 92.

54. Catherine W. Bishir, "A Spirit of Improvement: Changes in Building Practice, 1830–1860," in Bishir et al., *Architects and Builders in North Carolina: A History of the Practice of Building* (Chapel Hill: University of North Carolina Press, 1990), 155.

55. See Carl R. Lounsbury, "The Wild Melody of Steam: The Mechanization of the Manufacture of Building Materials, 1850–1890," 193–239, in Bishir et al., *Architects and Builders in North Carolina*; Stephen C. Gordon, "House Building by Machinery: The Cincinnati Experience, 1850–1870," and Greg Koos, "Lumber and Mill Work: Builders Supplies in Pre-1880 Bloomington, Illinois," both in *Pioneer America Society Transactions* 11 (1988): 33–43 and 44–53, respectively; J. Ritchie Garrison, "Carpentry in Northfield, Massachusetts: The Domestic Architecture of Calvin Stearns and Sons, 1799–1856," in Thomas Carter and Bernard L. Herman, eds., *Perspectives in Vernacular Architecture*, vol. 4 (Columbia: University of Missouri Press, 1991), 9–22.

56. Reckman, "Carpentry," 86–87.

57. Robert F. Fries, *Empire in Pine: The Story of Lumbering in Wisconsin, 1830–1900* (Madison: State Historical Society of Wisconsin, 1951), 65; William Cronon, *Nature's Metropolis: Chicago and the Great West* (New York: Norton, 1991), 198; see esp. chap. 4, "The Wealth of Nature: Lumber."

58. Bernhard E. Fernow, "American Lumber," in Chauncey M. Depew, ed., *One Hundred Years of American Commerce*, 2 vols. (New York: Haynes, 1895), 1:196–203; Lounsbury, "Wild Melody," 212–26.

59. Thomas R. Cox, *Mills and Markets: A History of the Pacific Coast Lumber Industry to 1900* (Seattle: University of Washington Press, 1974).

60. Ibid., 238.

61. William Sellers, "Machinery Manufacturing Interests," in Depew, *One Hundred Years of American Commerce*, 2:350.

62. Jules Tygiel, "Workingmen in San Francisco, 1880–1901," Ph.D. diss., University of California, Los Angeles, 1977, 105; Thomas J. Suhrbur, "The Economic Transformation of Carpentry in Late-Nineteenth-Century Chicago," *Illinois Historical Journal* 81 (summer 1981): 109–24.

63. Thomas R. Brooks, *The Road to Dignity: A Century of Conflict, A History of the United Brotherhood of Carpenters and Joiners of American, AFL-CIO, 1881–1981* (New York: Atheneum, 1981), 17.

64. Walter Galenson, *The United Brotherhood of Carpenters: The First Hundred Years* (Cambridge: Harvard University Press, 1983), 229. Ironically, in the 1920s concern about high construction costs led to an investigation of seasonal unemployment. The fact that builders' off-season work had been replaced by mechanized production, controlled by a few large lumber companies, was forgotten by that time. Proposals for addressing the problem consisted of facilitating year-round construction by developing materials and techniques that would be impervious to weather conditions. See *Seasonal Operation in the Construction Industries: The Facts and Remedies* (New York: McGraw-Hill, 1924), sponsored by Secretary of Commerce Herbert Hoover.

65. Richard Rutledge Myers, "The Building Workers: A Study of an Industrial Sub-Culture," Ph.D. diss., University of Michigan, 1945, 167; Upton, "Pattern Books and Professionalism," 109–11.

66. Catherine Bishir, "Jacob W. Holt: An American Builder," in Dell Upton and John Michael Vlach, eds., *Common Places: Readings in American Vernacular Architecture* (Athens: University of Georgia Press, 1986), 447–81, originally published in *Winterthur Portfolio* (spring 1981). Preindustrial relations of production, as well as preindustrial practices, persisted in more isolated areas and in small-scale building enterprises.

67. This account is based on Robert A. Christie, *Empire in Wood: A History of the Carpenters' Union*, Cornell Studies in Industrial and Labor Relations, vol. 7 (Ithaca, N.Y.: Cornell University Press, 1956), 21–22.

68. Ibid. Also see Catherine W. Bishir, "A Proper Good Nice and Workmanlike Manner: A Century of Traditional Building Practice, 1730–1830," in Bishir et al., *Architects and Builders in North Carolina*, 110; Bishir, "Spirit of Improvement," 145–61; Gabrielle Lanier, "Samuel Wilson's Working World: Builders and Building in Chester County, Pennsylvania, 1780–1827," in Carter and Herman, 23–30; Allison Carll White, "Monuments to Their Skill: Urbana-Champaign Carpenters, Contractors, and Builders, 1850–1900," *Illinois Historical Journal* 85 (spring 1992): 37–45.

69. Christie, *Empire in Wood*, 39. The centennial of the founding of the union was the occasion for a number of histories, including Brooks, *Road to Dignity*, and Galenson, *United Brotherhood of Carpenters*. Local histories include Mark Ehrlich, *With Our Hands: The Story of Carpenters in Massachusetts* (Philadelphia: Temple University Press, 1986), and Paul Bullock et al., *Building California: The Story of the Carpenters' Union* (Los Angeles: University of California, Center for Labor Research and Education, Institute of Industrial Relations, 1982).

70. Christie, *Empire in Wood*, 39.

71. Galenson, *United Brotherhood of Carpenters*, 41; the quotation is from the general executive board's minutes, March 1885.

72. Brooks, *Road to Dignity*, 66.

73. Galenson, *United Brotherhood of Carpenters*, 77.

74. Brooks, *Road to Dignity*, 92, quoting President Hutcheson.

75. Galenson, *United Brotherhood of Carpenters*, 113, citing the general executive board's minutes, 24 February 1915.

76. Reckman, "Carpentry," 97.

77. Christie, *Empire in Wood*, 60. For an example of opposition between contractors and building workers in Chicago in 1899 and 1900, see Wright, *Moralism and the Model Home*, 181–82.

78. Myers, "Building Workers," 79–80, 150 ff.

79. As Wright notes, the general contractor emerged as an organizer of complex building processes in the 1880s in response to the demands of skyscraper construction. His logistical expertise was subsequently applied to large-scale residential projects. See Wright, *Moralism in the Model Home*, 307 n. 21. On residential contractors, see Michael J. Doucet and John C. Weaver, "Material Culture and the North American House: The Era of the Common Man, 1870–1920," *Journal of American History* 72 (December 1985): 565–67, subsequently published in idem, *Housing the*

North American City (Montreal: McGill-Queen's University Press, 1991), chap. 5.

80. Christie, *Empire in Wood*, 71; Wright, *Moralism and the Model Home*, 94.

81. Zunz, *The Changing Face of Inequality*.

82. Robert Lacey, *Ford: The Men and the Machine* (New York: Ballantine, 1986).

83. Hicks, "Houses by General Motors," 32–39; Joan M. Meister, "Civic Park: General Motors' Solution for the Housing Shortage," in *A Wind Gone Down: Smoke into Steel* (Lansing: Michigan History Division, Michigan Department of State, 1978), 5–14. My thanks to Gail Radford for the Meister reference.

84. "General Motors Will Build 1000 Houses Here At Once," *Flint Daily Journal*, 24 March 1919, 1, cited in Meister, "Civic Park," 6.

85. Examples of housing produced by the United States Shipping Board and by the Department of Labor can be found in *Homes for Workmen* (New Orleans: Southern Pine Association, 1919). For federal war-housing projects, see also Edith Elmer Wood, *Recent Trends in American Housing* (New York: Macmillan, 1931); Miles L. Colean, *Housing for Defense* (New York: Twentieth Century Fund, 1940); the bibliography in Giorgio Ciucci et al., *The American City: From the Civil War to the New Deal* (Cambridge: MIT Press, 1979), 282–84; Christian Topalov, "Scientific Urban Planning and the Ordering of Daily Life: The First 'War Housing' Experiment in the United States, 1917–1919," *Journal of Urban History* 17 (November 1990): 14–45.

86. Milton Dana Morrill, "Standardized Small Houses," *Building Age* (June 1920): 19.

Chapter 2. Brightmoor

1. David A. Levine, *Internal Combustion: The Races in Detroit 1915–1926* (Westport, Conn.: Greenwood Press, 1976), 39.

2. Robert G. Barrows, "Beyond the Tenement: Patterns of American Urban Housing, 1970–1930," *Journal of Urban History* 9 (August 1983): 410, table 5, "Excess of Families over Dwellings as a Percentage of Total Families." For discussion of the housing shortage nationwide beginning with World War I, see Edith Elmer Wood, *Recent Trends in American Housing* (New York: Macmillan, 1931), 84–85. For photographic docu-

mentation of workers' housing in Detroit, see Kevin Boyle and Victoria Getis, *Muddy Boots and Ragged Aprons: Images of Working-Class Detroit, 1900–1930* (Detroit: Wayne State University Press, 1997).

3. Sidney Glazer, *Detroit: A Study in Urban Development* (New York: Bookman, 1965), 95.

4. Michigan Planning Commission (MPC), *A Study of Suburban Development in the Detroit Metropolitan Area* (Lansing: MPC, 1939), 1.

5. Ibid., 13.

6. "Survey of 15 Years Reveals Jump in Land Subdividing," *Northwestern Business Booster* 1 (October 1925): 24.

7. MPC, *Suburban Development*, 10.

8. Exceptions are the contributions of Levine, *Internal Combustion*, and Olivier Zunz, *The Changing Face of Inequality: Urbanization, Industrial Development and Immigrants in Detroit, 1880–1920* (Chicago: University of Chicago Press, 1982). Their works help to provide a broader historical context within which to situate specific housing initiatives.

9. E. M. Heermans, "$55,000,000 Expended for 11,000 Suburban Homes Here in 1923," *Detroit Free Press*, 6 January 1924, real estate sec., 1.

10. Clarence M. Burton, *The City of Detroit, Michigan, 1701–1922* (Detroit: Clarke Publishing, 1922), 3:206.

11. Brightmoor Community Center, Inc., *Brightmoor, A Community in Action* (Detroit: Brightmoor Community Center, 1940), in the Burton Historical Collection of the Detroit Public Library.

12. B. E. Taylor, "Building a New Town," *Proceedings of the First Annual Convention Conferences of the Homebuilders' and Subdividers' Division of the National Association of Real Estate Boards* (Omaha, Neb.: NAREB, 1923), 107–10.

13. Brightmoor Community Center, quoting "B. E. Taylor's Official Brightmoor Census," April 1925.

14. Ibid.

15. MPC, *Suburban Development*, 25. Nor is this unique to working-class housing in Michigan; see Margaret M. Mulrooney, "A Legacy of Coal: The Coal Company Towns of Southwestern Pennsylvania," in Thomas Carter and Bernard L. Herman, eds., *Perspectives in Vernacular Architecture*, vol. 4 (Columbia: University of Missouri Press, 1991), 130–37. For the larger economic context, indicating that possibly 40 percent of the population lived in poverty, see Frank Stricker, "Affluence for Whom?

Another Look at Prosperity and the Working Class in the 1920s," in Daniel J. Leab, ed., *The Labor History Reader* (Urbana: University of Illinois Press, 1985), 288–316.

16. Ronald Edsforth, *Class Conflict and Cultural Consensus: The Making of a Mass Consumer Society in Flint, Michigan* (New Brunswick, N.J.: Rutgers University Press, 1987), 260 n. 50.

17. William S. Worley, *J. C. Nichols and the Shaping of Kansas City: Innovation in Planned Residential Communities* (Columbia: University of Missouri Press, 1990), 180.

18. Walter H. Kilham, "The Planning of the Low-Cost House," in National Conference on Housing, *Housing Problems in America: Proceedings of the Fourth Annual Conference on Housing* (New York: National Housing Association, 1915), 175–85.

19. Jon C. Teaford, *City and Suburb: The Political Fragmentation of Metropolitan America 1850–1970* (Baltimore: Johns Hopkins University Press, 1979), 87.

20. H. C. L. Jackson, "Building a Bungalow City in 18 Months," *Building Age* (April 1924): 83.

21. *Detroit Free Press*, 6 April 1924, real-estate sec., 5.

22. Elmer Akers, *Southern Whites in Detroit* (Ann Arbor: University Microfilms, 1979), 3.

23. Levine, *Internal Combustion*, 12.

24. Akers, *Southern Whites in Detroit*, 2. One source mentions Paducah, Kentucky, and Jonesboro, Tennessee, as particular areas from which migrants came to Detroit. See Erdmann Beynon, "The Southern White Laborer Migrates to Michigan," *American Sociological Review* 3 (June 1938): 339 n. 14; Philip E. Balla, "Appalachia and Detroit," Ph.D. diss., University of Michigan, 1977.

25. *Detroit Free Press*, 6 April 1924, real-estate sec., 5. For the context of American nativism, see John Higham, *Strangers in the Land: Patterns of American Nativism 1860–1925* (New York: Atheneum, 1963).

26. The countries of origin of the foreign-born in Brightmoor were Canada or the United Kingdom. Donald S. Hecock and Harry A. Trevelyan, *Detroit Voters and Recent Elections* (Detroit: Bureau of Governmental Research, School of Public Affairs and Social Work, Wayne University, 1938), maps 1 and 2. The foreign-born population of Detroit as a whole was slightly more than 25 percent in 1930. See also Citizens Research

Council of Michigan, *Population (1930 Census) and Other Social Data for Detroit by Census Tracts* (Detroit: Detroit Bureau of Governmental Research, 1937).

27. Citizens Research Council of Michigan, *A Social Study of Brightmoor, a Community of Detroit* (Detroit: Wayne University School of Public Affairs and Social Work, 1941).

28. B. E. Taylor, "Building a New Town," 111.

29. Frederick W. DesAutels, *The Township of Redford, Its Heritage and History* (n.p., 1975), 39.

30. Michael J. Doucet, "Urban Land Development in Nineteenth-Century North America: Themes in the Literature," *Journal of Urban History* 8 (May 1982): 306, 312–16.

31. Allan Nevins, *Ford: The Times, the Man, the Company* (New York: Scribner's, 1954), 517.

32. Nine out of ten migrants from the South were from rural areas. Akers, *Southern Whites in Detroit*, 4, 6.

33. The source for biographical material on Taylor is Burton, *City of Detroit*, 3:206, 209, unless otherwise noted.

34. Personal communication from Burt Eddy Taylor Jr., 25 September 1985.

35. Pearl Janet Davies, *Real Estate in American History* (Washington, D.C.: Public Affairs Press, 1958), 50; Worley, *J. C. Nichols*, 19–20; Anne Durkin Keating, *Building Chicago: Suburban Developers and the Creation of a Divided Metropolis* (Columbus: Ohio State University Press, 1988), 71; Emily Clark and Patrick Ashley, "The Merchant Prince of Cornville," *Chicago History* 21 (December 1992): 4–19. Ross Paterson argues that the introduction of the installment plan had a far-reaching impact on real-estate development in "Creating the Packaged Suburb: The Evolution of Planning and Business Practices in the Early Canadian Land Development Industry, 1900–1914," in Barbara M. Kelly, ed., *Suburbia Reexamined* (New York: Greenwood Press, 1989), 119–32.

36. Allan Nevins and Frank Ernest Hill, *Ford: Expansion and Challenge, 1915–1933* (New York: Scribner's, 1957), 147.

37. Personal communication from B. E. Taylor Jr., who had no further information on their locations, January 1986.

38. DesAutels, *Township of Redford*, 39; personal communication from B. E. Taylor Jr., 14 December 1985.

39. Brightmoor clipping file, Burton Historical Collection, Detroit Public Library.

40. See B. E. Taylor, "Building a New Town," 93–106, discussion 106–12; idem, "Developing a Community of Inexpensive Homes by Motor Bus Transportation," *Home Building and Subdividing: Proceedings and Reports of the Home Builders and Subdividers Division* (Chicago: NAREB, 1925), 85–99.

41. List provided to the author by B. E. Taylor Jr.

42. Personal communication from B. E. Taylor Jr., 25 September 1985.

43. Taylor, "Developing a Community," 85–86.

44. "Detroit Plans Its Future," *American Society of Planning Officials Newsletter* 19 (October 1953): 73–74; W. Hawkins Ferry, *The Buildings of Detroit: A History*, rev. ed. (Detroit: Wayne State University Press, 1980), 358.

45. The city limit lies half a block east of Telegraph Road.

46. *Polk's Redford, Brightmoor, and Rosedale Park Directory* (Detroit: Polk, 1925).

47. Bruce H. Wark, "Subsidizing Transportation by the Subdivider," *Annals of Real Estate Practice* (Chicago: NAREB, 1928), 641–43; Taylor, "Developing a Community," 91–94.

48. Harold M. Mayer and Richard C. Wade, *Chicago: Growth of a Metropolis* (Chicago: University of Chicago Press, 1969), 326.

49. The plat books are located in the Wayne County Real Estate Index Department, City-County Building, Detroit.

50. Michael Southworth and Peter M. Owens, "The Evolving Metropolis: Studies of Community, Neighborhood, and Street Form at the Urban Edge," *Journal of the American Planning Association* 59 (summer 1993): 273.

51. Jackson, "Bungalow City," 83.

52. Taylor, "Building a New Town," 110.

53. John B. Spiker, *Real Estate Business as a Profession* (Cincinnati: Stewart Kidd, 1923), 212.

54. Taylor, "Building a New Town," 107–8; idem, "Developing a Community," 90.

55. Taylor, "Building a New Town," 111.

56. Roy Lubove, "Homes and 'A Few Well Placed Fruit Trees': An Object Lesson in Federal Housing," *Social Research* 27 (winter 1960): 478.

57. By comparison, the original Levitt house measured less than 800

square feet. George Sternlieb, "Residential Construction," in Lisa Taylor, ed., *Housing: Symbol, Structure, Site* (New York: Cooper-Hewitt Museum, 1990), 97; Christian Topalov, "Scientific Urban Planning and the Ordering of Daily Life: The First 'War Housing' Experiment in the United States, 1917–1919," *Journal of Urban History* 17 (November 1990): 24.

58. MPC, *Suburban Development*, 25.

59. See Gwendolyn Wright, *Moralism and the Model Home: Domestic Architecture and Cultural Conflict in Chicago, 1873–1913* (Chicago: University of Chicago Press, 1980); Andrew Saint, *The Image of the Architect* (New Haven: Yale University Press, 1983); Spiro Kostof, ed., *The Architect: Chapters in the History of the Profession* (New York: Oxford University Press, 1977); Judith R. Blau, Mark E. LaGory and John S. Pipkin, eds., *Professionals and Urban Form* (Albany: State University of New York Press, 1983), esp. Magali Sarfatti Larson, "Emblem and Exception: The Historical Definition of the Architect's Professional Role," 49–86; Robert Twombly, *Power and Style: A Critique of Twentieth Century Architecture in the United States* (New York: Hill & Wang, 1995).

60. See, for example, Alberto Perez Gomez, *Architecture and the Crisis of Modern Science* (Cambridge: MIT Press, 1983).

61. Henry S. Saylor, *The A.I.A.'s First Hundred Years* (Washington, D.C.: Octagon, 1957), 32.

62. William P. P. Longfellow, "The Architect's Point of View," *Scribner's Magazine* 9 (January 1891): 119–20.

63. Saint, *Image of the Architect*, 72.

64. Wright, *Moralism and the Model Home*, chaps. 1, 2.

65. Quoted in Gwendolyn Wright, "On the Fringe of the Profession: Women in American Architecture," in Kostof, *The Architect*, 282.

66. Wright, *Moralism and the Model Home*, 205, 203.

67. Saint, *Image of the Architect*, 90–91; Wright, *Moralism and the Model Home*, 212–13.

68. Wright, *Moralism and the Model Home*, 213.

69. Larson, "Emblem and Exception," 81 n. 26.

70. Robert Gutman, *The Design of American Housing: A Reappraisal of the Architect's Role* (New York: Center for Cultural Resources, 1985), 51.

71. For insight into the flexible approach to work and professionalism needed by an architect on the Midwestern frontier in the second half of the nineteenth century, see George Ehrlich and Peggy E. Schrock, "The A. B. Cross Lumber Company, 1858–1871," *Missouri Historical Review* 80

(October 1985): 14–32. The decision not to participate in the profession was made by architects in other countries as well. Auguste Perret, for example, never took his diploma for his studies at the Academie because doing so would automatically have precluded his working as a building contractor. Peter Collins, *Concrete: The Vision of a New Architecture, A Study of Auguste Perret and His Precursors* (New York: Horizon Press, 1959), 160.

72. Robert Gutman, "Architects in the Home-Building Industry," in Blau, LaGory, and Pipkin, *Professionals*, 208–23; Dell Upton, "Pattern Books and Professionalism: Aspects of the Transformation of Domestic Architecture in America, 1800–1860," *Winterthur Portfolio* 19 (summer/autumn 1984): 107–50; Michael J. Crosbie, "From 'Cookbooks' to 'Menus': The Transformation of Architecture Books in Nineteenth-Century America," *Material Culture* 17 (spring 1985): 1–23; Mary Woods, "The First American Architectural Journals: The Profession's Voice," *Journal of the Society of Architectural Historians* 48 (June 1989): 117–38.

73. And for social ideas as well; see Wright, *Moralism and the Model Home*, chap. 1; Linda Smeins, "National Rhetoric, Public Discourse, and Spatialization: Middle Class America and the Pattern Book House," *Nineteenth-Century Contexts* 16 (1992): 135–64.

74. Larson, "Emblem and Exception," 79 n. 21.

75. Arthur C. Holden, "Outside Business Factors as Competitors of the Architect," *Journal of the American Institute of Architects* 8 (1925): 308–10; Gutman, in Blau, LaGory, and Pipkin, *Professionals*, 211. On the history of the ASHSB, also see Thomas Harvey, "Mail-Order Architecture in the Twenties," *Landscape* 25 (1981): 1–9. For another example of opposition to stock plans, see Leland M. Roth, "Getting the Houses to the People: Edward Bok, *The Ladies' Home Journal*, and the Ideal House," in Thomas Carter and Bernard L. Herman, eds., *Perspectives in Vernacular Architecture*, vol. 4 (Columbia: University of Missouri Press, 1991), 189.

76. Robert T. Jones, ed., *Authentic Small Houses of the Twenties* (New York: Dover, 1987), "Endorsements," reprint of *Small Homes of Architectural Distinction: A Book of Suggested Plans Designed by the Architects' Small House Service Bureau* (New York: Harper & Bros., 1929).

77. Introduction, ibid.

78. Wright, *Moralism and the Model Home*, chaps. 2, 9.

79. For examples of early-twentieth-century architects who were inter-

ested in large-scale housing solutions, see Richard M. Candee and Greer Hardwicke, "Early Twentieth-Century Reform Housing by Kilham and Hopkins, Architects of Boston," *Winterthur Portfolio* 22 (spring 1987): 47–80; T. William Booth, "Design for a Lumber Town by Bebb and Gould, Architects: A World War I Project in Washington's Wilderness," *Pacific Northwest Quarterly* 82 (October 1991): 132–39.

80. Lubove, "Homes and 'A Few Well Placed Fruit Trees,'" 483.

81. Saint, *Image of the Architect*, 91–94.

82. Editorial, *Michigan Architect and Engineer* 1 (April 1919): 3. For AIA opposition to the office of state architect in California, see the editorial, "Official Competence," *Journal of the American Institute of Architects* 1 (March 1913): 111–12.

83. Gutman, *The Design of American Housing*, 29; Lubove, "Homes and 'A Few Well Placed Fruit Trees,'" 477–78; Frederick Law Olmsted Jr., "Planning Residential Subdivisions," in National Conference on City Planning, *Proceedings of the Tenth National Conference on City Planning* (Baltimore: Norman, Remington, 1924).

84. Gutman, *The Design of American Housing*, 4.

85. Alfred H. Granger, "The Architect of Tomorrow," *American Architect* 115 (15 January 1919): 93.

86. Frank Weitenkampf, "Art and Architecture After the War, A List of References," *Architectural Record* 46 (November 1919): 485.

87. Lubove, "Homes and 'A Few Well Placed Fruit Trees,'" 482.

88. Zunz, *The Changing Face of Inequality*, 161 ff. For other discussions of owner-builder housing, see Richard Harris, *Unplanned Suburbs: Toronto's American Tragedy, 1900–1950* (Baltimore: Johns Hopkins University Press, 1996), and Richard Harris and Matt Sendbuehler, "The Making of a Working-Class Suburb in Hamilton's East End, 1900–1945," *Journal of Urban History* 20 (August 1994): 486–511.

89. Keating, *Building Chicago*.

90. Leifur Magnusson, "Housing by Employers in the United States," in *Homes for Workmen* (New Orleans: Southern Pine Association, 1919), 39–48.

91. Henry Glassie, "The Types of the Southern Mountain Cabin," in Jan Harold Brunvard, *The Study of American Folklore: An Introduction* (New York: Norton, 1968), appendix C, 338–70; see illus. at 356–57. On the origins of this type, see the same author's "The Appalachian Log Cabin," in W. K. McNeil, ed., *Appalachian Images in Folk and Popular*

Culture (Ann Arbor, Mich.: UMI Research Press, 1989), 307–14, originally published in *Mountain Life and Work* 39 (winter 1963): 5–14. Also see John Morgan, *The Log House in East Tennessee* (Knoxville: University of Tennessee Press, 1990); Henry Glassie, *Pattern in the Material Folk Culture of the Eastern United States* (Philadelphia: University of Pennsylvania Press, 1968). For a discussion of mail-order versions based on this house type, which he calls "southern cabin," see Alan Gowans, *The Comfortable House: North American Suburban Architecture 1890–1930* (Cambridge: MIT Press, 1986), 156; the rusticity of this type lent itself to use as summer cottages.

92. Charles E. Martin, *Hollybush: Folk Buildings and Social Change in an Appalachian Community* (Knoxville: University of Tennessee Press, 1984). Further reflections on the evolution of forms in the upland South can be found in Michael Ann Williams, "Rethinking the House: Interior Space and Social Change," in McNeil, *Appalachian Images*, 323–36.

93. Glassie, "Types of Southern Mountain Cabin," 342; Martin, *Hollybush*, 28–31. Papering served to keep out drafts as well as to decorate the walls.

Chapter 3. Westwood Highlands

1. The most detailed discussions of the early history of these districts can be found in Anita Day Hubbard, "Cities within the City," *San Francisco Bulletin*, 12 and 13 September 1924, also in collected volumes, San Francisciana Collection, San Francisco Public Library, 1 (August–November 1924); Mel Scott, *The San Francisco Bay Area: A Metropolis in Perspective* (Berkeley: University of California Press, 1959); and Sally Woodbridge and John M. Woodbridge, *Architecture San Francisco: The Guide* (San Francisco: American Institute of Architects, San Francisco Chapter, and 101 Productions, 1982), 160–75.

2. In *The Rise of the Community Builders: The American Real Estate Industry and Urban Land Planning* (New York: Columbia University Press, 1987), Marc A. Weiss maintains that the real-estate industry in California developed faster and with a clearer sense of purpose than anywhere else in the nation, especially regarding the interests of large-scale developers. He focuses on the state realty association and on the Los Angeles Realty Board in chaps. 4 and 5.

3. Scott, *San Francisco Bay Area*, 167.
4. Hubbard, "Cities within the City," 1:66.
5. Scott, *San Francisco Bay Area*, 167; Woodbridge and Woodbridge, *Architecture San Francisco*, 160.
6. Hubbard, "Cities within the City," 1:66.
7. Mansel Blackford, *The Lost Dream: Businessmen and City Planning on the Pacific Coast, 1890-1920* (Columbus: Ohio State University Press, 1992), 55, citing *Merchants' Association Review* (October 1911).
8. Margaret Goddard King, "The Growth of San Francisco, Illustrated by Shifts in the Density of Population," 2-vol. master's thesis, University of California, Berkeley, 1928, 2: map 15.
9. Scott, *San Francisco Bay Area*, 167.
10. Blackford, *Lost Dream*, 57.
11. Michael M. O'Shaughnessy, "The Hetch-Hetchy Water and Power Project, the Municipal Railway, and Other Notable Civic Improvements of San Francisco," n.p., n.d., quoted in Scott, *San Francisco Bay Area*, 167; Robert W. Cherny, "City Commercial, City Beautiful, City Practical: The San Francisco Visions of William C. Ralston, James D. Phelan, and Michael M. O'Shaughnessy," *California History* 73 (winter 1994/95): 305-7.
12. Richard Longstreth, *On the Edge of the World: Four Architects in San Francisco at the Turn of the Century* (Cambridge: MIT Press, 1983), 145-49.
13. Blackford, *Lost Dream*, 56-57.
14. John Bernard McGloin, *San Francisco: The Story of a City* (San Rafael, Calif.: Presidio Press, 1978), 178-79.
15. "Twin Peaks Bore Opened for Regular Traffic: First Car over Line Greeted by Thousands," *San Francisco Examiner*, 4 February 1918, 11; McGloin, *San Francisco*, 178-79.
16. James E. Vance Jr., *Geography and Urban Evolution in the San Francisco Bay Area* (Berkeley: Institute of Governmental Studies, University of California, 1964), 52.
17. McGloin, *San Francisco*, 178-79.
18. Prentice Duell, "The New Era of California Architecture," 2: "San Francisco," *Western Architect* 32 (November 1923): 127.
19. The phrase derives from Sam Bass Warner Jr., *Streetcar Suburbs: The Process of Growth in Boston, 1870-1900* (Cambridge: Harvard University Press, 1962; 2nd ed. 1978).

20. Woodbridge and Woodbridge, *Architecture San Francisco*, 171.

21. F. J. Glunk, "Westwood Park and Westwood Highlands," *The Home Designer and Garden Beautiful* 8 (March 1925): 194.

22. Scott, *San Francisco Bay Area*, 167.

23. Woodbridge and Woodbridge, *Architecture San Francisco*, 173.

24. Z. A. Battu, "Merchandising Serviced Homes," *Building Age and National Builder* (February 1927): 112.

25. "Westwood Park Building Up Solid," *San Francisco Chronicle*, 19 January 1924, 7.

26. William H. Wilson, *The City Beautiful Movement* (Baltimore: Johns Hopkins University Press, 1989).

27. *Attractive Bungalows of Moderate Cost for Westwood Park* (San Francisco: Baldwin & Howell, 1917).

28. Battu, "Merchandising Serviced Homes," 153.

29. Ibid., 110.

30. The national average cost for a new single-family house in 1927 was $4,830. Blanche Halbert, ed., *The Better Homes Manual* (Chicago: University of Chicago Press, 1931), 53, citing an April 1931 report in the *Monthly Labor Review*. The average cost of houses bought by the families of streetcar men in San Francisco from 1924 to 1929 was $4,500. E. H. Huntington and M. G. Luck, *Living on a Moderate Income* (Berkeley: University of California Press, 1937), 72, cited in John P. Dean, *Home Ownership: Is It Sound?* (New York: Harper & Bros., 1945), 97.

31. Woodbridge and Woodbridge, *Architecture San Francisco*, 171.

32. William Issel and Robert W. Cherny, *San Francisco, 1865–1932: Politics, Power, and Urban Development* (Berkeley: University of California Press, 1986), 79.

33. Battu, "Merchandising Serviced Homes," 112.

34. *Crocker-Langley San Francisco City Directory* (San Francisco: Polk, 1910–1928); *Polk's Crocker-Langley San Francisco City Directory* (San Francisco: Polk, 1929–1957). No obituary has been located for Nelson in the local press.

35. "Charles Strothoff, Architect, Dies," *San Francisco Chronicle*, 6 March 1963, 28. Most of the facts concerning Strothoff's career derive from this obituary.

36. *The Wilmerding School of Industrial Arts* (Berkeley: University Press, 1901), 5.

37. *Crocker-Langley San Francisco City Directory*, 1912–13.

38. Kevin Starr, *Americans and the California Dream, 1850–1915* (New York: Oxford University Press, 1973), 222.

39. A brief biography of Albert Farr (1871–1945) can be found in Sally B. Woodbridge, ed., *Bay Area Houses* (New York: Oxford University Press, 1976), 318–19. In addition to a discussion of his work in an essay in this volume by John Beach, "The Bay Area Tradition, 1890–1918," examples of his work can be seen in *Architect and Engineer* (June 1919): 48–49; *The Western Architect* (December 1927): plates 199–202; *Keith's Magazine on Home Building* (April 1928): 173. Also see Longstreth, *On the Edge of the World*, 307–8.

40. George S. Koyl, *American Architects Directory* (New York: Bowker, 1962).

41. This photograph album was made available to the author by James T. Hughes of San Francisco, a descendant of one of the Baldwin & Howell principals.

42. A photo of another house that illustrates this siting strategy can be found in Woodbridge and Woodbridge, *Architecture San Francisco*, 173. It was designed by Strothoff.

43. See Kirk Peterson, "Eclectic Stucco," in Charles W. Moore, Kathryn Smith, and Peter Becker, eds., *Home Sweet Home: American Domestic Vernacular Architecture* (New York: Rizzoli; Los Angeles: Craft and Folk Art Museum, 1983), 112–17, for similar examples.

44. Battu, "Merchandising Serviced Homes," 110.

45. Anne Bloomfield, "The Real Estate Associates: A Land and Housing Developer of the 1870s in San Francisco," *Journal of the Society of Architectural Historians* 37 (March 1978): 17. For examples of similar organizations see, for Hamilton, Ontario, Michael Doucet and John Weaver, *Housing the North American City* (Montreal: McGill-Queen's University Press, 1991); for Chicago, Ann Durkin Keating, *Building Chicago: Suburban Developers and the Creation of a Divided Metropolis* (Columbus: Ohio State University Press, 1988).

46. Bloomfield, "Real Estate Associates," 17.

47. See Bloomfield, "Real Estate Associates"; see also Anne Vernez Moudon, *Built for Change: Neighborhood Architecture in San Francisco* (Cambridge: MIT Press, 1986).

48. Dell Upton, "Pattern Books and Professionalism: Aspects of the Transformation of Domestic Architecture in America, 1800–1860," *Winterthur Portfolio* 19 (summer/autumn 1984): 144.

49. Moudon, *Built for Change*, 69–71.

50. Ibid., 56 ff.

51. Drummond Buckley, "A Garage in the House," in Martin Wachs and Margaret Crawford, eds., *The Car and the City: The Auto, the Built Environment, and Daily Urban Life* (Ann Arbor: University of Michigan Press, 1992), 124–40.

52. The best general history of land as a commodity in the United States remains A. M. Sakolski, *The Great American Land Bubble: The Amazing Story of Land-Grabbing, Speculations, and Booms from Colonial Days to the Present Time* (New York: Harper & Bros., 1932; reprint, New York: Johnson Reprint, 1966). See also Peter Wolf, *Land in America: Its Value, Use and Control* (New York: Pantheon, 1981). For a comprehensive survey of works dealing with real-estate history, see Marc A. Weiss, "Real Estate History: An Overview and Research Agenda," *Business History Review* 63 (summer 1989): 241–82.

53. R. E. Sherman, "The Realtor," *National Real Estate Journal* 23/24 (20 November 1922): 20.

54. Magali Sarfatti Larson, *The Rise of Professionalism: A Sociological Analysis* (Berkeley: University of California Press, 1977). The phrase *professional project* derives from Larson's work.

55. Richard T. Ely, "The Economics of Real Estate," in Blake Snyder, ed., *Real Estate Handbook* (New York: McGraw-Hill, 1925), 7.

56. The original name of the organization founded in 1908 was the National Association of Real Estate Exchanges; the name used here was adopted in 1916. The source for factual information concerning early NAREB activities, unless otherwise noted, is Pearl Janet Davies, *Real Estate in American History* (Washington, D.C.: Public Affairs Press, 1958), written on the occasion of the fiftieth anniversary of NAREB's founding.

57. As late as 1921, real-estate professionals felt that an advertising campaign was necessary to familiarize the public with the word *realtor* and what it stood for. See the remarks of NAREB President Fred E. Taylor, "Wants College Courses in Real Estate," *National Real Estate Journal* 22 (18 July 1921): 27, and the article on this theme, ibid.: 29–30. A Minneapolis realtor, C. N. Chadbourn, is cited as the inventor of the term by Weiss, *Rise of the Community Builders*, 170 n. 17.

58. Eliot Freidson, *Profession of Medicine* (New York: Dodd & Mead, 1970), 360, quoted in Larson, *Rise of Professionalism*, 57.

59. John B. Spilker, *Real Estate Business as a Profession* (Cincinnati: Stewart Kidd, 1923), 21.

60. According to Weiss, *Rise of the Community Builders*, 13, the California licensing act was signed into law in 1917, whereas Davies provides the date as 1919. For an expanded account of the mechanisms NAREB used in its professionalizing effort, see Weiss, ibid., 19–27.

61. Davies, *Real Estate in American History*, 114–15.

62. Ross Paterson, "Creating the Packaged Suburb: The Evolution of Planning and Business Practices in the Early Canadian Land Development Industry, 1900–1914," in Barbara M. Kelly, ed., *Suburbia Re-examined* (New York: Greenwood Press, 1989), 122.

63. Larson, *Rise of Professionalism*, chaps. 3 and 4.

64. Davies, *Real Estate in American History*, 116.

65. Larson, *Rise of Professionalism*, chap. 4. This concept derives ultimately from Karl Marx; see, for example, *The German Ideology* (New York: International Publishers, 1970).

66. Davies, *Real Estate in American History*, 121.

67. Marc A. Weiss, "Richard T. Ely and the Contribution of Economic Research to National Housing Policy, 1920–1940," *Urban Studies* 26 (1989): 117 n. 10; Garnett Laidlaw Eskew, *Of Land and Men: The Birth and Growth of an Idea* (Washington, D.C.: Urban Land Institute, 1959).

68. Larson, *Rise of Professionalism*, chaps. 3, 4, and 9.

69. Ibid., 70.

70. Weiss, *Rise of the Community Builders*, 27.

71. Davies, *Real Estate in American History*, 135.

72. Weiss, *Rise of the Community Builders*, 28.

73. Christian Topalov, "Scientific Urban Planning and the Ordering of Daily Life: The First 'War Housing' Experiment in the United States, 1917–1919," *Journal of Urban History* 17 (November 1990): 26. Also see chap. 2 in David Barry Cady, "The Influence of the Garden City Ideal on American Housing and Planning Reform, 1900–1940," Ph.D. diss., University of Wisconsin, 1970.

74. In addition to Larson, see Samuel Haber, *Efficiency and Uplift: Scientific Management in the Progressive Era* (Chicago: University of Chicago Press, 1964); Samuel P. Hays, *The Response to Industrialism: 1885–1914* (Chicago: University of Chicago Press, 1957); Gabriel Kolko, *The Triumph of Conservatism* (New York: Free Press, 1963); James Weinstein, *The Corporate Ideal In the Liberal State: 1900–1918* (Boston: Beacon Press,

1968); M. Christine Boyer, *Dreaming the Rational City: The Myth of American City Planning* (Cambridge: MIT Press, 1983).

75. On the relationship of planners to urban development in the decades around the turn of the century, see Richard Fogelsong, *Planning the Capitalist City: The Colonial Era to the 1920s* (Princeton: Princeton University Press, 1986); John D. Fairfield, "The Scientific Management of Urban Space: Progressive City Planning and the Legacy of Progressive Reform," *Journal of Urban History* 20 (February 1994): 179–204, and, by the same author, *The Mysteries of the Great City: The Politics of Urban Design 1877–1937* (Columbus: Ohio State University Press, 1993).

76. Editorial, *Buffalo Real Estate and Financial News*, 1892, quoted in Davies, *Real Estate in American History*, 39.

77. Davies, *Real Estate in American History*, 36.

78. Ibid., 72.

79. Weiss, *Rise of the Community Builders*, 6.

80. Ibid., 42.

81. Davies, *Real Estate in American History*, 50. William E. Harmon was one of the earliest developers to champion the creation of playground areas in subdivisions; see Suzanne Braley, "Philanthropy and Finance in the Development of the Modern Subdivision: A Study of the Harmon Company," in Laurence Gerckens, comp., *Proceedings of the Fifth National Conference on American Planning History* (Hilliard, Ohio: Society for American City and Regional Planning History, 1993), 650–68.

82. Davies, *Real Estate in American History*, 68.

83. For a contemporary account of this development, see Waldon Fawcett, "Roland Park, Baltimore County, Maryland: A Representative American Suburb," *House and Garden* 3 (April 1903): 174–96.

84. Davies, *Real Estate in American History*, 75. For plans of Roland Park, the Country Club District, River Oaks, and other developments, see Keller Easterling, *American Town Plans, A Comparative Timeline* (New York: Princeton Architectural Press, 1993).

85. Eskew, *Of Land and Men*, 10–11.

86. A. D. Theobald, *Financial Aspects of Subdivision Development* (Chicago: Institute for Economic Research, 1930), 77.

87. J. C. Nichols, "The Responsibilities of Realtors in City Planning," *City Planning* 1 (April 1925): 34.

88. Editorial, *Chicago Tribune*, May 1908, quoted in Davies, *Real Estate in American History*, 55. For a recent discussion of the commitment of

community builders to "the creation of complete communities with a mix of uses, planned for internal coherence and with the requisite connections to an urban region," see Greg Hise, *Magnetic L.A.: Planning the Twentieth-Century Metropolis* (Baltimore: Johns Hopkins University Press, 1997), quote from 4.

89. Weiss, *Rise of the Community Builders*, 57, 180 n. 5. See also Thomas S. Ingersoll, "How the Real Estate Man Can Help," in National Conference on City Planning, *Proceedings of the Ninth National Conference on City Planning* (Baltimore: Norman, Remington, 1924).

90. Weiss, *Rise of the Community Builders*, 55. Duncan McDuffie, as one of the principals in the San Francisco firm Mason-McDuffie, was the developer of Saint Francis Wood in the West of Twin Peaks district.

91. Ibid., 72–78.

92. J. C. Nichols, "Responsibilities and Opportunities of Real Estate Boards in Building Cities," *National Real Estate Journal* 25 (30 June 1924): 25.

93. Leo Grebler, David M. Blank, and Louis Winnick, *Capital Formation in Residential Real Estate: Trends and Prospects* (Princeton: Princeton University Press, 1956), 10–14.

94. Weiss, *Rise of the Community Builders*, 40.

95. B. E. Taylor, "Building a New Town," *Proceedings of the First Annual Convention Conferences of the Homebuilders' and Subdividers' Division of the National Association of Real Estate Boards* (Omaha, Neb.: NAREB, 1923), 110. This was true for Nichols's projects, too, according to William S. Worley, *J. C. Nichols and the Shaping of Kansas City: Innovation in Planned Residential Communities* (Columbia: University of Missouri Press, 1990), 207.

96. Weiss, *Rise of the Community Builders*, 2.

97. For a contemporary architect's acknowledgement of this trend, see George F. Root III, "Can the Architect Serve the Speculative Builder?" *Architectural Forum* (January 1928): 122–26.

98. Weiss, *Rise of the Community Builders*, 3.

99. Ibid., 68.

100. J. C. Nichols, "Financial Effect of Good Planning in Land Subdivision," in National Conference on City Planning, *Proceedings of the Eighth National Conference on City Planning* (Baltimore: Norman, Remington, 1924), 105.

101. Baldwin & Howell were general brokers, engaging in individual

sales transactions, property management, and other activities. See Weiss, *Rise of the Community Builders*, chap. 2, for an overview of the facets of realtors' enterprises.

Chapter 4. The Home-Ownership Network

1. The record of the 1920s was broken, of course, in the period following World War II. For a discussion of urban housing starts from 1890 to 1930, see Robert G. Barrows, "Beyond the Tenement: Patterns of American Urban Housing, 1870–1930," *Journal of Urban History* 9 (August 1983): 398–400.

2. Kenneth T. Jackson, *Crabgrass Frontier: The Suburbanization of the United States* (New York: Oxford University Press, 1985), 175.

3. Jules Tygiel, "Housing in Late Nineteenth-Century American Cities: Suggestions for Research," *Historical Methods* 12 (spring 1979): 88.

4. Barrows, "Beyond the Tenement," 402–3 and 414, table 6.

5. U.S. Bureau of the Census, *Housing Construction Statistics, 1889 to 1964* (Washington, D.C.: GPO, 1966), table A-1, "U. S.—New Housing Units Started: Annually 1889–1964"; also Richard A. Walker, "The Suburban Solution: Urban Geography and Urban Reform in the Capitalist Development of the United States," Ph.D. diss., Johns Hopkins University, 1977, 695, fig. 71.

6. See for example Gwendolyn Wright, *Moralism and the Model Home: Domestic Architecture and Cultural Conflict in Chicago, 1873–1913* (Chicago: University of Chicago Press, 1980); Clifford Edward Clark Jr., *The American Family Home, 1800–1960* (Chapel Hill: University of North Carolina Press, 1986).

7. Olivier Zunz, *The Changing Face of Inequality: Urbanization, Industrial Development, and Immigrants in Detroit, 1880–1920* (Chicago: University of Chicago Press, 1982), 152 ff. There was a certain amount of promotional literature aimed toward immigrant groups through their community and foreign-language presses. See Guy A. Szuberla, "*Dom, Namai, Heim:* Images of the New Immigrant's Home," in Jack Salzman, ed., *Prospects: An Annual of American Cultural Studies* (New York: Cambridge University Press, 1985), 139–68. For an example of advertising aimed at an immigrant market, see the 1883 ad in German for Samuel E. Gross's Chicago cottages, reproduced in Harold M. Mayer and Richard C.

Wade, *Chicago: Growth of a Metropolis* (Chicago: University of Chicago Press, 1969), 155.

8. Michael H. Lang, "The Design of Yorkship Garden Village," in Mary Corbin Sies and Christopher Silvers, eds., *Planning the Twentieth-Century American City* (Baltimore: Johns Hopkins University Press, 1996), 120–44.

9. Kenneth Baar, citing the proceedings of the National Housing Association, in "The National Movement to Halt the Spread of Multifamily Housing, 1890–1926," *Journal of the American Planning Association* 58 (winter 1992): 43.

10. David R. Contosta, *Suburb in the City: Chestnut Hill, Philadelphia, 1850–1990* (Columbus: Ohio State University Press, 1992).

11. U.S. Bureau of the Census, *Historical Statistics of the United States, Colonial Times to 1957* (Washington, D.C.: GPO, 1960), "Owner-Occupied Dwellings"; Barrows, "Beyond the Tenement," 416, table 7.

12. Michael E. Stone, "The Housing Problem in the United States: Origins and Prospects," *Socialist Review* 10 (July/August 1980): 80.

13. On investment funds available to developers in this period, see Gail Radford, "New Building and Investment Patterns in 1920s Chicago," *Social Science History* 16 (spring 1992): 12–16.

14. Josephine H. Ewalt, *A Business Reborn: The Savings and Loan Story, 1930–1960* (Chicago: American S&L Institute Press, 1962), 4. On the early history of the savings and loan association up to the 1930s, see also Horace Russell, *Savings and Loan Associations*, 2nd ed. (New York: Bender, 1960), 23–31; M. J. Daunton, "Home Loans versus Council Houses: The Formation of American and British Housing Policy, 1900–1920," *Housing Studies* 3 (1988): 232–46.

15. John P. Dean, *Home Ownership: Is It Sound?* (New York: Harper & Bros., 1945), 68.

16. For a discussion of period practices, see, for example, Forrest Adair Jr., "Housing Loans," *Real Estate Finance: Committee Reports, Addresses, Discussions, and Special Bulletins* (Chicago: NAREB, Mortgage and Finance Division, 1923), 54–55. A summary of these developments can be found in Marc A. Weiss, "Marketing and Financing Home Ownership: Mortgage Lending and Public Policy in the United States, 1918–1989," *Business and Economic History* 2nd ser., 18 (1989): 109–12.

17. Russell, *Savings and Loan Associations*, 23–31.

18. Marc A. Weiss, "Richard T. Ely and the Contribution of Economic Research to National Housing Policy, 1920–1940," *Urban Studies* 26 (1989): 118.

19. J. C. Nichols, "Housing and the Real Estate Problem," *Annals of the American Academy of Political and Social Science* 51 (January 1914): 134.

20. Irenaeus Shuler, "Subdivisions," chap. 14 of Blake Snyder, ed., *Real Estate Handbook* (New York: McGraw-Hill, 1925), 128.

21. Cited in Daunton, "Home Loans versus Council Houses," 243.

22. Ellis W. Hawley, *The Great War and the Search for a Modern Order: A History of the American People and Their Institutions, 1917–1933* (New York: St. Martin's, 1979), 71. Fears about social unrest had periodically fueled housing reforms from at least the 1860s; see Peter Marcuse, "Housing in Early City Planning," *Journal of Urban History* 6 (February 1980): 168–71.

23. Robert F. Bingham and Elmore L. Andrews, *Financing Real Estate* (Cleveland: McMichael, 1924), 307.

24. Charles Abrams, "The Residential Construction Industry," in Walter Adams, ed., *The Structure of American Industry, Some Case Studies* (New York: Macmillan, 1950), 116.

25. Abrams, "Residential Construction Industry," 115.

26. Walker, chaps. 1, 2, and 5.

27. Michael Sumichrast, *Profile of the Builder and His Industry* (Washington, D.C.: National Association of Home Builders, 1970), 8.

28. Jackson, *Crabgrass Frontier*, 129–30.

29. Marc A. Weiss, *The Rise of the Community Builders: The American Real Estate Industry and Urban Land Planning* (New York: Columbia University Press, 1987), 62.

30. Patrick J. Ashton, "Toward a Political Economy of Metropolitan Areas," M.A. thesis, Michigan State University, 1975, 1–2; Patrick J. Ashton, "The Political Economy of Suburban Development," and David M. Gordon, "Capitalist Development and the History of American Cities," in William K. Tabb and Larry Sawers, eds., *Marxism and the Metropolis* (New York: Oxford University Press, 1978).

31. See, for example, John J. Murphy, Edith Elmer Wood, and Frederick J. Ackerman, *The Housing Famine: How to End It* (New York: Dutton, 1920) for a debate among three writers over such issues.

32. Dean, *Home Ownership*, 41. On the "cooperative state" in the

1920s, see M. Christine Boyer, *Dreaming the Rational City: The Myth of American City Planning* (Cambridge: MIT Press, 1983), chap. 7.

33. Fred A. Bjornstad, "'A Revolution in Ideas and Methods': The Construction Industry and Socioeconomic Planning in the United States, 1915–1933," Ph.D. diss., University of Iowa, 1991, 33.

34. On the origins and roles of these organizations, see Robert A. Christie, *Empire in Wood: A History of the Carpenters' Union* (Ithaca, N.Y.: Cornell University Press, 1956); Pearl Janet Davies, *Real Estate in American History* (Washington, D.C.: Public Affairs Press, 1958); National Lumber Manufacturers Association, *High Lights of a Decade of Achievement* (n.p., 1929); Bjornstad "'A Revolution'"; Eugenie Ladner Birch, "Advancing the Art and Science of Planning: Planners and Their Organizations, 1909–1980," *APA Journal* 46 (January 1980): 22–49; Michael Doucet and John Weaver, "Material Culture and the North American House: The Era of the Common Man, 1870–1920," *Journal of American History* 72 (December 1985): 560–87; Booth Mooney, *Builders for Progress: The Story of the Associated General Contractors of America* (New York: McGraw-Hill, 1965); Mel Scott, *American City Planning since 1890* (Berkeley: University of California Press, 1969); Henry H. Saylor, *The A.I.A.'s First Hundred Years* (Washington, D.C.: Octagon, 1957); William H. Wilson, *The City Beautiful Movement* (Baltimore: Johns Hopkins University Press, 1989, chap. 2, "Municipal Improvement and Beautifying the Entire Community."

35. Doucet and Weaver, "Material Culture and the North American House," 576–79.

36. Ibid., 578. On the controversy over whether such compilations of statistics promoted monopolistic control or were beneficial forms of cooperation, see Robert F. Himmelberg, *The Origins of the National Recovery Administration: Business, Government, and the Trade Association Issue, 1921–1933* (New York: Fordham University Press, 1976).

37. National Lumber Manufacturers Association, *High Lights*, 16.

38. United States Congress Subcommittee on Housing and Community Development, *Evolution of Role of the Federal Government in Housing and Community Development: A Chronology of Legislative and Selected Executive Actions, 1892–1974* (Washington, D.C.: GPO, 1975).

39. Tygiel, "Housing in Late Nineteenth-Century American Cities," 87–88, discusses the changes in census information relating to housing.

40. Davies, *Real Estate in American History*, 126.

41. Hoover, in a letter to national and state trade associations, 1 April 1923, cited in Craig Lloyd, *Aggressive Introvert: A Study of Herbert Hoover and Public Relations Management 1912–1932* (Columbus: Ohio State University Press, 1972), 109. Also see Bjornstad, "'A Revolution,'" chap. 1.

42. Cited in Lloyd, *Aggressive Introvert*, 56 n. 33.

43. Ibid., 101–2, citing a public statement by Hoover headlined "Neighborhood (Settlement) Houses Help Solve Social Problems." The reference is undated but the statement was made in 1919 or 1920.

44. Bjornstad "'A Revolution'"; William Leach, *Land of Desire: Merchants, Power, and the Rise of a New American Culture* (New York: Pantheon, 1993), esp. chap. 12, "Herbert Hoover's Emerald City and Managerial Government."

45. *Seasonal Operation in the Construction Industries: The Facts and Remedies* (New York: McGraw-Hill, 1924).

46. Lloyd, *Aggressive Introvert*, 124–25.

47. Guy Alchon, *The Invisible Hand of Planning: Capitalism, Social Science, and the State in the 1920s* (Princeton: Princeton University Press, 1985), 63–67; Samuel Haber, *Efficiency and Uplift: Scientific Management in the Progressive Era, 1890–1920* (Chicago: University of Chicago Press, 1964), 156–59.

48. Miles L. Colean, *American Housing: Problems and Prospects* (New York: Twentieth Century Fund, 1949); National Lumber Manufacturers Association, *High Lights*.

49. "Report on House Building Issued by Commerce Department," *National Real Estate Journal* 24 (12 March 1923): 35; "Recommended Minimum Requirements for Small House Construction," *National Real Estate Journal* 24 (12 March 1923): 40. The first is a press release, datelined Washington, D.C., that describes the constitution of the committee and quotes Hoover's praise of its endeavors. The second piece, in the same issue, reports on the general outlines of the recommendations. This citation illustrates the method of dissemination of such recommendations, which could be enforced only at the local level. The organizations within the national network informed their members of these recommendations, encouraging their adoption as mainstream practice. Local leadership could then design regulations to enforce such practices.

50. Weiss, *Rise of the Community Builders*, 67; also Harvey S. Perloff,

"Education of City Planners: Past, Present and Future," *Journal of the American Institute of Planners* 22 (fall 1956): 213.

51. John M. Gries and James S. Taylor, *How to Own Your Home: A Handbook for Prospective Home Owners* (Washington, D.C.: Department of Commerce, 1923), vi.

52. "Home Owning Move Launched," *Detroit Free Press,* 6 January 1924, real-estate news section, 4.

53. Ibid.

54. "Teaching Good Citizenship and Home Ownership," *National Real Estate Journal* 23 (20 November 1922): 15.

55. William S. Worley, *J. C. Nichols and the Shaping of Kansas City: Innovation in Planned Residential Communities* (Columbia: University of Missouri Press, 1990), 280.

56. See movement publications such as *Midas Gold* (New York: Butterick Publishing, 1925); *Guidebook for Better Homes Campaigns* (Washington, D.C.: Better Homes in America, 1929); Blanche Halbert, ed., *The Better Homes Manual* (Chicago: University of Chicago Press, 1931). Also, Janet Hutchison, "The Cure for Domestic Neglect: Better Homes in America, 1922–1935," in Camille Wells, ed., *Perspectives in Vernacular Architecture*, vol. 2 (Columbia: University of Missouri Press, 1986), 168–78; Bjornstad, "'A Revolution,'" 182–88.

57. This house was an evocation of "Home Sweet Home," the seventeenth-century Long Island birthplace of the author of the song "Home Sweet Home," written in 1822. See Donn Barber, "Our First National Better Home: The Modern Version of Home Sweet Home," *Delineator* (September 1923): 2; also Hutchison, 169–73.

58. Cited in Lloyd, *Aggressive Introvert,* 132.

59. Ibid., 133.

60. From a 1924 letter from Hoover to President Coolidge, cited in Lloyd, *Aggressive Introvert,* 133.

61. Lloyd, *Aggressive Introvert,* 133; Ellis W. Hawley, "Herbert Hoover, the Commerce Secretariat, and the Vision of the 'Associative State,' 1921–1928," *Journal of American History* 61 (June 1974): 133–34.

62. Obituary, *New York Times,* 13 May 1944, 19; Scott, *American City Planning,* 20; Bjornstad, "'A Revolution,'" 31–32. In the 1930s, Ford's work focused on slum clearance.

63. James Ford, "Some Fundamentals of Housing Reform," *American City* 8 (1913): 473–80, cited in Baar, "National Movement," 43.

64. Later, Gries served on the Federal Home Loan Board; obituary, *New York Times*, 25 September 1953, 21.

65. William Starr Myers and Walter H. Newton, *The Hoover Administration: A Documented Narrative* (New York: Scribner's, 1936), 448.

66. E. G. S. Elliot, "American Housing Before the New Deal," *Town Planning Review* 16 (June 1935): 247–48.

67. John M. Gries and James Ford, eds., *Home Ownership, Income, and Types of Dwellings* (Washington, D.C.: President's Conference on Home Building and Home Ownership [hereafter HBHO], 1932), 145.

68. Gries and Ford, *Home Ownership*, xi.

69. Ibid., 3.

70. John M. Gries and James Ford, eds., *House Design, Construction, and Equipment* (Washington, D.C.: President's Conference HBHO, 1932), 97–98.

71. Gries and Ford, *House Design, Construction, and Equipment*, 15.

72. Ibid., 21.

73. This committee was one of six correlating committees whose mandates complemented the tasks of the twenty-five fact-finding committees. The report of the correlating committee on technological development is published in John M. Gries and James Ford, *Housing Objectives and Programs* (Washington, D.C.: President's Conference HBHO, 1932), 27–100.

74. See John M. Gries and James Ford, eds., *Home Finance and Taxation* (Washington, D.C.: President's Conference HBHO, 1932). The other resolution passed unanimously by those at the conference supported continuing the work of the conference.

75. Frederick L. Olmsted Jr., "Lessons from Housing Developments of the United States Housing Corporation," *Monthly Labor Review* 8 (May 1919): 27–38.

76. Weiss, *Rise of the Community Builders*, 28.

77. Weiss, "Marketing and Financing Home Ownership," 109–12; Bjornstad, "'A Revolution,'" 71–72.

78. Hawley, *The Great War and Search for a Modern Order*, 100.

79. Lewis Mumford, "Mass Production and Housing," in *City Development: Studies in Disintegration and Renewal* (New York: Harcourt, Brace & World, 1945), 70. This essay originally appeared in *Architectural Record*, issues of January 1930: 13–20 and February 1930: 110–16.

80. Editorial, *National Real Estate Journal* 22 (28 March 1921): 22.

81. Sam Bass Warner Jr., *Streetcar Suburbs: The Process of Growth In Boston, 1870–1900*, 2nd ed. (Cambridge: Harvard University Press, 1978), 117.

82. Emily Clark and Patrick Ashley, "The Merchant Prince of Cornville," *Chicago History* 21 (December 1992): 4–19; Ann Durkin Keating, *Building Chicago: Suburban Developers and the Creation of a Divided Metropolis* (Columbus: Ohio State University Press, 1988), 70–71; Perry R. Duis and Glen E. Holt, "Little Boxes, Big Fortunes," *Chicago* (November 1977): 116–17.

83. Worley, *J. C. Nichols*, 264–65; J. C. Nichols, "Suburban Subdivisions with Community Features," *American City* 31 (October 1924): 335–38.

84. Gries and Ford, *Housing Objectives and Programs*, 159. For the beginnings of this notion, see also John Archer, "Country and City in the American Romantic Suburb," *Journal of the Society of Architectural Historians* 42 (May 1983): 139–56.

85. On Downing, see David Schuyler, *Apostle of Taste: Andrew Jackson Downing, 1815–1852* (Baltimore: Johns Hopkins University Press, 1996); on Llewellyn Park, see Richard Guy Wilson, "Idealism and the Origin of the First American Suburb: Llewellyn Park, New Jersey," *American Art Journal* 11 (October 1979): 79–90; on Riverside, see Walter L. Creese, *The Crowning of the American Landscape: Eight Great Spaces and Their Buildings* (Princeton: Princeton University Press, 1985), 219–40. For summaries of these developments, and further bibliography, see David Schuyler, *The New Urban Landscape: The Redefinition of City Form in Nineteenth Century America* (Baltimore: Johns Hopkins University Press, 1986) and Jackson, *Crabgrass Frontier*, chaps. 3 and 4.

86. On the history of garden-suburb design, see Walter L. Creese, *The Search for Environment* (New Haven: Yale University Press, 1966); David Barry Cady, "The Influence of the Garden City Ideal on American Housing and Planning Reform, 1900–1940," Ph.D. diss., University of Wisconsin, 1970.

87. William Smythe, *City Homes on Country Lanes* (New York: Macmillan, 1922), 60, cited in Peter J. Schmitt, *Back to Nature: The Arcadian Myth in Urban America* (New York: Oxford University Press, 1969), xvii.

88. Worley stresses that Nichols could not have seen garden-city de-

velopments on his trip since it predated these; see *J. C. Nichols*, 93. On Nichols's early years, see also "Portrait of a Salesman: Jesse Clyde Nichols," *National Real Estate Journal* 40 (February 1939): 19; Richard Longstreth, "J. C. Nichols, the Country Club Plaza, and Notions of Modernity," *Harvard Architecture Review* 5 (1986): 123.

89. J. C. Nichols, *Real Estate Subdivisions: The Best Manner of Handling Them* (Washington, D.C.: American Civic Association, 1912), 15.

90. Jesse Clyde Nichols, "Town Planning," in Blake Snyder, ed., *Real Estate Handbook* (New York: McGraw-Hill, 1925), 363–64.

91. Michael Southworth and Eran Ben-Joseph, "Street Standards and the Shaping of Suburbia," *Journal of the American Planning Association* 61 (winter 1995): 67.

92. On the history and background of Perry's neighborhood unit plan, see James Dahir, *The Neighborhood Unit Plan, Its Spread and Acceptance: A Selected Bibliography with Interpretive Comments* (New York: Sage, 1947). For an overview of concepts of neighborhood in planning history, from settlements to the present, see Christopher Silver, "Neighborhood Planning in Historical Perspective," *Journal of the American Planning Association* 51 (spring 1985): 161–74. Greg Hise develops the concept of "modern community planning," which embraces ideas derived from both garden-city ideals and the neighborhood unit plan, in *Magnetic L.A.: Planning the Twentieth-Century Metropolis* (Baltimore: Johns Hopkins University Press, 1997).

93. Clarence Arthur Perry, "The Local Community as a Unit in the Planning of Urban Residential Areas," in Ernest W. Burgess, ed., *The Urban Community* (Chicago: University of Chicago Press, 1926), 238–41.

94. Clarence A. Perry, "The Neighborhood Unit, a Scheme of Arrangement for the Family Community," *Regional Plan of New York and Its Environs*, vol. 7 (New York: Regional Plan of New York and Its Environs, 1929). Perry's final statement of the plan appears in his last work, *Housing for the Machine Age* (New York: Sage, 1939).

95. Perry studied at Stanford University, Cornell University, and Teachers College, Columbia University. He taught in the Philippines, was a high school principal in Puerto Rico, and worked for the U.S. Immigration Commission before joining the staff of the Russell Sage Foundation, where he worked until his retirement in 1937. For biographical information on Perry, see John M. Glenn, Lilian Brandt, and F. Emerson Andrews, *Russell Sage Foundation, 1907–1946*, 2 vols. (New York: Sage, 1947), and Patricia

Mooney Melvin, ed., *American Community Organizations: A Historical Dictionary* (New York: Greenwood Press, 1986), 146–47.

96. Glenn, Brandt, and Andrews, *Russell Sage Foundation*, 72.

97. Clarence A. Perry, *Wider Use of the School Plant* (New York: Sage, 1910).

98. Luther Halsey Gulick, introduction to Perry, *Wider Use of the School Plant*, viii. Gulick was the first president of the Playground Association of America, founded in 1906 and funded by the Russell Sage Foundation.

99. Allen F. Davis, *Spearheads for Reform: The Social Settlements and the Progressive Movement, 1890–1914* (New York: Oxford University Press, 1967), 77.

100. John C. Teaford, *The Twentieth-Century American City: Problem, Promise, and Reality* (Baltimore: Johns Hopkins University Press, 1986), 31.

101. Cooley's principal works were *Human Nature and the Social Order* (1902) and *Social Organization* (1909). On Cooley's ideas, see Jean B. Quandt, *From the Small Town to the Great Community: The Social Thought of Progressive Intellectuals* (New Brunswick, N.J.: Rutgers University Press, 1970), chap. 4. For discussions of the impact of Cooley's ideas on Perry and others, see Perry, *Housing for the Machine Age*, 217; Dahir, *Neighborhood Unit Plan*; Lewis Mumford, "The Neighborhood and the Neighborhood Unit," *Town Planning Review* 24 (January 1954): 256–70.

102. Perry, *Housing for the Machine Age*, 205.

103. Patricia Mooney Melvin, *The Organic City: Urban Definition and Community Organization, 1880–1920* (Lexington: University Press of Kentucky, 1987), 23–24; Sidney Dillick, *Community Organization for Neighborhood Development—Past and Present* (New York: Woman's Press and William Morrow, 1953), 65; Robert M. Fisher, *Let the People Decide: Neighborhood Organizing in America* (Boston: Twayne, 1984), 13–20; Ronald M. Johnson, "Forgotten Reformer: Edward J. Ward and the Community Center Movement, 1907–1921," *Mid-America* 74 (January 1992): 17–35.

104. Samuel Howe's "Town Planning on a Large Scale," in *House Beautiful* 36 (October 1914): 130–36, provides a contemporary view of this project.

105. Perry, *Housing for the Machine Age*, 211.

106. Ibid.

107. Mumford, "Neighborhood and Neighborhood Unit," 262.

108. Scott, *American City Planning*, 72–74; Howard Gillette Jr., "The Evolution of Neighborhood Planning from the Progressive Era to the 1949 Housing Act," *Journal of Urban History* 9 (August 1983): 423–24.

109. Alfred B. Yeomans, ed., *City Residential Land Development: Studies in Planning. Competitive Plans for Subdividing a Typical Quarter Section of Land in the Outskirts of Chicago* (Chicago: University of Chicago Press, 1916).

110. Yeomans, *City Residential Land Development*, 37–44. This was the plan submitted by Prairie School architect William Drummond.

111. Clarence Arthur Perry, *The Rebuilding of Blighted Areas* (New York: Regional Plan Association, 1933).

112. Stanley Buder, *Visionaries and Planners: The Garden City Movement and the Modern Community* (New York: Oxford University Press, 1990), 64.

113. Ibid., 158.

114. Ibid., 64.

115. Mumford, "Neighborhood and Neighborhood Unit," 263. The conclusions of the 1929 White House Conference on Child Health and Protection also seem to register the impact of Perry's ideas. See Leach, *Land of Desire*, 370–71.

116. Report on the Michigan State Convention, *National Real Estate Journal* (10 October 1921).

117. Weiss, *Rise of the Community Builders*, 6–12.

118. Report on the Home Builders and Subdividers Division meetings, *National Real Estate Journal* 25 (16 June 1924): 50. This talk was published as an essay with the same title, "Suburban Subdivisions with Community Features," in *American City* 31 (October 1924): 335–38.

119. J. C. Nichols, "Responsibilities and Opportunities of Real Estate Boards in Building Cities," *National Real Estate Journal* 25 (30 June 1924): 25.

120. Ellis W. Hawley refers to Hoover as an "associational progressive" in his untitled contribution to J. Joseph Huthmacher and Warren I. Susman, eds., *Herbert Hoover and the Crisis of American Capitalism* (Cambridge, Mass.: Schenkman, 1973), 27.

121. Ellis W. Hawley, "Herbert Hoover, the Commerce Secretariat, and the Vision of an 'Associative State,' 1921–1928," *Journal of American History* 61 (June 1974): 121. See also William Appleman Williams, *The Contours of American History* (Cleveland: World Publishing, 1961), esp.

"The Central Role of Herbert Hoover in the Maturation of an Industrial Gentry," 425–38.

122. Grosvenor Atterbury, "Model Towns in America," *Scribner's Magazine* 52 (July 1912): 27. On Atterbury's ideas, also see David Handlin, *The American Home: Architecture and Society, 1815–1915* (Boston: Little, Brown, 1979), 285–88.

123. Warner, *Streetcar Suburbs*, 158.

124. Dolores Hayden, *The Grand Domestic Revolution: A History of Feminist Designs for American Homes, Neighborhoods, and Cities* (Cambridge: MIT Press, 1981), 23. In *The Great War and Search for a Modern Order*, Hawley observed a similar parallel on a wider scale: "The period from 1922 through 1928 really stands as a kind of premature spring for the capitalist adaptations of our own time" (81).

Chapter 5. Architectural Style

1. Peter G. Rowe, *Making a Middle Landscape* (Cambridge: MIT Press, 1991), 96. Also see Alan Colquhoun, "Form and Figure," *Oppositions* 12 (spring 1978): 29–37.

2. For example, "Grouping Houses to Get Ideal Homes," *Building Age* (August 1921): 58; "Beauty by Grouping Homes," ibid. (September 1922): 25–27. Some of the interest in bungalow courts in this period stemmed from this emphasis on grouping houses; see Albert Marple, "The Modern Bungalow Court," ibid. (March 1920): 19–22: 40, among numerous examples. For an analysis of these, see Stefanos Polyzoides et al., *Courtyard Housing in Los Angeles* (Berkeley: University of California Press, 1982).

3. William B. Bragdon, "Inside and Outside the Modern Colonial House," *House and Garden* 32 (August 1917): 58.

4. See William B. Rhoads, "The Colonial Revival and American Nationalism," *Journal of the Society of Architectural Historians* 35 (December 1976): 239–54, and idem, *The Colonial Revival* (New York: Garland, 1977); Karal Ann Marling, *George Washington Slept Here: Colonial Revivals and American Culture, 1876–1986* (Cambridge: Harvard University Press, 1988).

5. William B. Rhoads, "Roadside Colonial: Early American Design for the Automobile Age, 1900–1940," *Winterthur Portfolio* 21 (summer/autumn 1986): 136–38; James S. Walmsley, *American Ingenuity: Henry*

Ford Museum and Greenfield Village (New York: Abrams, 1985); Marling, *Washington Slept Here*, 269–70, 283–90.

6. Marling, *Washington Slept Here*, 288.

7. Rhoads, "The Colonial Revival and American Nationalism;" David Gebhard, "The American Colonial Revival in the 1930s," *Winterthur Portfolio* 22 (summer/autumn 1987): 109–48.

8. William B. Rhoads, "The Colonial Revival and the Americanization of Immigrants," in Alan Axelrod, ed., *The Colonial Revival in America* (New York: Norton, 1985), 341–61. For historical background on Americanization, see John Higham, *Strangers in the Land: Patterns of American Nativism, 1860–1925* (New York: Atheneum, 1963).

9. Talbot Hamlin, *The American Spirit In Architecture* (New Haven: Yale University Press, 1926), 267.

10. "A Style That Never Grows Old," *Popular Mechanics* 52 (November 1929): 879, cited in Gebhard, "American Colonial Revival," 109.

11. Jean Gordon and Jan McArthur, "Popular Culture, Magazines, and American Domestic Interiors, 1898–1940," *Journal of Popular Culture* 22 (spring 1989): 47, 49. The authors survey *Good Housekeeping, Ladies' Home Journal,* and *House Beautiful*.

12. Alan Gowans, *The Comfortable House: North American Suburban Architecture, 1890–1930* (Cambridge: MIT Press, 1986), 156. See also the discussion of Henry Glassie's work and its relevance to Brightmoor in chap. 2.

13. Kevin Starr, *Americans and the California Dream, 1850–1915* (New York: Oxford University Press, 1973), chap. 12, "An American Mediterranean," 396–411; Harold Kirker, *California's Architectural Frontier: Style and Tradition in the Nineteenth Century* (Santa Barbara, Calif.: Peregrine Smith, 1973); and the following articles by David Gebhard: "The Spanish Colonial Revival in Southern California, 1895–1930," *Journal of the Society of Architectural Historians* 26 (May 1967): 131–47; "Architectural Imagery, the Mission, and California," *Harvard Architecture Review* 1 (spring 1980): 137–45; and "Tile, Stucco Walls, and Arches: The Spanish Tradition in the Popular American House," in Charles W. Moore, Kathryn Smith, and Peter Becker, eds., *Home Sweet Home: American Domestic Vernacular Architecture* (New York: Rizzoli, 1983), 104–11.

14. John Beach, "The Bay Area Tradition, 1890–1918," in Sally B. Woodbridge, ed., *Bay Area Houses* (New York: Oxford University Press, 1976), 80.

15. William B. Bragdon, "Defining Colonial Architecture: The Colonial Plan," *House and Garden* 31 (June 1917): 48–49; see also David Gebhard, "Learning from the 1920s: The Ideals of Romance, Charm, and Personality," *Review* (School of Architecture, Tulane University) (1984–85): 50–55, and Gebhard, "American Colonial Revival."

16. Rexford Newcomb, *The Spanish House for America* (Philadelphia: Lippincott, 1927), and idem, *Mediterranean Domestic Architecture in the United States* (Cleveland: Jansen, 1928).

17. "Local Materials and Local Labor," *House and Garden* 43 (April 1923): 90.

18. Gowans, *Comfortable House,* 211–12. See also Gwendolyn Wright, *Building the Dream: A Social History of Housing In America* (New York: Pantheon, 1981), chap. 11.

19. Quoted in A. Lawrence Kocher, "The Country House," *Architectural Record* 62 (1927): 342, cited in Jonathan Lane, "The Period House in the Nineteen-twenties," *Journal of the Society of Architectural Historians* 20 (December 1961), 171. Also see Richard Longstreth, *On the Edge of the World: Four Architects in San Francisco at the Turn of the Century* (Berkeley: University of California Press, 1983), chap. 1. This form of "modernism"—historicism—has, of course, been a feature of Western architecture since the nineteenth century.

20. Written in relation to the manufacture of furniture, this statement reflects the current standpoint toward architectural design as well. *Furniture: As Interpreted by the Century Furniture Company* (Grand Rapids, Mich.: Century Furniture Co., 1928), 10, as quoted in Candace M. Volz, "The Modern Look of the Early Twentieth-Century House: A Mirror of Changing Lifestyles," in Jessica H. Foy and Thomas J. Schlereth, eds., *American Home Life, 1880–1930: A Social History of Spaces and Services* (Knoxville: University of Tennessee Press, 1992), 27.

21. Daniel Platt Gregory, "Magazine Modern: A Study of the American Architectural Press, 1919–1930," Ph.D. diss., University of California, Berkeley, 1982, 85 ff.

22. Alessandro Falassi and Edward Tuttle, "California's Houses in Costume," *Journal of American Folklore* 103 (October–December 1990): 502.

23. Rowe, *Making a Middle Landscape,* 105.

24. Quoted in Karal Ann Marling, "From the Quilt to the Neocolonial Photograph: The Arts of the Home in an Age of Transition," in Jessica H.

Foy and Karal Ann Marling, eds., *The Arts and the American Home, 1890–1930* (Knoxville: University of Tennessee Press, 1994), 8.

25. Gowans, *Comfortable House*, 213.

26. Clifford Edward Clark Jr., *The American Family Home, 1800–1960* (Chapel Hill: University of North Carolina Press, 1986), 82.

27. Gwendolyn Wright, *Moralism and the Model Home: Domestic Architecture and Cultural Conflict in Chicago, 1973–1913* (Chicago: University of Chicago Press, 1980), esp. chap. 8. See also Lane, "The Period House in the Nineteen-twenties," 169–78. Lane's pioneering article was the first to look beyond the eclecticism of 1920s designs to note the innovative features of open plans, informality, and outdoor living areas.

28. Bridget A. May, "Progressivism and the Colonial Revival: The Modern Colonial House, 1900–1920," *Winterthur Portfolio* 26 (summer/autumn 1991): 107–22.

29. Robert T. Jones, ed., *Authentic Small Houses of the Twenties* (New York: Dover, 1987), 23, reprint of *Small Houses of Architectural Distinction: A Book of Suggested Plans Designed by The Architects' Small House Service Bureau, Inc.* (New York: Harper & Bros., 1929).

30. William B. Bragdon, "The Exterior of Colonial Houses," *House and Garden* 32 (July 1917): 22.

31. Leo Grebler, David M. Blank, and Louis Winnick, *Capital Formation in Residential Real Estate: Trends and Prospects* (Princeton: Princeton University Press, 1956), 8–15.

32. David E. Nye, *Electrifying America: Social Meanings of a New Technology* (Cambridge: MIT Press, 1990), 260.

33. Ibid., 267. According to Thomas J. Schlereth in "Conduits and Conduct: Home Utilities in Victorian America, 1876–1915," the All-Electric Home at the 1893 Chicago Exposition was the first separate building to be devoted to electricity at a world's fair; in Foy and Schlereth, *American Home Life*, 233. For an example of the introduction of new technologies to residential subdivisions—in this case, to J. C. Nichols's Country Club District—see Mark H. Rose, *Cities of Light and Heat: Domesticating Gas and Electricity in Urban America* (University Park: Penn State University Press, 1995).

34. Ruth Schwartz Cowan, *More Work for Mother: The Ironies of Household Technology from the Open Hearth to the Microwave* (New York: Basic Books, 1983). On the rapid spread of new household technologies and equipment, see the classic studies *Zanesville, Ohio, and 36 Other Ameri-*

can *Communities* (New York: Eastman, 1927), and Robert S. Lynd and Helen M. Lynd, *Middletown: A Study of American Culture* (New York: Harcourt, Brace, 1929).

35. Sally E. Davidson, "Electricity Comfort Key," *Detroit Free Press* 6 January 1924, 6.

36. Dorothy M. Brown, *Setting a Course: American Women in the 1920s* (Boston: Twayne, 1987), 7.

37. Daniel Horowitz, *The Morality of Spending: Attitudes Toward the Consumer Society in America, 1875–1940* (Baltimore: Johns Hopkins University Press, 1985), esp. chap. 7, "Double Digits: World War I, the Red Scare, and Attitudes to Consumption," 109–33; Jackson Lears, *Fables of Abundance: A Cultural History of Advertising in America* (New York: Basic Books, 1994).

38. Tamara K. Hareven, "The Home and the Family in Historical Perspective," in Arien Mack, ed., *Home: A Place in the World* (New York: New York University Press, 1993), 227–59; Marilyn Ferris Motz and Pat Browne, eds., *Making the American Home: Middle-Class Women and Domestic Material Culture, 1840–1940* (Bowling Green, Ohio: Bowling Green State University Popular Press, 1988); Ellen M. Plante, *The American Kitchen, 1700 to the Present: From Hearth to Highrise* (New York: Facts on File, 1995).

39. Benjamin R. Andrews, "The Home Woman as Buyer and Controller of Consumption," *Annals* 143 (May 1929): 41, cited in Brown, *Setting a Course*, 105.

40. Margaret Marsh, "From Separation to Togetherness: The Social Construction of Domestic Space in American Suburbs, 1840–1915," *Journal of American History* 76 (September 1989): 506–27; also see the same author's *Suburban Lives* (New Brunswick, N.J.: Rutgers University Press, 1990); Cheryl Robertson, "Male and Female Agendas for Domestic Reform: The Middle-Class Bungalow in Gendered Perspective," *Winterthur Portfolio* 26 (summer/autumn 1991): 123–41; Daphne Spain, *Gendered Spaces* (Chapel Hill: University of North Carolina Press, 1992), chap. 5, "From Parlor to Great Room."

41. See, for example, John Modell, "Dating Becomes the Way of American Youth," in Leslie Page Moch and Gary D. Stark, eds., *Essays on the Family and Historical Change* (College Station: Texas A&M University Press, 1983), 91–126; Elaine Tyler May, "The Pressure to Provide: Class, Consumerism, and Divorce in Urban America, 1880–1920," in Mel Al-

bin and Dominick Cavallo, *Family Life in America, 1620–2000* (St. James, N.Y.: Revisionary Press, 1981), 279–89; Beth L. Bailey, *From Front Porch to Back Seat: Courtship in Twentieth-Century America* (Baltimore: Johns Hopkins University Press, 1988); Christopher Lasch, *Haven in a Heartless World: The Family Besieged* (New York: Basic Books, 1979).

42. Laura J. Miller, "Family Togetherness and the Suburban Ideal," *Sociological Forum* 10 (September 1995): 395; Anne Scott MacLeod, "Reading Together: Children, Adults, and Literature at the Turn of the Century," in Foy and Marling, *Arts and the American Home*, 111–23; Katherine C. Grier, "The Decline of the Memory Palace: The Parlor after 1890," and Karin Calvert, "Children in the House, 1890–1930," in Foy and Schlereth, *American Home Life*, 49–74 and 75–93, respectively.

43. On this theme, see, for example, Richard Longstreth, "The Diffusion of the Community Shopping Center Concept during the Interwar Decades," *Journal of the Society of Architectural Historians* 56 (September 1997): 268–93.

44. A. D. Theobald, *Financial Aspects of Subdivision Development* (Chicago: Institute for Economic Research, 1930), 59–60.

45. Jones, *Authentic Small Houses of the Twenties*, 91.

46. Cited in Mark H. Rose, "'There is Less Smoke in the District': J. C. Nichols, Urban Change, and Technological Systems," *Journal of the West* 25 (January 1986): 48.

47. Gowans, *Comfortable House*, 212.

48. Marling, *Washington Slept Here*, 290. Paula S. Fass refers to the "personal plasticity" cultivated in this period in *The Damned and the Beautiful: American Youth in the 1920s* (New York: Oxford University Press, 1977).

49. Jones, *Authentic Small Houses of the Twenties*, 93.

50. Ibid., 236.

51. Emily Post, *The Personality of a House: The Blue Book of Home Design and Decoration* (New York: Funk & Wagnalls, 1930).

52. Raymond Williams, *Keywords: A Vocabulary of Culture and Society* (New York: Oxford University Press, 1976), 195.

53. Warren I. Susman, "'Personality' and Twentieth-Century Culture," in *Culture as History: The Transformation of American Society in the Twentieth Century* (New York: Pantheon, 1984), 271–85.

54. Karen Halttunen, "From Parlor to Living Room: Domestic Space, Interior Decoration, and the Culture of Personality," in Simon J. Bronner,

ed., *Consuming Visions: Accumulation and Display of Goods in America, 1880–1920* (New York: Norton, 1989), 157–89. Also see Gordon and McArthur, "Popular Culture and American Domestic Interiors." On *personality* as referring both to the house and the woman of the house in the 1920s, see Beverly Gordon, "Woman's Domestic Body: The Conceptual Conflation of Women and Interiors in the Industrial Age," *Winterthur Portfolio* 31 (winter 1996): 281–301.

Conclusion

1. Ellis W. Hawley, "Herbert Hoover, the Commerce Secretariat, and the Vision of an 'Associative State,' 1921–1928," *Journal of American History* 61 (June 1974): 138.

2. See chap. 4, note 107.

3. Dell Upton, "Vernacular Buildings," in Diane Maddex, ed., *Built in the U.S.A.: American Buildings from Airports to Zoos* (Washington, D.C.: Preservation Press, 1985), 167–68. On architecture as a social process, also see Henri Lefebvre, *The Production of Space*, trans. Donald Nicholson-Smith (Oxford: Blackwell, 1991); Reinhard Bentmann and Michael Mueller, *The Villa as Hegemonic Architecture*, trans. Tim Spence and David Craven (Atlantic Highlands, N.J.: Humanities Press, 1992).

4. J. C. Nichols, "A Developer's View of Deed Restrictions," *Journal of Land and Public Utility Economics* 5 (May 1929): 134; "Planning for Permanence" is the title of Nichols's address to the forty-first annual convention of NAREB in 1948, cited in Garnett Laidlaw Eskew, *Of Land and Men: The Birth and Growth of an Idea* (Washington, D.C.: Urban Land Institute, 1959), 161.

5. Frederick L. Allen, "Suburban Nightmare," *Independent* 114 (13 June 1925): 671.

6. On use and exchange values in relation to real estate, see John R. Logan and Harvey L. Molotch, *Urban Fortunes: The Political Economy of Place* (Berkeley: University of California Press, 1987); David Harvey, *The Limits to Capital* (Chicago: University of Chicago Press, 1982).

7. Peter G. Rowe, *Making a Middle Landscape* (Cambridge: MIT Press, 1991), 52.

8. Marc A. Weiss, "Richard T. Ely and the Contributions of Economic Research to National Housing Policy, 1920–1940," *Urban Studies* 26 (1989): 122–23.

9. Daniel Horowitz, *The Morality of Spending: Attitudes Toward the Consumer Society in America, 1875–1940* (Baltimore: Johns Hopkins University Press, 1985), 116.

10. Constance Perin, *Everything in Its Place: Social Order and Land Use in America* (Princeton: Princeton University Press, 1977), 66.

11. Ibid., 77, 66.

12. Robert Fishman, *Bourgeois Utopias: The Rise and Fall of Suburbia* (New York: Basic Books, 1987), 49; John Archer, "Ideology and Aspiration: Individualism, the Middle Class, and the Genesis of the Anglo-American Suburb," *Journal of Urban History* 14 (February 1988): 240–41. Both of these authors draw on Raymond Williams, *The Country and the City* (London: Chatto & Windus, 1973).

BIBLIOGRAPHICAL NOTE

Periodicals that provide valuable materials on developments during the 1920s include *Architect and Engineer* (San Francisco), *Architectural Forum* (Boston), *Architectural Record* (New York), *Building Age* (New York), *Building Review* (San Francisco, 1919–23), *Home Designer and Garden Beautiful* (Oakland, Calif., 1921–28), *Keith's Magazine on Home Building* (Minneapolis), *Michigan Architect and Engineer* (Detroit), *National Real Estate Journal* (Cedar Rapids, Iowa), *Pacific Coast Architect* (San Francisco, 1924–29), and *Western Architect* (Minneapolis).

Resources dating from the 1920s that are relevant to developments in Dearborn, Detroit, and San Francisco are available in the collections of the Dearborn Historical Society, the Henry Ford Museum and Greenfield Village (Dearborn), the Burton Historical Collection of the Detroit Public Library, the Bancroft Library and the Environmental Design Library at the University of California, Berkeley, and the San Franscisciana Collection at the San Francisco Public Library. Period materials of a broader geographical scope can be found in the libraries of the National Association of Realtors (Chicago) and the Engineering Societies (New York City), at the Avery Architectural and Fine Arts Library at Columbia University, and at the Clarke Historical Library at Central Michigan University.

Bibliographies, newsletters, journals, and published conference proceedings of the following organizations are excellent guides to the wealth of related recent scholarship in the fields of architectural, planning, and urban history: MARHO: the Radical Historians' Organization; the Society for American City and Regional Planning History; the Urban History Association; and the Vernacular Architecture Forum.

ILLUSTRATION CREDITS

Frontispiece: *Building Age* (Feb. 1927).
Figure 1: Based on a graph in Michael Sumichrast, *Profile of the Builder and His Industry* (Washington, D.C.: National Association of Home Builders, 1970).
Figure 2: Based on a map of Brightmoor in the Burton Historical Collection of the Detroit Public Library.
Figure 3: Reproduced with the permission of Mari Shaw.
Figures 4 through 13: Reproduced with permission from the Collections of Henry Ford Museum and Greenfield Village (photographs N.189.857, N.189.543, N.189.492, N.189.540, N.189.537, N.189.850, N.189.495, N.189.493, N.189.494, and N.189.292).
Figure 14: *Building Age* (Apr. 1923).
Figures 15 through 21: *Building Age* (Apr. 1924).
Figure 22: Photograph from *Hollybush: Folk Buildings and Social Change in an Appalachian Community* (Knoxville: University of Tennessee Press, 1984).
Figure 23: Based on a map in Frederick M. Wirt, *Power in the City: Decision-making in San Francisco* (Berkeley: University of California Press, 1974).
Figure 24: Based on a map from the U.S. Department of the Interior, Geological Survey, 1956, revised 1980.
Figures 25 and 26: Courtesy of James T. Hughes.
Figures 27 and 28: The author.
Figure 29: Reproduced with the permission of the Bancroft Library, University of California, Berkeley.
Figures 30 through 32: Courtesy of James T. Hughes.
Figures 33 through 36: The author.
Figure 37: *Building Age* (Feb. 1927).
Figure 38: The author.

ILLUSTRATION CREDITS

Figure 39: Reproduced with the permission of the Bancroft Library, University of California, Berkeley.
Figure 40: The author.
Figure 41: *Building Age* (Feb. 1927).
Figures 42 and 43: Reproduced with the permission of the Bancroft Library, University of California, Berkeley.
Figure 44: *National Real Estate Journal* (12 March 1923).
Figure 45: *Building Age* (June 1920).
Figure 46: Reproduced from *Regional Plan of New York and Its Environs*, vol. 7, New York: Regional Plan of New York and Its Environs, 1929, with permission of the Regional Plan Association.

INDEX

Page numbers in italics refer to illustrations.

Allen, Frederic Lewis, 209
alternative housing. *See* housing, alternative
American City Planning Institute, 150
American Civic Association, 150, 158
"American Dream," as built form, 10
American Farm Bureau Federation, 158
American Federation of Labor, 49, 150, 158
American Home Economics Association, 158
American Institute of Architects (AIA), 71, 75, 76, 77, 78, 80, 150, 158
  founding of, 71
  membership in, 30, 103
American Sociological Society, 169
Appalachia, housing in, 84–86, *85*
architects, 14, 71–81, 120, 145
  conflict among, 74–75, 78
  education of, 75
  and licensing, 75, 76
  and planning, 77, 78–79, 80
  and rationalization, 137–38
  relationship to realtors, 6, 7, 14, 80, 81, 103, 161
  role of, in subdivision development, 4, 6, 12, 13, 55, 74, 88, 102, 205
  and small-house design, 4, 12, 67, 74, 81
Architects' Small House Service Bureau, 76, 77, 78, 150, 161
architectural style, 77, 180–203, 209
  and personality, 198–99, 202
  role of, in subdivisions, 15, 107–8
  See also colonial revival style; Mediterranean revival style; stylistic pluralism
assembly-line production, 11, 40, 137
Associated General Contractors of America, 150
associational progressivism, 176, 177, 207. *See also* experts; voluntary associations
Association of General Contractors, 158
Association of Life Insurance Presidents, 158
Atterbury, Grosvenor, 176

Baldwin, A. S., 91
  Residential Development Co., 90, 94

263

INDEX

Baldwin & Howell, 13, 88, 89, 94, 120, 123, 139
balloon frame, *44*, 183, 193
  history, 43
  and standardization, 45, 47, 52
bankers
  financing strategies of, 209
  relationships with home owners, 210
basements, 33, 40, 58, 66, 67, 120
bathrooms, 32–33, *38*, 58, 66, 67
Bauer, Catherine, 7, 10, 213
Beaux Arts, 71, 74, 75, 76, 78
bent house, *111*, 115
Better Homes in America, Inc., 14, 155–57, 158, 206
Bouton, Edward H., 131, 132, 134
Brightmoor, 10, 55–87, *64*
  community center, 57, 60
  community services in, 83
  history of, 57, 58, 62, 63
  housing: construction of, 65–66; cost of, 59; design, 71, 81, 84–86; dimensions of, 67, 86; exteriors, *70, 72*; features of, 58, 59, 81; and health, 57–58, 60, 67; interiors, *68, 69*; market for, 12, 55, 59, 60, 62, 63, 82; plans, 66, *70, 72, 73*; standards of, 12, 58, 60; style, 186–87, 191
  lay-out of, 63–65
  location of, *22*, 62, 63
  lot dimensions in, 63
  neighborhood identity in, 67, 82, 177–78
  as object of study, 57, 59–60
  settlement house in, 57, 80, 177–78
builder, definition of, 19, 47–48. *See also* building-craftsmen

building
  codes, 66, 164
  craft traditions in, 43
  industrialization of, 6, 11, 12, 20, 30, 42, 43–47, 54, 87, 88, 194–95
  materials supply network, 41, 45, 46, 76, 149, 151
  rationalization in, 41
  trades, 50, 51
  See also construction industry; residential construction
building-craftsmen
  deskilling of, 11, 19, 47, 48, 194–95
  history of, 43–51
  loss of livelihood, 49
  relationship to realtors, 5, 7, 14, 51–52
  role of, in construction, 41, 73, 74, 76
  role of, in subdivision development, 4, 11, 12, 13, 20, 55, 102, 177, 205
  and small house design, 4, 81
building and loan association. *See* savings and loan association
Building Trades Councils, 50

carpenters, 43, 45, 46, 48, 49, 50, 65–66
Chamber of Commerce of the United States, 158
City Beautiful movement, 95, 166
civic activism, desire to foster, 27, 212
civic improvement. *See* public good
colonial revival style, 53, 103, 182, 183–86
  characteristics of, 32, 195–96, 199, 200

INDEX

design needs and, 183
history of, 183–84
industrialized production and, 183, 186, 189
national identity and, 184–85
commodity
  design as, 77
  household appliances as, 148, 197–98
  housing as, 209–10
community
  and continuity, 5
  design, 11
  idea of, 165
  and reformers, 14, 206–7
  role of, in housing market, 5, 144, 165, 211
  services, 12, 27, 29, 53, 67
community-builders, 79, 128–36, 139
  realtors' self-description as, 13, 25, 81, 83, 87, 165, 208–9
community center movement, 171, 208
"Community Homes," 24–27, *26*, 54, 78
company towns, 9, 11, 20, 27, 53, 79, 83
construction industry, 12
  changes in, 4, 7, 41, 42, 43, 47, 49, 50, 51, 52, 54, 207
  cost-reduction in, 46, 63, 192
  division of labor in, 19, 42, 47–51, 52
  greenhands, 46, 49
  mechanization in, 52
  piecework in, 46, 49, 51
  rationalization in, 52, 53
  See also building; residential construction

continuity
  architectural style and, 191, 198–99, 208
  image of, 3, 13, 138, 181, 192, 200–201
  and risk, 144, 203, 211–12
contractors, 48, 50, 51
Cooley, Charles Horton, 170, 171, 183, 207
cult of domesticity, 198
curbstoners, 130, 132

data collection, 128, 129, 150–51, 176
Davis, Alexander Jackson, 165
Dearborn, Michigan, 11, 21, 23
Dearborn Realty & Construction Company, 11
  aims of, 33, 54
  demise of, 21
  establishment of, 19, 21, 33
  organization of, 28
  and right to buy-back, 28
deed restrictions, 138, 174, 199
Delano, William, 192
deskilling, 52. *See also* building-craftsmen, deskilling of
developers. *See* realtors
Dewey, John, 170
diversity of housing design. *See* subdivision development, design, balance in
division of labor, 194–95. *See also* construction industry, division of labor in
Downing, Andrew Jackson, 165, 167
dual-housing market, 82
Durant, W. C., 53

INDEX

economy. *See* national economy
Edison, Thomas, 23, 184
efficiency, 20, 21, 23, 25, 28, 33, 40, 80, 129, 137, 138
Ely, Richard, 124, 127
engineers, 14, 73, 80, 145, 149, 163, 205
entrepreneurial vernacular, 2–6, 10, 15, 209–13
  design, 180, 181, 191
  explanation of, 5, 211
  success of, 10
exchange value. *See* housing, as commodity
experts, 9, 10, 124, 143, 158
  network of, 176, 177
  See also associational progressivism; voluntary associations

federal government
  housing for war-workers, 53, 80
  housing standards, 66
  recognition of realtors, 127
  support for home-ownership network, 14, 149, 153, 154, 155
Federal Home Loan Bank System, 162
financiers
  historic role of, in building, 48
  organizational interactions of, 206
  and residential construction, 14, 149, 163
financing, 61, 65, 146–47, 154, 164
  alternative, 212
  federal involvement in, 149, 162
  new strategies for, in 1920s, 209
Flint, Michigan, 28, 53, 58
Ford, Edsel, 33

Ford, Henry, 19, 20, 24, 40
  and application of production principles, 21, 23, 54
  colonial revival and, 184, 185–86
  design ideas of, in Ford Homes, 30, 31
  support for Ford Homes, 21, 23, 27
Ford, James, 157, 158, 159
Ford Homes, 19–54
  community services in, 29
  design of, 31
  history of, 21, 23, 24, 31, 33
  housing: construction of, 31, 33, 40–41, *42*, 54; cost of, 11, 28; design, 32; exteriors, *34, 35, 36, 37;* interiors, *38, 39;* middle-class purchasers of, 11; plans, 32–33; restrictions on owners of, 28; style, 182–87, 188, 191
  location of, 21, *22*
  lot dimensions in, 31
  as model construction project, 11, 33, 40, 53, 54
  residents of, 27–28
  workforce at, 19, 40–41, 52
Fordson Village, 23
Forest Hills Gardens, 79, 132, 207

garages, 27, 29, 93
garden-suburb, 2, 13, 78, 83, 166, 167, 171, 172, 173, 204
  influence on neighborhood unit plan, 14, 207
General Electric, 162
General Federation of Women's Clubs, 155, 158
General Motors, 58, 162
Gould, A. Warren, 30

INDEX

Gries, John, 154, 157, 158, 159
Gross, Samuel Eberly, 163
Gutterson, Henry, 95

Hamlin, Talbot, 185, 191
historicist styles, 191
   function of, 190, 200
   geographic appropriateness of, 41, 191
   as picturesque, 185, 189, 191
   See also stylistic pluralism
home owners, 93, 97, 102
   community of, 101, 211
   debt of, in 1920s, 144
   and design decisions, 41, 183, 188
   individuality of, 41, 202
   investment of, 209–10, 211
   lot purchase required of, 57, 65
   needs of, 67
   restrictions on, 97, 108, 109
   role of market in decisions of, 209
   targeted sub-group of, 186–87
home ownership
   and citizenship, 154, 159, 210
   and class conflict, 147–48
   and morals, 159–60
   as necessity, 210
   promotion of, 60, 114, 131, 147, 148, 159, 175, 205
   symbolic meaning of, 210
   trends in, 146, 149, 164
home-ownership network, 2, 4, 5, 6, 9–10, 14, 139, 143–70, 204, 212
   and architectural style, 180–81
   creation of, 149
   proposals of, 205, 206
   social concerns of, 206, 207
   standards of, 206
   and transmission of expertise, 10, 14, 207
Hoover, Herbert
   as commerce secretary, 9, 143, 151, 153, 154, 155, 162, 176, 177, 206
   at Food Administration, 152
   management style of, 9, 151–57, 207
   as president, 9, 157, 163
housing
   alternative proposals for, 2, 6–7, 25, 78, 145, 212
   amenities, 12, 81, 82, 83, 120
   class-segregation in, 82, 83, 109, 133
   as commodity (*see* commodity, housing as)
   construction (*see* residential construction)
   cost of, 21, 24, 25, 28, 59, 99, 109
   experts (*see* home-ownership network)
   folk-traditional, 82, 84
   health aspects of, 25, 58, 60, 67
   impact of social changes on, 198–99
   impact of technology on, 196–98
   industry (*see* residential construction)
   market, 83, 87, 97 (*see also* dual-housing market)
   marketability of, 209–10, 211
   middle-class, 28, 82
   network (*see* home-ownership network)
   professionals (*see* home-ownership network)
   provision of, 5, 6, 13, 24–25, 53, 212

housing (*cont.*)
    reformers, 5, 14, 145, 167, 212
    shortage, 5, 6, 15, 54, 56, 144, 205–6, 207
    single-family, 145, 146 (*see also* single-family detached houses)
    social transformations in, 207
    standards, 12, 33, 58, 60, 66–67, 206
    types, in 1920s, 6, 145
    wartime (*see* World War I)
    working-class, 12, 58, 59, 73, 147
Howard, Ebenezer, 173
Howard, John Galen, 95
Hull House. *See* settlement houses

individualization of housing design. *See* subdivision development, design, balance in
infrastructure for subdivisions, 82, 83, 105, 130. *See also* municipal government
Institute for Research in Land Economics and Public Utilities, 127, 132
investment security, 5, 126, 144, 149, 174, 175, 179, 194, 199–200, 201, 202, 211–12. *See also* property values; risk

labor
    disputes, 48, 50
    reduction in hours of, 49, 51
    unions, 49–51, 160–61
landscaping, 165, 166, 167, 175, 179, 208, 211
land-sharks, 123, 124
large-scale residential projects, 28, 42, 53, 56, 82
    design of, 164, 165, 174, 175

    importance in housing industry, 11
    role of architects in, 79, 80
    role of realtors in, 10, 51, 79, 80
    stratification of workers in, 51
legal instruments, role in housing patterns, 5, 145. *See also* deed restrictions; zoning
licensing. *See* architects, licensing; realtors, licensing
Liebold, E. G., 24, 33, 40, 41
    design ideas of, in Ford Homes, 30, 31
Llewellyn Park, 1, 165, 167
local services. *See* community, services
lot sales. *See* speculation, and lot sales
lumber industry. *See* building, materials supply network

Magnusson, Leifur, 28, 83, 84
management, bureaucratic, 206, 211
market forces, 5, 56, 77, 149
marketing innovation, 139
mass production
    of building supplies, 43, 45, 82
    of design details, 183, 189
    in Ford Homes, 11, 23, 40
McDuffie, Duncan, 134
McKim, Mead & White, 80
mechanization, 43, 45, 50
Mediterranean revival style, 104, 107, 188–90, 191, 199
    history of, 189
    and regional identity, 189–90, 191
Michigan Planning Commission, 56, 68

middle class, 13, 73, 78, 88, 97, 105, 145
minimal house, 195–96, 200
mission style. *See* Mediterranean revival style
model subdivisions, 52, 53, 131–33, 174, 176, 177, 179
  Country Club District, 131, 136, 175
  as critique of status quo, 6–7
  European, 212
  and home-ownership network, 180, 196, 206
  model suburb competition, 78, 172
  Radburn, 7, 173
  River Oaks, 131
  Roland Park, 131, 132
modern design, 192–93, 196, 200
modular system, 14, 88, 137, 196
  and design, 32, 53, 117–18
  in Ford Homes, 25, 32, 33
  in Westwood Highlands, 112, 115, 187
module, definition of, 112
moral environment, 166, 174
morality
  appeals to, 206
  housing's influence on, 25, 27, 83
mortgage. *See* financing
Mumford, Lewis, 172, 207, 212
municipal government, 91, 93
  development annexation by, 59, 62
  role in development, 88, 129, 130, 139

National Association of Builders' Exchanges, 158
National Association of Building Trades Employers, 150
National Association of Real Estate Boards (NAREB), 124–28, 130, 131, 132, 138, 139, 143, 150
National Builders' Association, 51
National Conference on City Planning, 134
National Congress of Parents and Teachers, 158
national economy, 137, 148, 149, 152
National Farmers' Union, 158
National Federation of Construction Industries, 150
National Grange, 158
National Lumber Manufacturers Association, 150, 151, 153
National Real Estate Association, 131
neighborhood identity, 12, 13, 107
  design of, 15, 88, 110
  role of community amenities in, 208, 211
  role of, in risk management, 5, 208–9
  successful creation of, at Brightmoor, 57, 67
neighborhood unit plan, 167–69, *168*, 171–74, 207
Nelson, Hans, 97, 102
Nelson Brothers, 97, 101, 102
new vernacular, 205–8. *See also* entrepreneurial vernacular
Nichols, Jesse Clyde, 58, 61, 133, 136, 138, 147, 155, 165, 166–67, 177, 208–9, 211

INDEX

Olmsted, Frederick Law, Jr., 132, 162, 167, 176
O'Shaughnessy, Michael M., 91
owner-builders, 13, 52, 75, 82, 83, 84
Own Your Home, 14, 128, 154–55, *156*

Perry, Clarence A., 167–74. *See also* neighborhood unit plan
plan book, 202. *See also* stock plans
planlessness, apparent, 9, 206, 211
planners, 5, 14, 149, 163, 205
   relationship to realtors, 89, 133–36, 138
planning
   architects and, 30, 78
   devices, 174, 182
   ideals of, 7, 9
   real estate practices and, 166
   and standardization, 66
   in subdivisions, 9, 207
platform frame. *See* Western frame
population growth
   in Detroit, 10, 20, 21, 55, 57, 59, 83
   in San Francisco, 91, 130
Potter, Hugh, 131
power tools, impact on building, 47
President's Conference on Home Building and Home Ownership, 14, 157–63, 164, 165, 167–69, 174, 177
   organizations participating in, 158
professionalization, rise of, 4, 13
property values, 13, 132, 133, 138, 209, 210–11. *See also* investment security; risk
public good, 120, 129, 159, 174

public space, 109, 111, 118
public transportation, 13, 93, 94, 97, 99, 130, 178
Punnett, John M., 94, 95, 138

realtor-developers. *See* realtors
realtors
   appearance of term, 124–25
   attitude of critics toward, 7
   as community builders, 87, 88, 128–36, 139, 174, 208–9
   education of, 127, 130
   emergence of, 51
   as home owner's community, 211–12
   licensing of, 123, 125, 127
   professionalization of, 4, 9, 13, 20, 65, 77, 89, 123–28, 129, 132, 133, 134, 136, 143, 147, 176
   rationalization and, 129, 138–39
   relationship to architects, 6, 7, 14, 80, 81, 103, 161
   relationship to building-craftsmen, 5, 7, 14, 51–52
   relationship to planners, 89, 133–36, 138
   role in subdivision development, 4, 5, 10, 51, 204, 205, 206, 211
   skills of, 4, 5, 126, 137
   and small house design, 4
recreation
   activities for, 60, 167
   areas, 165, 166, 167, 169, 175
   parks as, 29, 131, 167
reformers. *See* housing, reformers
Reid, John, Jr., 95
residential construction
   cost reduction in, 63, 131, 137, 161–62, 192
   federal policy of, 159

mass production in, 23, 53
  and national economy, *8*, 148, 149
  rationalization of, 20, 21, 67; in planning, 9; in practices, 11, 12, 42, 137
  role of architects in, 80
  role of building-craftsmen in, 74
  trends in, 6, 14, 144–45, 148, 149
residential development. *See* subdivision development
Riis, Jacob, 170
risk, 5, 144, 187, 211
romantic suburb, 13, 167. *See also* garden-suburb
"rus in urbe," 165
Russell Sage Foundation, 79, 158, 169

savings and loan association, 146–47
Savings Bank Division of the American Bankers' Association, 158
school center movement, 170
schools, 167, 169, 170, 171, 175
science, appeals to, 206
segregation in housing, 60
settlement houses, 25, 57, 60, 170, 173, 177, 178
Shuler, Irenaeus, 147
single-family detached houses, 2, 5, 6, 25, 144, 145, 146, 160, 204
skills, 13, 51, 52, 137. *See also* de-skilling
small-house design, 4, 12, 54, 75, 76, 77, 147, 161, 185, 194, 201, 204
social services. *See* community services

specialization of labor. *See* construction industry, division of labor
speculation, 2, 48, 53, 54, 83, 133, 137, 139
  attitude of critics toward, 7, 25, 28
  and lot sales, 56, 57, 65, 130, 131
stability. *See* national economy; continuity
standardization, 11
  in construction, 160, 190
  in design, 161, 191
  Hoover's program of, 153
  national trend towards, 45
  opposition to, 161
Stein, Clarence, 173
stock plans, 76, 77, 78
streets, 14, 29, 58, 59, 109
  contour, 131, 175
  curvilinear, 14, 94, 95, 107, 110, 165, 166, 167
  pattern of, 169, 172, 179, 208
Strothoff, Charles, 97, 102–3, 108, 120
stucco, 107–8, 190
stylistic pluralism, 15, 191–94, 211
  plasticity of, 201, 202–3
  reasons for reliance on, 194–200
subdivision development
  attitude of critics toward, 57
  characterization of, as vernacular, 1, 3
  commercial services in, 12, 59, 67, 81, 94
  design, 29, 32, 108–9, 112, 163–67, 174–75, 178; balance in, 31–32, 104, 112, 115, 120, 138, 163, 181, 182, 183, 186, 188, 190, 202; house clusters in, 25, *26*, 31, 182, 183

271

INDEX

subdivision development (*cont.*)
    features of, 2, 11, 131, 181, 204
    guidelines for, 206, 211
    of inexpensive homes, 62
    influences on, 1, 13
    innovation in, 104–5
    market relationships and, 213
    models of, 131–36, 137
    pattern of, 9, 13, 88, 143, 205, 207–8
    planning of, 10, 14, 205
    promotion of, 90, 91, 93
    reduction of costs in, 163
    and regional considerations, 208
    success of, 2, 5, 7
    as synthesis, 207, 208
suburban community, desire for, 160
suburbanization, and land availability, 148–49

Taylor, Burt Eddy, 12, 25, 57, 58, 60, 61–62, 67, 83, 87
Taylor, James S., 154
The Real Estate Associates (TREA), 109
Twin Peaks, *89*, 93, 94, 97, 190
    Property Owners Association, 91, 130

U.S. Bureau of Labor Statistics, 151
U.S. Census Bureau, 151
U.S. Department of Commerce, 134
U.S. Department of Labor, 147
U.S. Housing Corporation, 67, 80, 127, 128
unions. *See* labor, unions; United Brotherhood of Carpenters and Joiners

United Brotherhood of Carpenters and Joiners, 49–50
United States League of Building and Loan Associations, 158
unity. *See* subdivision development, design, balance in
urban reform and subdivision development, 134, 136, 204–5
utilities, 29, 58, 59, 197, 200

Veiller, Lawrence, 145
vernacular, definition of, 2–4, 207–8
Victorian style, 90, 107–8, 117, 118, 188, 189, 195
voluntary associations, 9, 124, 151, 152, 163, 164, 206, 207. *See also* associational progressivism; experts

Ward, Edward J., 171
Western frame, definition of, 43
Westwood Highlands, 10, 13, 14, 88–139, *89*, *101*
    design of, 14, *100*, 108–20
    history of, 95, 97
    housing: construction of, 88, 102; cost of, 99; design, 88, 109, 110–11, 112–15, 118; exteriors, *104*, *105*, *106*, *110*, *111*, *113*, *114*, *116*, *117*, *121*; interiors, *116*, 118–20, *121*, *122*; market for, 88, 101, 105; plans, *116*, 118, *119*, 120; style, 107–8, 187–90, *191*
    location of, 88, *89*
    neighborhood identity of, 88, 178
    street pattern of, 92
Westwood Park, 13, 94–97, *99*
Women's National Farm and Garden Association, 158

INDEX

Wood, Albert, 24, 25, 27, 30–31, 33, 53, 55, 182, 186, 212
Wood, Edith Elmer, 7, 149
Woodcrest, 94–95, *96*, 97, *98*
wood products, 45, 46, 47
wood-working machinery, 45, 46, 47, 49, 50
working class, 82, 83. *See also* housing, standards; housing, working class; owner-builders
World War I, impact on housing, 6, 7, 21, 24, 53, 81, 127, 128
Wright, Henry, 7, 10, 161, 173

zoning, 138, 153, 154, 164, 174, 175

About the Author

Carolyn Loeb was born and raised, and attended public schools, in New York City. She studied at the University of California, Berkeley (B.A.), and San Francisco State University (M.A.) and received a Ph.D. in Art History from the Graduate Center, City University of New York. She is an associate professor in the Art Department at Central Michigan University, where she teaches modern and contemporary art and architectural history. She has written articles on subdivisions for *The Encyclopedia of Urban America* and *The Encyclopedia of Chicago History* and contemporary art reviews for the *New Art Examiner* and other periodicals, and she is currently writing on social housing, urban planning, and public sculpture in Central Europe.